Employment Trends and Master Index

Editorial Advisory Board

The Career Information Center includes:

Employment Trends and Master Index

Ninth Edition

MACMILLAN REFERENCE USA
An imprint of Thomson Gale, a part of The Thomson Corporation

Detroit • New York • San Francisco • New Haven, Conn. • Waterville, Maine • London

THOMSON

GALE

™

Career Information Center, Ninth Edition

Paula Kepos, Series Editor

Project Editor
Mary Rose Bonk

Editorial
Jennifer Greve

© 2007 Thomson Gale, a part of The Thomson Corporation.

Thomson, Star Logo and Macmillan Reference USA are trademarks and Gale is a registered trademark used herein under license.

For more information, contact
Macmillan Reference USA
An imprint of Thomson Gale
27500 Drake Rd.
Farmington, Hills, MI 48331-3535
Or you can visit our Internet site at
http://www.gale.com

ALL RIGHTS RESERVED
No part of this work covered by the copyright hereon may be reproduced or used in any form or by any means—graphic, electronic, or mechanical, including photocopying, recording, taping, Web distribution, or information storage retrieval systems—without the written permission of the publisher.

Imaging
Lezlie Light, Daniel Newell, Christine O'Bryan

Permissions
Kelly A. Quin, Tim Sisler, Andrew Specht

For permission to use material from this product, submit your request via Web at http://www.gale-edit.com/permissions, or you may download our Permissions Request form and submit your request by fax or mail to:

Permissions
Thomson Gale
27500 Drake Rd.
Farmington Hills, MI 48331-3535
Permissions Hotline:
248-699-8006 or 800-877-4253 ext. 8006
Fax: 248-699-8074 or 800-762-4058

Manufacturing
Rhonda Dover

Since this page cannot legibly accommodate all copyright notices, the acknowledgments constitute an extension of the copyright notice.

While every effort has been made to ensure the reliability of the information presented in this publication, Thomson Gale does not guarantee the accuracy of the data contained herein. Thomson Gale accepts no payment for listing; and inclusion in the publication of any organization, agency, institution, publication, service, or individual does not imply endorsement of the editors or publisher. Errors brought to the attention of the publisher and verified to the satisfaction of the publisher will be corrected in future editions.

ISBN 0-02-866047-1 (set)
ISBN 0-02-866048-X (v.1)
ISBN 0-02-866049-8 (v.2)
ISBN 0-02-866050-1 (v.3)
ISBN 0-02-866051-X (v.4)
ISBN 0-02-866052-8 (v.5)
ISBN 0-02-866053-6 (v.6)
ISBN 0-02-866054-4 (v.7)
ISBN 0-02-866055-2 (v.8)
ISBN 0-02-866056-0 (v.9)
ISBN 0-02-866057-9 (v.10)
ISBN 0-02-866058-7 (v.11)
ISBN 0-02-866059-5 (v.12)
ISBN 0-02-866060-9 (v.13)
ISSN 1082-703X

This title is also available as an e-book.
ISBN 0-02-866099-4
Contact your Thomson Gale representative for ordering information.

Printed in the United States of America
10 9 8 7 6 5 4 3 2 1

Contents

Comprehensive Job Summary Chart

Job	Salary	Education/ Training	Employment Outlook	Volume: Page
Job Profiles—No Specialized Training				
Admitting Interviewer	Median—$11.94 per hour	High school	Good	**7:33**
Aerospace Engineering and Operations Technician	Median—$52,250 per year	High school plus training	Good	**6:31**
⭐ **Air-Conditioning, Heating, and Refrigeration Mechanic and Installer**	Median—$17.43 per hour	Trade school, apprenticeship, or on-the-job training	Very good	**4:27**
Airline Baggage and Freight Handler	Median—$21,570 per year	High school	Good	**12:27**
Airline Reservations Agent	Median—$27,750 per year	High school	Poor	**12:28**
Airline Ticket Agent	Median—$28,420 per year	High school	Poor	**12:30**
Airport Utility Worker	Median—$21,570 per year	High school	Fair	**12:31**
Alternative Fuels Vehicle Technician	Median—$38,000 per year	High school plus training	Very good	**6:33**
Amusement and Recreation Attendant	Median—$7.69 per hour	Varies—see profile	Very good	**8:29**
Animal Caretaker	Median—$8.39 per hour	High school plus training	Good	**8:31**
Apparel Worker	Varies—see profile	None	Poor	**9:29**
Armed Services Career	Varies—see profile	Varies—see profile	Good	**11:31**
Assembler and Fabricator	Varies—see profile	None	Poor	**9:31**
⭐ **Auto Body Repairer**	Median—$16.68 per hour	High school	Good	**12:32**
Auto Parts Counter Worker	Median—$15.16 per hour	High school plus training	Poor	**10:29**
Auto Sales Worker	Median—$18.61 per hour	High school plus training	Very good	**10:31**
Baker	Median—$21,330 per year	High school	Good	**1:31**
Bank Clerk	Median—$23,317 to $27,310 per year	High school	Poor	**3:33**
Bank Teller	Median—$21,120 per year	High school	Fair	**3:34**
⭐ **Bartender**	Median—$7.42 per hour plus tips	Voc/tech school plus training	Good	**8:33**
Bicycle Mechanic	Median—$9.76 per hour	None	Good	**12:34**
Billing Clerk	Median—$27,040 per year	High school	Fair	**3:37**
Bookbinder	Median—$13.71 per hour	High school	Poor	**2:31**
Bookkeeper	Median—$28,570 per year	High school	Fair	**3:38**
Bricklayer	Median—$20.07 per hour	Apprenticeship	Good	**4:30**
Bridge and Lock Tender	Median—$37,050 per year	High school plus training	Poor	**12:35**
Brokerage Clerk	Median—$35,235 per year	High school	Fair	**3:40**
Building Custodian	Median—$23,414 per year	Training	Good	**11:33**

⭐ **High-growth job**

Job	Salary	Education/ Training	Employment Outlook	Volume: Page
Bulldozer, Grader, or Paving Machine Operator	Varies—see profile	High school and training	Good	4:32
Business Machine Operator	Varies—see profile	High school	Poor	3:42
Cable Television and Telecommunications Technician	Median—$17.36 per hour	High school plus training	Poor	6:35
★ Cafeteria Attendant	Median—$7.10 per hour	Training	Good	8:35
Candy Manufacturing Worker	Median—$21,420 per year	High school	Poor	1:32
Car Wash Worker	Median—$8.41 per hour	None	Good	12:37
Carpenter	Average—$16.90 per hour	Apprenticeship	Good	4:34
Cashier	Median—$7.81 per hour	Training	Fair	10:34
Ceiling Tile Installer	Median—$16.67 per hour	High school	Fair	4:36
Cement Mason	Median—$15.10 per hour	Apprenticeship	Good	4:38
★ Chauffeur	Median—$9.41 per hour	License	Good	5:27
Cheese Industry Worker	Starting—$8.50 per hour	None	Poor	1:34
Chemical Technician	Median—$18.35 per hour	High school plus training	Fair	6:37
Child Care Worker, Private	Median—$8.06 per hour	None	Good	5:28
Companion	Median—$8.12 per hour	None	Excellent	5:30
Comparison Shopper	Average—$24,643 per year	High school plus training	Fair	10:36
Construction Electrician	Median—$20.33 per hour	Apprenticeship or on-the-job training	Good	4:40
Construction Equipment Mechanic	Median—$18.34 per hour	Trade school or on-the-job training	Fair	4:42
Construction Laborer	Median—$12.14 per hour	None	Fair	4:45
Construction Millwright	Average—$21.24 per hour	High school plus training	Poor	4:46
Correspondence Clerk	Median—$29,340 per year	High school	Poor	3:44
Costume Attendant	Average—$12.04 per hour	On-the-job training	Very good	2:33
Credit Authorizer, Checker, and Clerk	Median—$29,058 per year	High school	Poor	3:46
Credit Collector	Median—$27,456 per year	High school	Very good	3:48
Customer Service Representative	Median—$27,020 per year	High school	Very good	3:49
Dairy Industry Worker	Average—$16.60 per hour	High school	Poor	1:36
Data Entry Keyer	Median—$23,250 per year	High school	Poor	3:51
Day Care Worker	Average—$9.76 per hour	High school plus training	Very good	11:35
Demolition Worker	Varies—see profile	None	Fair	4:48
★ Dental Assistant	Median—$13.62 per hour	High school plus training	Excellent	7:34
Dialysis Technician	$25,682 to $32,413 per year	High school	Very good	7:36
Dining Room Attendant	Median—$7.17 per hour	Training	Fair	8:36
Direct Sales Worker	Average—$12.92 per hour	Training	Poor	10:37

★ High-growth job

Job	Salary	Education/ Training	Employment Outlook	Volume: Page
Dishwasher	Median—$7.35 per hour	Training	Good	**8:38**
Diver	Varies—see profile	Varies—see profile	Good	**1:38**
Dockworker	Median—$9.67 per hour	None	Poor	**12:38**
Doorkeeper	Varies—see profile	Training	Fair	**8:40**
Dry Cleaning Worker	Median—$8.28 per hour	None	Poor	**5:32**
Drywall Installer and Taper	Varies—see profile	On-the-job training	Fair	**4:51**
Electric Power Service Worker	Median—$16.60 to $25.27 per hour	None	Poor	**11:36**
Electric Power Transmission and Distribution Worker	Median—$23.61 per hour	Varies—see profile	Poor	**11:37**
★ Electrical and Electronics Engineering Technician	Median—$46,310 per year	High school plus training	Good	**6:39**
Electrical and Electronics Installer and Repairer	$15.54 to $25.86 per hour	High school plus training	Fair to Good	**6:42**
Electromechanical Engineering Technician	Median—$41,440 per year	High school plus training	Good	**6:44**
Electronic Home Entertainment Equipment Installer and Repairer	Median—$13.44 per hour	High school	Poor	**6:46**
Elevator Installer and Repair Worker	Median—$28.23 per hour	High school plus apprenticeship	Good	**4:53**
Farm Laborer	Varies—see profile	None	Fair	**1:40**
★ Fast Food Franchise Worker	Median—$7.06 per hour	Training	Good	**8:42**
File Clerk	Median—$21,029 per year	High school	Poor	**3:53**
Firefighter	Median—$18.43 per hour	High school plus training	Very good	**11:39**
Fisher	Median—$8.19 per hour	None	Poor	**1:42**
Floor Covering Installer	Varies—see profile	High school plus apprenticeship or training	Good	**4:54**
Floor Sander and Finisher	Median—$12.88 per hour	None	Fair	**4:57**
Food Canning and Freezing Worker	Varies—see profile	None	Fair	**1:45**
Gaming Cage Worker	Median—$10.74 per hour	Training	Fair	**8:44**
★ Gaming Dealer	Median—$14,340 per year plus tips	High school plus certification	Good	**8:46**
Garage Door Mechanic	Median—$15.17 per hour	On-the-job training	Good	**4:59**
Gardener and Groundskeeper	Median—$25,881 per year	None	Very good	**5:34**
Gas Station Cashier	Median—$7.54 per hour	None	Good	**12:40**
★ Geriatric Aide	Median—$8.47 to $9.11 per hour	Training	Very good	**11:41**
Glazier	Median—$15.63 per hour	Apprenticeship	Good	**4:61**
Gunsmith	$18,000 to $35,000 per year	High school plus training	Good	**9:33**
★ Highway Maintenance Worker	Median—$14.21 per hour	High school plus training	Very good	**11:43**

★ High-growth job

Job	Salary	Education/ Training	Employment Outlook	Volume: Page
Home Caterer	Median—$28,800 to $65,000 per year	None	Good	5:36
★ Home Health Aide	Median—$8.81 per hour	Varies—see profile	Excellent	7:37
Homemaker	None	None	Excellent	5:38
Hospitality Cashier	Median—$7.81 per hour	High school plus training	Fair	8:48
Hotel Bellhop and Porter	Median—$8.69 per hour plus tips	Training	Good	8:50
★ Hotel Housekeeper	Median—$16,900 per year	Training	Good	8:52
★ Hotel, Motel, and Resort Desk Clerk	Median—$17,700 per year	High school plus training	Good	8:54
Housekeeper, Domestic	Median—$16,900 per year	None	Good	5:40
Human Resources Assistant	Median—$31,750 per year	High school	Good	3:55
Hydraulic and Pneumatic Technician	$20,000 to $50,000 per year	High school plus training	Good	6:48
Industrial Machinery Maintenance Worker	Median—$15.79 per hour	Varies—see profile	Poor	9:35
Industrial Truck Operator	Median—$12.78 per hour	None	Poor	12:41
Inspector and Tester	Varies—see profile	None	Poor	9:37
★ Institutional Housekeeper	Median—$16,900 per year	Training	Good	11:44
★ Insulation Worker	Median—$14.57 to $16.03 per hour	On-the-job training	Excellent	4:63
★ Intercity Bus Driver	Median—$14.30 per hour	Training; license	Good	12:43
Interviewer	Median—$23,670 to $33,114 per year	High school	Fair	3:56
Laboratory Animal Care Worker	Median—$7.86 per hour	High school	Very good	7:39
Lather	Average—$16.36 per hour	Apprenticeship or on-the-job training	Poor	4:65
Laundry Worker	Median—$8.28 per hour	None	Poor	5:42
Lithographic Worker	Varies—see profile	High school	Poor	2:34
Local Transit Operator	Varies—see profile	Training; license	Good	12:45
★ Local Truck Driver	Median—$11.80 per hour	License	Good	12:47
Logger	Varies—see profile	None	Poor	1:46
★ Long-Haul Truck Driver	Median—$16.11 per hour	License	Good	12:48
Lumber Mill Worker	Median—$11.59 per hour	High school	Fair	1:48
Machine Operator and Tender	Varies—see profile	None	Poor	9:38
Mail Clerk	Median—$23,650 per year	None	Poor	3:58
Mail Service Worker	Varies—see profile	High school	Fair	3:59
Makeup Artist	Median—$32,630 per year	Varies—see profile	Good	2:37
Manufactured Home Assembler	Median—$11.64 per hour	None	Poor	4:67
Marble, Tile, and Terrazzo Worker	Varies—see profile	Apprenticeship or on-the-job training	Good	4:69
Marine Technician	Average—$32,000 to $40,000 per year	None	Good	12:51
Meat Packing Worker	Varies—see profile	High school	Fair	1:50

★ High-growth job

Job	Salary	Education/ Training	Employment Outlook	Volume: Page
★ Mechanical Engineering Technician	Median—$43,400 per year	High school plus training	Good	6:50
Merchandise Displayer and Window Trimmer	Median—$22,280 per year	High school	Good	2:38
Messenger Service Worker	Median—$20,190 per year	None	Poor	3:61
Metallurgical Technician	Median—$43,400 per year	High school plus training	Fair	6:53
Miner, Coal	Average—$21.57 per hour	None	Poor	1:52
Miner, Metal	Average—$21.95 per hour	Varies—see profile	Poor	1:55
Model	Varies—see profile	None	Good	2:40
Motion Picture Projectionist	Median—$8.32 per hour	High school and/or training	Poor	8:56
Motorboat Mechanic	Median—$14.74 per hour	High school plus training	Fair	12:52
Motorcycle Mechanic	Median—$13.70 per hour	Training	Good	12:54
Mover	Median—$9.67 per hour	None	Good	12:56
Nuclear Technician	Median—$28.46 per hour	High school plus training	Fair	6:55
★ Nursing Aide and Orderly	Average—$10.09 per hour	High school	Very good	7:40
Office Clerk	Median—$22,770 per year	High school	Fair	3:63
Optometric Assistant	$12,000 to $30,000 per year	High school	Excellent	7:42
Painter and Paperhanger	Median—$14.55 per hour	Apprenticeship or on-the-job training	Good	4:71
Painting and Coating Worker	Median—$12.64 per hour	None	Fair	9:40
Parking Attendant	Median—$16,820 per year	License	Poor	12:57
Parking Cashier	Median—$7.81 per hour	None	Poor	12:59
Payroll Clerk	Median—$30,350 per year	High school	Good	3:64
Personal Service Worker	Average—$5.15 to $25 per hour	None	Good	5:44
Personal Shopper	Median—$30,000 to $57,500 per year	None	Good	5:45
Pest Control Worker	Median—$12.61 per hour	High school	Very good	5:47
Pesticide Handler, Sprayer, and Applicator, Vegetation	Median—$12.30 per hour	None	Good	1:56
Pet Care Worker	Median—$8.39 per hour	None	Very good	5:49
Petroleum and Natural Gas Exploration and Production Worker	Varies—see profile	None	Fair	1:58
Pharmaceutical Technician	$15.97 to $18.35 per hour	High school plus training	Very good	6:57
Photographic Processing Machine Operator	Median—$9.33 per hour	On-the-job training	Poor	2:43
Photonics Technician	Median—$55,000 per year	High school plus training	Excellent	6:59
Plasterer and Stucco Mason	Median—$15.88 per hour	Apprenticeship or on-the-job training	Fair	4:73
★ Plumber and Pipe Fitter	Median—$19.85 per hour	Voc/tech school or apprenticeship	Very good	4:75

★ High-growth job

Job	Salary	Education/ Training	Employment Outlook	Volume: Page
Postal Service Worker	Varies—see profile	High school plus training	Poor	**11:46**
Power Plant Worker	Median—$52,530 per year	High school plus training	Poor	**11:48**
Power Tool Repairer	Median—$32,960 per year	High school plus training	Fair	**4:78**
Precision Instrument and Equipment Repairer	$13.47 to $21.25 per hour	High school plus training	Fair to Good	**6:62**
Prepress Worker	Median—$15.30 per hour	High school	Poor	**2:45**
Printing Machine Operator	Median—$14.38 per hour	High school	Fair	**2:47**
Professional Organizer	Starting—$25 to $35 per hour	None	Very good	**5:51**
Psychiatric Aide	Median—$11.19 per hour	High school plus training	Fair	**7:44**
Railroad Clerk	Median—$22,770 per year	High school	Poor	**12:60**
Railroad Maintenance Worker	Varies—see profile	High school	Poor	**12:62**
Railroad Signal or Switch Operator	Median—$21.46 per hour	High school plus training	Poor	**12:63**
Railroad Track Worker	Median—$19.03 per hour	None	Poor	**12:65**
Receiving, Shipping, and Traffic Clerk	Median—$24,400 per year	High school plus training	Poor	**10:40**
Receptionist	Median—$21,840 per year	High school	Very good	**3:66**
Refuse Worker	Median—$13.87 per hour	High school plus training	Poor	**11:50**
Reinforcing Ironworker	Median—$16.90 per hour	Apprenticeship	Good	**4:79**
⭐ Rental Clerk	Median—$8.79 per hour	Training	Very good	**10:42**
⭐ Restaurant Host or Hostess	Median—$7.52 per hour	High school and/or training	Good	**8:57**
Retail Store Sales Worker Supervisor	Median—$32,720 per year	Training	Fair	**10:46**
⭐ Retail Store Sales Worker	Median—$8.98 per hour	Training	Good	**10:44**
Rigger	Median—$17.27 per hour	Apprenticeship	Fair	**4:81**
Robotics Technician	$30,400 to $50,500 per year	High school plus training	Excellent	**6:64**
Roofer	Median—$14.83 per hour	On-the-job training	Good	**4:83**
⭐ Route Delivery Driver	Median—$9.96 per hour	High school; license	Good	**12:67**
Rug and Carpet Cleaner	Median—$15,320 to $24,420 per year	None	Good	**5:52**
Sailor	Median—$14 per hour	None	Poor	**12:68**
⭐ Sales Demonstrator and Product Promoter	Median—$9.95 per hour	High school plus training	Good	**10:47**
⭐ School Bus Driver	Median—$11.18 per hour	License	Good	**12:70**
Security Guard	Median—$20,320 per year	High school plus training	Good	**11:52**
Semiconductor Processor	Median—$13.85 per hour	High school plus training	Poor	**6:66**
Septic Tank Installer and Servicer	Median—$30,120 per year	High school and on-the-job training	Varies—see profile	**4:85**
Service Station Attendant	Median—$8.33 per hour	None	Poor	**12:71**

⭐ High-growth job

Job	Salary	Education/Training	Employment Outlook	Volume: Page
Sheet Metal Worker	Median—$17.09 per hour	High school and apprenticeship	Good	**4:87**
Shoe Repairer	Median—$9.29 per hour	High school plus training	Poor	**5:54**
⭐ Short-Order Cook	Median—$8.11 per hour	Training	Good	**8:59**
Special Service Bus Driver	Median—$10.81 per hour	High school; license	Good	**12:73**
Stagehand	Varies—see profile	None	Poor	**2:49**
Statistical Assistant	Median—$31,390 per year	High school	Fair	**3:68**
Stock Clerk	Median—$9.66 per hour	Training	Poor	**10:49**
Stonemason	Median—$16.82 per hour	Apprenticeship or on-the-job training	Very good	**4:90**
Structural Steelworker	Median—$20.40 per hour	Apprenticeship	Good	**4:92**
Substance Abuse Counselor	Median—$32,960 per year	High school	Very good	**7:45**
Supermarket Worker	Median—$7.90 to $15.08 per hour	Training	Fair	**10:51**
Surveying Technician	Median—$30,380 per year	High school	Good	**4:93**
Swimming Pool Servicer	Median—$9.82 to $16.99 per hour	High school	Very good	**5:55**
Taxi Dispatcher	Median—$30,920 per year	High school plus training	Good	**12:75**
⭐ Taxi Driver	Median—$10.68 per hour	Licenses	Good	**12:76**
Telecommunications Central Office Technician	Median—$23.96 per hour	Varies—see profile	Poor	**6:68**
Telemarketer	Average—$23,520 per year	Training	Poor	**10:54**
Telephone Operator	Median—$28,392 per year	High school	Poor	**3:70**
Telephone Service Representative	Median—$27,020 per year	High school	Good	**3:72**
Telephone Service Technician	Median—$23.96 per hour	Varies—see profile	Poor	**6:70**
Ticket Taker	Median—$7.30 per hour	Training	Good	**8:61**
Tire Changer and Repairer	Median—$9.99 per hour	None	Poor	**12:78**
Tobacco Industry Worker	Varies—see profile	None	Poor	**1:61**
Tour Escort	Median—$9.27 per hour	High school and/or training	Fair	**8:63**
Tow Truck Dispatcher	Median—$30,920 per year	High school	Good	**12:79**
Tow Truck Operator	Average—$18,000 to $25,000 per year	High school plus training	Good	**12:80**
⭐ Truck and Bus Dispatcher	Median—$30,920 per year	High school plus training	Good	**12:82**
Usher	Median—$7.35 per hour	Training	Good	**8:65**
Vending Machine Servicer and Repairer	Median—$26,333 per year	Training	Fair	**10:56**
⭐ Waiter	Median—$6.75 per hour including tips	Training	Good	**8:67**
Ward Clerk	$24,320 to $28,167 per year	High school	Good	**7:47**
Warehouse Worker	Varies—see profile	Training	Good	**10:57**
Wastewater Treatment Plant Operator	Median—$34,960 per year	High school	Good	**1:63**

⭐ High-growth job

Job	Salary	Education/ Training	Employment Outlook	Volume: Page
Welder	Median—$14.72 per hour	On-the-job training	Fair	**4:95**
Window Cleaner	Median—$18,790 per year	None	Good	**5:57**
Wireless Communications Technician	Average—$45,000 per year	High school plus training	Good	**6:72**
Word Processor	Median—$28,030 per year	High school	Poor	**3:74**

Job Profiles—Some Specialized Training/Experience

Job	Salary	Education/ Training	Employment Outlook	Volume: Page
Actor	Varies—see profile	Varies—see profile	Good	**2:52**
Administrative Assistant	Median—$34,970 per year	High school plus training	Fair	**3:76**
Agricultural Technician	Average—$13.74 per hour	2-year college	Good	**1:65**
AIDS Counselor	Median—$34,820 per year	Varies—see profile	Varies—see profile	**7:49**
Air Pollution Control Technician	Starting—$16.98 per hour	2-year college or voc/tech school	Good	**1:67**
Aircraft Dispatcher	Varies—see profile	Some college; certification	Fair	**12:84**
⭐ Aircraft Mechanic	Median—$21.77 per hour	High school plus training	Good	**12:86**
⭐ Airline Flight Attendant	Median—$43,440 per year	High school plus training	Good	**12:88**
Ambulance Driver	Median—$24,722 per year	License plus training	Excellent	**7:51**
Animal Trainer	Median—$10.60 per hour	Varies—see profile	Good	**1:69**
Announcer	Median—$10.64 per hour	Varies—see profile	Poor	**2:55**
Appliance Service Worker	Median—$32,180 per year	High school plus training	Fair	**5:59**
Architectural Drafter	Median—$39,190 per year	High school plus training	Fair	**4:98**
Architectural Model Maker	Varies—see profile	Varies—see profile	Poor	**4:100**
Artist	Varies—see profile	Varies—see profile	Fair	**2:57**
Auctioneer	Average—$46,062 per year	Varies—see profile	Varies—see profile	**10:60**
Automobile Driving Instructor	Varies—see profile	Varies—see profile	Good	**12:90**
Automotive Exhaust Emissions Technician	Median—$15.68 per hour	High school plus training	Fair	**12:92**
⭐ Automotive Mechanic	Median—$15.60 per hour	Varies—see profile	Good	**12:93**
Avionics Technician	Median—$21.30 per hour	High school plus training; license	Fair	**12:95**
Barber and Hairstylist	Varies—see profile	Voc/tech school; license	Good	**5:60**
Biological Technician	Median—$15.97 per hour	2- or 4-year college	Good	**6:75**
Biomedical Equipment Technician	Median—$17.90 per hour	High school plus training	Good	**7:53**
⭐ Boilermaker	Median—$21.68 per hour	High school	Good	**9:43**
Border Patrol Agent	Average—$55,000 per year	College plus training	Good	**11:54**
Broadcast News Analyst	Varies—see profile	High school plus training	Poor	**2:60**
Broadcast Technician	Median—$28,010 per year	High school plus training	Fair	**2:62**

⭐ High-growth job

Job	Salary	Education/Training	Employment Outlook	Volume: Page
⭐ Building Inspector	Median—$43,670 per year	High school plus training	Very good	**4**:102
Camera Operator	Median—$37,610 per year	Varies—see profile	Varies—see profile	**2**:65
⭐ Car Rental or Leasing Agent	Varies—see profile	Varies—see profile	Very good	**12**:96
Cardiac Monitor Technician	Median—$26,513 per year	High school plus training	Poor	**7**:55
Cardiology Technologist	Median—$38,690 per year	High school plus training	Excellent	**7**:56
Cartoonist and Animator	Varies—see profile	Varies—see profile	Good	**2**:67
Caterer	Varies—see profile	Varies—see profile	Good	**8**:70
Choreographer	Median—$33,670 per year	Varies—see profile	Good	**2**:70
Claims Adjuster	Median—$44,080 per year	High school; license	Good	**3**:78
Claims Examiner	Median—$33,669 per year	2- or 4-year college	Good	**3**:80
Clinical Laboratory Technician	Median—$30,840 per year	High school plus training	Excellent	**7**:58
Computer and Office Machine Repairer	Median—$35,152 per year	High school plus training	Fair	**3**:82
Computer Control Operator	Median—$14.75 per hour	Varies—see profile	Good	**9**:45
Computer Operator	Median—$31,070 per year	High school plus training	Poor	**3**:84
Construction Equipment Dealer	Varies—see profile	Varies—see profile	Varies—see profile	**4**:104
Construction Supervisor	Average—$50,980 per year	High school, training, and experience	Good	**4**:106
⭐ Consumer Credit Counselor	Median—$34,436 per year	High school plus training	Very good	**5**:62
⭐ Cook and Chef	Varies—see profile	High school plus training	Good	**8**:72
Correctional Officer	Median—$33,600 per year	Varies—see profile	Very good	**11**:56
Cosmetologist	Median—$19,800 per year	Voc/tech school; license	Good	**5**:64
Court Clerk	Median—$27,300 per year	Varies—see profile	Very good	**11**:58
Court Reporter	Median—$42,920 per year	High school plus training	Good	**11**:59
Craftsperson	Varies—see profile	Varies—see profile	Good	**2**:72
Crane Operator	Median—$17.99 per hour	High school plus training	Good	**4**:108
Crime Laboratory Technician	Median—$21.16 per hour	2- or 4-year college	Very good	**11**:61
Custom Tailor and Dressmaker	Median—$10.79 per hour	High school plus training	Poor	**5**:66
Custom Upholsterer	Median—$12.35 per hour	Varies—see profile	Poor	**5**:68
Customs Worker	Median—$49,736 per year	College plus training	Good	**11**:63
Dancer	Varies—see profile	Varies—see profile	Good	**2**:74
Dental and Medical Secretary	Median—$26,540 per year	High school plus training	Good	**7**:64
⭐ Dental Hygienist	Median—$28.05 per hour	2-year college; license	Excellent	**7**:60
Dental Laboratory Technician	Median—$14.93 per hour	High school plus training	Fair	**7**:62
Detective	Varies—see profile	High school plus training	Very good	**11**:65
⭐ Diesel Mechanic	Median—$17.20 per hour	Varies—see profile	Good	**12**:98

⭐ **High-growth job**

Job	Salary	Education/ Training	Employment Outlook	Volume: Page
Dietetic Technician	Average—$10.99 per hour	College	Good	**5:**71
Dispensing Optician	Median—$27,950 per year	High school plus training	Good	**7:**66
Drafter	Median—$39,190 to $43,180 per year	High school plus training	Fair	**9:**47
Electrologist	Varies—see profile	Voc/tech school	Good	**5:**72
Electroneurodiagnostic Technologist	Median—$44,621 per year	High school plus training	Fair	**7:**68
☆ Emergency Medical Technician/ Paramedic	Median—$25,310 per year	High school plus training	Excellent	**7:**70
Employment Interviewer	Median—$40,970 per year	High school plus training	Very good	**3:**86
☆ Environmental Engineering Technician	Median—$38,550 per year	College	Very good	**1:**71
Environmental Health Specialist	$37,300 to $57,551 per year	Varies—see profile	Good	**7:**72
Environmental Science and Protection Technician	Median—$16.99 per hour	College	Good	**1:**73
Expediter	Median—$36,340 per year	Voc/tech school	Fair	**4:**110
Farm Equipment Mechanic	Median—$13.40 per hour	College	Poor	**1:**74
Farmer, Poultry	Varies—see profile	Varies—see profile	Poor	**1:**76
Farmer, Vegetable	Varies—see profile	Varies—see profile	Poor	**1:**78
Federal Government Worker	Varies—see profile	Varies—see profile	Fair	**11:**67
Film and Video Editor	Median—$43,590 per year	High school plus training	Good	**2:**76
First-Line Supervisor	Median—$21.51 per hour	Varies—see profile	Poor	**9:**50
Fish Hatchery Manager	Median—$47,680 per year	Varies—see profile	Good	**1:**80
Fitness Trainer and Aerobics Instructor	Median—$12.25 per hour	Varies—see profile	Very good	**8:**75
Floral Designer	Median—$20,450 per year	High school plus training	Good	**5:**74
Food Broker	Median—$45,400 to $46,829 per year	Varies—see profile	Good	**10:**62
Food Processing Technician	Varies—see profile	2-year college	Good	**1:**81
Food Science Technician	Median—$14.29 per hour	Varies—see profile	Good	**1:**83
Forestry Technician	Varies—see profile	High school plus training	Poor	**1:**85
Gaming Surveillance Officer	Median—$25,840 per year	High school plus certification	Good	**8:**76
Genetic Engineering Research Assistant	Median—$15.97 per hour	College	Good	**6:**77
Geological and Petroleum Technician	Median—$19.35 per hour	College plus training	Poor	**1:**87
Hazardous Waste Management Technician	Median—$15.90 per hour	Varies—see profile	Good	**1:**88
Highway Inspector	Varies—see profile	Varies—see profile	Good	**4:**113
Home Security Consultant	Varies—see profile	High school plus training	Fair	**5:**76

☆   High-growth job

Job	Salary	Education/ Training	Employment Outlook	Volume: Page
Hotel, Casino, and Resort Concierge	Median—$26,571 per year	High school plus training	Good	**8:77**
Industrial Machinery Mechanic	Median—$18.78 per hour	Varies—see profile	Fair	**9:52**
Institutional Child Care Worker	Median—$13.19 per hour	High school plus training	Very good	**11:68**
Insurance Agent and Broker	Median—$41,720 per year	High school plus training; license	Fair	**10:64**
Jeweler	Median—$27,400 per year	Varies—see profile	Poor	**5:78**
Legal Assistant, Corporate	Median—$39,130 per year	Varies—see profile	Very good	**11:70**
★ Licensed Practical Nurse	Median—$33,970 per year	High school plus training; license	Good	**7:74**
Lifeguard	Median—$7.95 per hour	Certification	Fair to good	**8:79**
Lighting Technician	Varies—see profile	High school plus training	Varies—see profile	**2:78**
Locksmith	Median—$31,331 per year	High school plus training	Good	**5:81**
Machine Setter	Varies—see profile	Varies—see profile	Poor	**9:54**
★ Machinist	Median—$16.33 per hour	Varies—see profile	Good	**9:56**
Maintenance Electrician	Median—$20.33 per hour	Apprenticeship or on-the-job training; license	Good	**4:115**
★ Manufacturers' Sales Worker	Median—$45,400 to $58,580 per year	College plus training	Good	**10:66**
★ Massage Therapist	Median—$15.36 per hour	Voc/tech school	Good	**5:82**
Medical Assistant	Median—$24,610 per year	High school plus training	Excellent	**7:76**
★ Medical Records and Health Information Technician	Median—$25,590 per year	2-year college	Very Good	**7:78**
Meeting Planner	Median—$39,620 per year	Varies—see profile	Very good	**3:89**
Merchant Marine Steward and Cook	Varies—see profile	Varies—see profile	Poor	**12:101**
Mining Technician	Varies—see profile	2-year college	Poor	**1:90**
Music Teacher	Varies—see profile	Varies—see profile	Good	**2:81**
Music Video Producer	Varies—see profile	Varies—see profile	Fair	**2:83**
Nanny	Median—$400 to $700 per week	High school plus training	Good	**5:84**
Nuclear Medicine Technologist	Median—$56,450 per year	Varies—see profile	Fair	**7:80**
Nursery/Greenhouse Manager	Median—$37,172 per year	College	Good	**1:92**
Nursery Worker	Median—$7.55 per hour	Varies—see profile	Poor	**1:93**
★ Occupational Therapist Assistant	Median—$38,430 per year	Varies—see profile	Very good	**7:82**
Ophthalmic Laboratory Technician	Median—$11.40 per hour	High school plus training	Fair	**7:83**
Outdoor Guide	$75 to $150 per day	Training; license	Fair	**8:81**
Paralegal Aide	Median—$39,130 per year	Varies—see profile	Very good	**11:71**
Parking Analyst	Median—$38,480 per year	Some college plus training	Varies—see profile	**12:102**
Party Planner	$20 to $40 per hour	High school	Good	**8:83**
Pastry Chef and Baker	Median—$21,330 per year	Training	Good	**8:84**

★ High-growth job

Job	Salary	Education/ Training	Employment Outlook	Volume: Page
Pharmaceutical Sales Representative	Median—$60,130 per year	2- or 4-year college plus training	Good	**7**:84
Photographer	Median—$26,080 per year	Varies—see profile	Varies—see profile	**2**:85
★ Physical Therapist Assistant	Median—$37,890 per year	2-year college	Very good	**7**:86
Piano and Organ Tuner and Technician	Median—$13.47 per hour	High school plus training	Poor	**5**:86
Pile-Driver Operator	Median—$21.29 per hour	Apprenticeship or on-the-job training	Good	**4**:117
Police Officer	Median—$45,210 per year	High school plus training	Good	**11**:72
Proofreader	Varies—see profile	High school plus training	Poor	**2**:87
Radiologic Technologist	Median—$43,350 per year	2- or 4-year college plus training	Good	**7**:88
Railroad Conductor	Median—$22.28 per hour	High school plus training	Poor	**12**:104
Railroad Engineer	Median—$24.30 per hour	High school plus training; license	Poor	**12**:106
Real Estate Developer	Varies—see profile	Varies—see profile	Good	**4**:119
Real Estate Sales Agent and Broker	Median—$35,670 to $58,720 per year	High school plus training; license	Good	**10**:69
Recreation Worker	Median—$19,320 per year	Varies—see profile	Good	**8**:86
Recycling and Reclamation Worker	Median—$12.38 per hour	High school plus training	Poor	**1**:95
Respiratory Therapist	Median—$43,140 per year	2- or 4-year college	Very good	**7**:90
Retail Butcher	Median—$27,030 per year	Training	Good	**10**:71
Secretary	Varies—see profile	Varies—see profile	Fair	**3**:90
Small Animal Breeder	Varies—see profile	Varies—see profile	Varies—see profile	**1**:97
Small Business Owner	Varies—see profile	Varies—see profile	Good	**10**:72
Software Quality Assurance Technician and Analyst	Varies—see profile	Varies—see profile	Good	**3**:92
Solar Energy Technician	Varies—see profile	Varies—see profile	Varies—see profile	**4**:121
Sound Engineering Technician	Median—$38,110 per year	High school plus training	Good	**2**:89
Sports Instructor	Median—$22,640 per year	Training; certification	Good	**8**:89
State Police Officer	Median—$23.55 per hour	High school plus training	Good	**11**:74
Stationary Engineer and Boiler Operator	Median—$44,150 per year	High school plus training	Poor	**9**:59
Surgical Technologist	Median—$34,010 per year	2-year college or voc/tech school	Very good	**7**:92
Swimming Instructor and Coach	Average—$40,000 per year	Training; certification	Good	**8**:90
Tax Preparer	Median—$32,000 per year	High school plus training	Good	**3**:94
Teacher Assistant	Median—$19,410 per year	Varies—see profile	Fair	**11**:76
Teacher, Vocational Education	Median—$45,830 per year	Varies—see profile	Good	**11**:78
Title Examiner	Average—$39,420 per year	High school plus training	Fair	**10**:75

★ High-growth job

Job	Salary	Education/Training	Employment Outlook	Volume: Page
Tool and Die Maker	Median—$20.55 per hour	High school plus training	Excellent	**9:62**
Traffic Technician	Median—$38,480 per year	College plus training	Good	**12:108**
⭐ Transportation Inspector	Median—$47,920 per year	Varies—see profile	Good	**12:109**
⭐ Truck Terminal Manager	Median—$32.36 per hour	Some college	Good	**12:111**
Umpire and Referee	Mean—$27,850 per year	High school plus training; certification	Very good	**8:92**
Union Business Agent	Varies—see profile	Varies—see profile	Fair	**3:96**
⭐ Veterinary Technician	Median—$11.99 per hour	College	Excellent	**1:99**
Watch Repairer	Median—$13.87 per hour	Varies—see profile	Poor	**5:88**
Water Treatment Plant and System Operator	Median—$34,960 per year	High school plus training	Good	**1:101**
Water Well Driller	Median—$33,570 per year	High school plus training	Fair	**4:123**
Wedding Consultant	Varies—see profile	None	Fair	**5:90**
⭐ Wholesale Sales Worker	Median—$45,400 to $58,580 per year	Varies—see profile	Good	**10:77**
Youth Organization Worker	Average—$16,000 to $18,000 per year	Varies—see profile	Fair	**11:79**

Job Profiles—Advanced Training/Experience

Job	Salary	Education/Training	Employment Outlook	Volume: Page
Accountant, Management	Median—$50,770 per year	College	Very good	**3:99**
Accountant, Public	Median—$50,770 per year	College	Very good	**3:101**
Actuary	Median—$76,340 per year	College	Very good	**3:103**
Acupuncturist	Median—$50,000 per year	Some college plus training	Good	**7:94**
Adult Education Worker	Median—$14.85 per hour	College	Very good	**11:82**
Advertising Account Executive	Median—$40,300 per year	College	Good	**10:80**
Advertising Copywriter	Median—$54,410 per year	College	Good	**2:92**
⭐ Advertising Manager	Median—$63,610 to $107,030 per year	College or advanced degree	Very good	**10:82**
Aerospace Engineer	Median—$79,100 per year	College	Good	**6:80**
Agricultural Engineer	Median—$56,520 per year	College	Good	**1:103**
Agricultural Inspector	Median—$14.92 per hour	College	Poor	**1:104**
Agronomist	Median—$51,200 per year	College	Fair	**1:106**
Air Traffic Controller	Median—$102,030 per year	Varies—see profile	Fair	**12:113**
Air-Conditioning Engineer	Median—$67,110 per year	College	Good	**6:82**
⭐ Airplane Pilot	Varies—see profile	Varies—see profile	Good	**12:115**
⭐ Airport Manager	Median—$47,450 per year	College	Good	**12:118**
Anatomist	Median—$65,110 per year	Advanced degree	Good	**6:84**
Anesthesiologist	Median—$321,686 per year	Advanced degree plus training	Very good	**7:95**

⭐ High-growth job

Job	Salary	Education/ Training	Employment Outlook	Volume: Page
Animal Scientist	Median—$49,920 per year	College	Fair	**1**:107
Anthropologist	Median—$43,890 per year	Advanced degree	Good	**6**:87
Appraiser	Varies—see profile	Varies—see profile	Good	**5**:93
Architect	Median—$60,300 per year	College plus training; license	Good	**4**:126
Art Director	Median—$63,750 per year	Varies—see profile	Good	**2**:94
Artificial Intelligence Specialist	Median—$74,980 per year	Advanced degree	Excellent	**6**:89
Astronomer	Median—$97,320 per year	Advanced degree	Fair	**6**:91
Athletic Coach	Mean—$32,780 per year	College or advanced degree; certification	Good	**8**:95
Athletic Trainer	Median—$33,940 per year	College plus training; certification	Very good	**8**:97
Audiologist	Median—$51,470 per year	Advanced degree	Good	**7**:98
Auditor	Median—$50,770 per year	College	Very good	**3**:105
Bank Officer and Manager	Varies—see profile	College	Poor	**3**:107
⭐ Biochemist	Median—$68,950 per year	Advanced degree	Good	**6**:93
Biologist	Average—$69,908 per year	Advanced degree	Good	**6**:96
⭐ Biomedical Engineer	Median—$67,690 per year	Advanced degree	Very Good	**6**:99
Botanist	Average—$62,207 per year	Advanced degree	Good	**6**:101
Business Family and Consumer Scientist	Varies—see profile	College	Good	**5**:95
Cable Television Engineer	Average—$64,416 per year	College plus training	Good	**6**:103
Cardiac Perfusionist	Median—$96,144 per year	College plus training	Excellent	**7**:100
Cartographer	Varies—see profile	College	Good	**1**:108
Ceramic Engineer	Median—$67,110 per year	College or advanced degree	Good	**6**:105
⭐ Chemical Engineer	Median—$76,770 per year	College or advanced degree	Good	**6**:107
Chemist	Median—$56,060 per year	Advanced degree	Fair	**6**:110
⭐ Chiropractor	Median—$69,910 per year	Advanced degree; license	Good	**7**:101
City Manager	Median—$88,695 per year	College	Fair	**11**:84
Civil Engineer	Varies—see profile	College plus training; license	Good	**4**:128
Civil Engineering Technician	Median—$38,480 per year	Two-year college	Good	**4**:131
Clinical Laboratory Technologist	Average—$45,730 per year	College plus training	Excellent	**7**:103
College Student Personnel Worker	Median—$45,636 to $75,245 per year	College	Good	**11**:86
College/University Administrator	Varies—see profile	Advanced degree	Good	**3**:109
Compensation and Benefits Analyst	Median—$47,490 per year	College	Very good	**3**:111
Composer	Median—$34,570 per year	Varies—see profile	Fair	**2**:96

⭐ High-growth job

Job	Salary	Education/ Training	Employment Outlook	Volume: Page
Computer and Information Systems Manager	Median—$92,570 per year	College plus training	Very good	**3:**113
Computer Consultant	Median—$85,904 per year	College	Excellent	**3:**115
Computer Control Programmer	Median—$19.31 per hour	Varies—see profile	Good	**9:**65
⭐ Computer Database Administrator	Median—$60,650 per year	College	Excellent	**3:**116
⭐ Computer Network Technician	Median—$60,600 per year	College	Excellent	**3:**118
Computer Programmer	Median—$62,890 per year	College	Fair	**3:**120
Computer Security Specialist	Varies —see profile	College	Very good	**3:**123
Computer Software Documentation Writer	Median—$53,490 per year	College	Very good	**3:**124
⭐ Computer Software Engineer	Median—$80,519 per year	College	Excellent	**3:**126
Computer Support Specialist	Median—$40,430 per year	Varies—see profile	Very good	**3:**129
⭐ Computer Systems Analyst	Median—$66,480 per year	College	Excellent	**3:**131
Conservation Scientist	Median—$52,480 per year	College	Poor	**1:**110
Consumer Advocate	Average—$30,000 to $70,000 per year	College	Varies—see profile	**5:**97
Controller	Median—$167,898 per year	College	Good	**3:**133
Corporate Travel Manager	Median—$72,540 per year	College plus training	Good	**8:**99
⭐ Cost Estimator	Median—$49,940 per year	College plus training	Very good	**4:**132
Credit Manager	Median—$72,329 per year	College	Good	**3:**135
Criminologist	Varies—see profile	Advanced degree	Poor	**11:**87
Crop Scientist	Median—$48,670 per year	College	Poor	**1:**113
Demographer	Average—$53,160 per year	Advanced degree	Good	**6:**112
⭐ Dentist	Median—$129,920 per year	Advanced degree	Good	**7:**105
Dermatologist	Median—$193,870 per year	Advanced degree plus training	Excellent	**7:**107
Desktop Publisher	Median—$32,340 per year	College plus training	Very good	**2:**97
⭐ Dietitian and Nutritionist	Median—$43,630 per year	College plus training	Very good	**5:**99
Director	Median—$52,840 per year	Varies—see profile	Good	**2:**100
⭐ Distribution Manager	Average—$73,050 per year	College or advanced degree plus training	Good	**10:**84
Divorce Mediator	Varies—see profile	College	Good	**5:**101
⭐ E-Commerce Marketing Manager	Median—$84,246 per year	College or advanced degree	Very good	**10:**85
Economist	Median—$72,780 per year	Advanced degree	Fair	**6:**114
Editor, Book	Median—$43,890 per year	College	Good	**2:**102
Editor, Copy	Varies—see profile	College	Varies—see profile	**2:**104
Editor, Magazine	Median—$43,620 per year	College	Good	**2:**106

⭐ High-growth job

Job	Salary	Education/ Training	Employment Outlook	Volume: Page
Editor, Newspaper	Median—$43,620 per year	College	Fair	2:108
⭐ Electrical and Electronics Engineer	Median—$71,610 to $75,770 per year	College or advanced degree	Good	6:117
Embalmer	Average—$34,690 per year	High school plus training; license	Good	5:103
Employee Benefits Manager	Median—$66,530 per year	College	Very good	3:137
Employment Counselor	Median—$45,570 per year	College	Very good	3:139
Entomologist	Median—$51,200 per year	Advanced degree	Good	6:120
⭐ Environmental Engineer	Median—$66,480 per year	College	Excellent	1:114
Environmental Scientist	Median—$51,080 per year	College	Good	1:116
Epidemiologist	Median—$54,800 per year	Advanced degree	Good	7:108
Ergonomist	$40,000 to $72,000 per year	Advanced degree	Very good	6:122
⭐ Executive Search Recruiter	Median—$70,192 per year	College	Very good	3:140
Family and Consumer Science Researcher	Median—$54,500 per year	College	Fair	5:105
Family and Consumer Science Teacher	Varies—see profile	College	Fair	5:107
Farm Manager	Median—$54,900 per year	College	Poor	1:118
Farmer, Cotton, Tobacco, and Peanut	Varies—see profile	Varies—see profile	Poor	1:119
Farmer, Dairy	Varies—see profile	Varies—see profile	Poor	1:121
Farmer, Fruit	Varies—see profile	Varies—see profile	Poor	1:123
Farmer, Grain	Varies—see profile	Varies—see profile	Poor	1:125
Farmer, Livestock	Varies—see profile	Varies—see profile	Poor	1:127
Fashion Designer	Median—$55,840 per year	Two-year or four-year degree	Fair	2:111
FBI Special Agent	Varies—see profile	College plus training	Fair	11:89
Fiction Writer	Varies—see profile	Varies—see profile	Fair	2:112
Financial Analyst	Median—$61,910 per year	College	Good	3:142
Financial Planner	Median—$62,700 per year	Varies—see profile	Very good	3:144
Fire Protection Engineer	Median—$80,000 to $100,000 per year	College or advanced degree	Very good	6:124
⭐ Fleet Manager	Varies—see profile	College	Good	12:120
Flight Engineer	Median—$129,250 per year	College plus training; license	Fair	12:121
Flight Instructor	Median—$31,530 per year	Varies—see profile	Good	12:123
Food Scientist	Median—$49,610 per year	College	Fair	1:129
Foreign Service Worker	Varies—see profile	Varies—see profile	Fair	11:91
Forensic Scientist	Varies—see profile	College or advanced degree	Good	6:126
Forester	Average—$48,230 per year	College	Poor	1:131
Fund-Raiser	Median—$60,259 per year	College	Good	11:93

⭐ High-growth job

Job	Salary	Education/Training	Employment Outlook	Volume: Page
Funeral Director	Median—$45,960 per year	Voc/technical school; license	Good	**5:**109
General Contractor	Median—$69,870 per year	Varies—see profile	Good	**4:**135
General Manager	Median—$77,420 per year	College	Good	**3:**146
Genetic Engineering Research Scientist	Median—$65,110 per year	Advanced degree	Very good	**6:**127
Geographer	Median—$58,970 per year	College	Fair	**1:**133
Geologist	Median—$68,570 per year	College	Fair	**1:**135
Geophysicist	Varies—see profile	College	Fair	**1:**136
Geriatric Social Worker	Median—$40,080 per year	Varies—see profile	Excellent	**7:**109
Geriatrician	Median—$166,420 per year	Advanced degree plus training	Excellent	**7:**111
Government Inspector and Examiner	Median—$32,000 to $40,000 per year	Varies—see profile	Good	**11:**95
Health and Safety Engineer	Median—$63,730 per year	College	Fair	**1:**138
Health Educator	Median—$52,639 per year	Advanced degree	Very good	**7:**113
Highway Engineer	Varies—see profile	College	Fair	**4:**137
Historian	Median—$44,490 per year	Advanced degree	Fair	**6:**130
Human Resources Manager	Median—$81,810 per year	College	Very good	**3:**148
⭐ Hydrologist	Median—$61,510 per year	Advanced degree	Excellent	**1:**140
Illustrator and Graphic Designer	Varies—see profile	College plus training	Varies—see profile	**2:**114
Import and Export Worker	Varies—see profile	Varies—see profile	Good	**10:**87
Industrial Designer	Median—$52,310 per year	College	Good	**9:**66
⭐ Industrial Engineer	Median—$65,020 per year	College	Good	**9:**68
Industrial Hygienist	Median—$69,103 per year	College	Good	**6:**132
Industrial Production Manager	Median—$73,000 per year	College	Fair	**9:**70
Industrial Traffic Manager	Median—$71,932 per year	College	Good	**12:**125
⭐ Instructional Designer	Varies—see profile	College	Very good	**2:**117
Insurance Underwriter	Median—$48,550 per year	College	Fair	**3:**150
Interior Designer	Median—$40,670 per year	College	Good	**5:**111
Internal Revenue Service Worker	Average—$36,963 to $81,417 per year	College plus training	Fair	**11:**97
Internet Entrepreneur	Varies—see profile	Varies—see profile	Varies—see profile	**3:**152
Investment Banker	Starting—$45,000 to $85,000 per year	Advanced degree plus training	Good	**3:**155
Judge	Median—$93,070 per year	Advanced degree	Good	**11:**98
Labor Relations Specialist	Starting—$36,967 per year	College	Very Good	**9:**74
Landscape Architect	Median—$53,120 per year	College	Very good	**4:**139
Lawyer	Median—$94,930 per year	Advanced degree	Good	**11:**100

⭐ High-growth job

Job	Salary	Education/ Training	Employment Outlook	Volume: Page
Lawyer, Corporate	Average—$50,000 to $90,000 per year	Advanced degree	Good	11:102
Lawyer, Public Service	Varies—see profile	Advanced degree	Good	11:104
Librarian, Public	Median—$42,500 per year	Advanced degree	Fair	11:106
Librarian, School	Varies—see profile	Varies—see profile	Fair	11:108
Librarian, Special	Median—$60,000 per year	Varies—see profile	Fair	11:110
Linguist	Varies—see profile	College or advanced degree	Good	6:135
Literary or Theatrical Agent	Varies—see profile	College plus training	Good	2:119
⭐ Lodging Manager	Median—$39,100 per year	College plus training	Good	8:101
Management Analyst and Consultant	Median—$63,450 per year	Advanced degree plus experience	Good	3:156
Marine Engineer	Median—$72,040 per year	College	Poor	1:142
Marketing Director	Median—$138,470 per year	Advanced degree plus training	Very good	10:89
⭐ Marketing Research Worker	Varies—see profile	College	Very good	10:91
Marriage and Family Counselor	Median—$38,980 per year	College	Very good	11:112
Mathematician	Median—$81,240 per year	Advanced degree	Poor	6:137
⭐ Mechanical Engineer	Median—$66,320 per year	College or advanced degree	Good	6:139
Media Buyer	Median—$56,279 per year	College plus training	Very good	10:94
Medical and Health Services Manager	Median—$67,430 per year	Advanced degree	Good	7:114
Medical Illustrator	Median—$59,000 per year	Advanced degree	Good	7:117
Medical Physicist	Median—$124,532 per year	Advanced degree	Good	7:119
Meeting and Convention Planner	Median—$39,620 per year	Varies—see profile	Very good	8:103
Merchant Marine Captain	Median—$24.20 per hour	Advanced degree	Poor	12:127
Merchant Marine Engineer	Median—$26.42 per hour	Academy	Poor	12:129
Merchant Marine Purser	Average—$30,514 per year	Varies—see profile	Poor	12:130
Merchant Marine Radio Officer	Median—$14 per hour	Varies—see profile	Fair	12:132
Metallurgical Engineer	Median—$67,110 per year	College or advanced degree	Fair	6:142
Meteorologist	Median—$70,100 per year	College	Good	1:144
Microbiologist	Median—$54,840 per year	Advanced degree	Good	6:145
Microwave Engineer	Median—$75,770 per year	College or advanced degree	Very good	6:148
Mining Engineer	Median—$64,690 per year	College	Poor	1:145
Multimedia Developer	Varies—see profile	College	Good	2:121
Museum Conservator	Median—$32,860 per year	Advanced degree plus training	Good	8:104
Museum Curator	Median—$43,920 per year	Advanced degree	Good	8:105
Musician	Varies—see profile	Varies—see profile	Good	2:123

⭐ High-growth job

Job	Salary	Education/ Training	Employment Outlook	Volume: Page
Natural Science Manager	Median—$88,660 per year	College	Good	1:147
Naval Architect	Median—$72,040 per year	College	Fair	1:149
☆ Network Administrator	Median—$58,190 per year	Varies—see profile	Excellent	3:159
News Reporter and Correspondent	Median—$31,320 per year	College	Poor	2:126
Nuclear Engineer	Median—$84,880 per year	College or advanced degree	Fair	6:150
Occupational Health and Safety Specialist	Median—$51,570 per year	College	Good	1:150
☆ Occupational Therapist	Median—$54,660 per year	Advanced degree	Excellent	7:121
Oceanographer	Varies—see profile	College	Good	1:152
Office Manager	Median—$41,030 per year	College	Fair	3:161
Office Planner	Median—$40,670 per year	College	Good	3:163
Operations Research Analyst	Median—$60,190 per year	College	Fair	3:166
Ophthalmologist	Median—$199,423 per year	Advanced degree plus training	Very good	7:122
Optometrist	Median—$88,410 per year	College plus training	Good	7:124
Organizational Developer	Median—$61,769 per year	College	Excellent	3:168
Orthoptist	Average—$45,000 to $50,000 per year	College plus training	Excellent	7:126
Orthotist and Prosthetist	Median—$59,540 per year	College degree	Good	7:128
Osteopathic Physician	Median—$156,010 per year	Advanced degree plus training	Very good	7:129
☆ Outplacement Consultant	Median—$52,800 per year	College	Excellent	3:170
Park Naturalist	Median—$43,118 per year	College	Poor	1:154
Park Ranger	Median—$30,000 per year	College	Poor	8:107
Parole Officer	Median—$39,600 per year	College plus training	Good	11:114
Pathologist	Varies—see profile	Advanced degree	Very good	6:152
☆ Personal Exercise Trainer	Median—$25,470 per year	High school and certification	Excellent	5:114
Petroleum Engineer	Median—$88,500 per year	College	Varies—see profile	1:155
Pharmacist	Median—$84,900 per year	Advanced degree	Very good	7:131
Pharmacologist	Average—$91,407 to $118,828 per year	Advanced degree	Very good	7:133
Photo Researcher	Varies—see profile	College	Good	2:129
Photonics Engineer	Varies—see profile	College or advanced degree	Excellent	6:155
☆ Physical Therapist	Median—$60,180 per year	Advanced degree	Very good	7:134
Physician	Varies—see profile	Advanced degree plus training	Good	7:136
☆ Physician Assistant	Median—$69,410 per year	Varies—see profile	Excellent	7:139
Physicist	Median—$87,450 per year	Advanced degree	Fair	6:158
Podiatrist	Median—$94,400 per year	Advanced degree	Good	7:140

☆ High-growth job

Job	Salary	Education/Training	Employment Outlook	Volume: Page
Political Consultant	Varies—see profile	Advanced degree	Very good	11:115
Political Scientist	Median—$86,750 per year	Advanced degree	Fair	6:160
Probation Officer	Median—$39,600 per year	College plus training	Good	11:117
Producer	Varies—see profile	Varies—see profile	Good	2:130
Product Manager	Median—$95,900 per year, including bonuses	College or advanced degree plus training	Very good	10:95
Professional Athlete	Median—$48,310 per year	Varies—see profile	Good	8:109
Property, Real Estate, and Community Association Manager	Median—$39,980 per year	College	Good	8:111
Psychiatrist	Median—$180,000 per year	Advanced degree plus training	Very good	7:142
Psychologist	Median—$54,950 per year	Advanced degree	Good	7:143
☆ Public Relations Manager	Median—$70,000 per year	College plus training	Very good	2:132
☆ Public Relations Specialist	Median—$43,830 per year	College	Excellent	2:135
Purchasing Agent	Median—$47,680 per year	College or advanced degree	Fair	10:97
Quality Control Manager	Median—$71,683 per year	College or advanced degree	Fair	9:76
Real Estate Appraiser	Median—$43,390 per year	2- or 4-year college plus training; license	Very good	10:99
Recreational Therapist	Median—$32,900 per year	College plus training	Fair	7:145
☆ Recruiter	Median—$41,190 per year	College	Very good	3:171
☆ Registered Nurse	Median—$52,330 per year	Varies—see profile	Excellent	7:147
☆ Rehabilitation Counselor	Median—$27,870 per year	College plus training	Very good	11:119
Religious Vocation	Varies—see profile	Advanced degree	Varies—see profile	11:120
☆ Restaurant Manager	Median—$41,490 per year	High school or college plus training	Good	8:113
Resume Writer	Varies—see profile	College	Fair	3:173
Retail Buyer	Median—$42,230 per year	College plus training	Fair	10:101
Robotics Engineer	$50,000 to $60,000	Advanced degree	Very Good	6:162
Safety Engineer	Median—$63,730 per year	College	Good	6:164
☆ Sales Engineer	Median—$70,620 per year	College plus training	Good	10:104
☆ Sales Manager	Median—$84,220 per year	College plus training	Very good	10:105
School Administrator	Median—$68,340 per year	Varies—see profile	Fair	11:122
School Counselor	Median—$45,570 per year	College plus training	Very good	11:124
School Media Specialist	Median—$45,900 per year	Advanced degree	Fair	11:126
Scriptwriter	Varies—see profile	Varies—see profile	Good	2:137
Securities Broker	Median—$69,200 per year	College plus training	Good	3:174
Set and Exhibit Designer	Median—$35,890 per year	2- or 4-year degree	Fair or poor	2:139

☆ High-growth job

Job	Salary	Education/ Training	Employment Outlook	Volume: Page
Sign Language and Oral Interpreter	Median—$16.28 per hour	Varies—see profile	Very good	**2:141**
Singer	Varies—see profile	Varies—see profile	Good	**2:143**
⭐ **Social Worker**	Median—$34,820 per year	Advanced degree	Excellent	**11:128**
Sociologist	Median—$57,870 per year	Advanced degree	Fair	**6:167**
Software Trainer	Median—$44,570 per year	College	Very good	**3:177**
Soil Scientist	Median—$51,200 per year	College	Fair	**1:157**
Specification Writer	Median—$45,015 per year	College plus training	Varies—see profile	**4:142**
Speech-Language Pathologist	Median—$52,410 per year	Advanced degree	Good	**7:150**
Sports Management Professional	Varies—see profile	Varies—see profile	Good	**10:107**
Statistician	Median—$58,620 per year	College	Fair	**3:179**
⭐ **Store Manager**	Median—$48,880 to $57,512 per year	Varies—see profile	Good	**10:109**
Surgeon	Median—$282,504 per year	Advanced degree plus training	Very good	**7:152**
Surveyor	Median—$42,980 per year	College; license	Good	**4:144**
Systems Engineer	Mean—$74,140 per year	College or advanced degree	Good	**6:169**
Teacher, College	Average—$51,800 per year	Advanced degree	Very good	**11:129**
Teacher, Preschool, Kindergarten, and Elementary	Varies—see profile	College plus training	Good	**11:132**
Teacher, Secondary School	Median—$41,400 to $45,970 per year	College plus training	Good	**11:134**
Technical Writer	Median—$53,490 per year	College	Very good	**2:146**
Telecommunications Consultant	Median—$65,130 per year	College	Excellent	**6:172**
Telecommunications Design Engineer	Median—$50,846 per year	Varies—see profile	Fair	**6:173**
Trade Show Manager	Median—$58,748 per year	Varies—see profile	Very good	**10:111**
Traffic Engineer	Median—$64,230 per year	College	Good	**12:133**
Training and Development Specialist	Median—$44,570 per year	College	Very good	**3:181**
Translator or Interpreter	Varies—see profile	College	Very good	**2:148**
Transportation Engineer	Median—$64,230 per year	College	Good	**12:135**
Travel Agent, Retail and Wholesale	Median—$27,640 per year	Varies—see profile	Poor to fair	**8:115**
⭐ **Urban and Regional Planner**	Median—$53,450 per year	Advanced degree	Very good	**11:136**
⭐ **Usability Researcher**	Varies—see profile	Varies—see profile	Very good	**2:151**
⭐ **Veterinarian**	Median—$66,590 per year	Advanced degree	Very good	**1:159**
Vocational Counselor	Median—$45,570 per year	College	Very good	**11:138**
⭐ **Web Designer**	Median—$59,894 per year	Varies—see profile	Excellent	**2:152**
⭐ **Webmaster**	Median—$66,105 per year	Varies—see profile	Excellent	**2:155**
Zookeeper	Median—$14 per hour	2- or 4-year college	Good	**8:117**
Zoologist	Median—$50,330 per year	Advanced degree	Good	**6:175**

⭐ **High-growth job**

The American Workforce: 2004-14

Bureau of Labor Statistics

The U.S. Department of Labor's Bureau of Labor Statistics (BLS) regularly predicts where future job growth is expected by industry and occupation—and what the demographic makeup of the labor force pursuing those jobs is likely to be. Becoming familiar with these projections can help you make decisions about your career.

PROJECTED CHANGES IN LABOR FORCE PARTICIPATION

Between 2004 and 2014 the U.S. labor force—those people working or looking for work—will continue to grow at a similar rate as during the previous ten-year period. By 2014, the supply of workers is expected to reach 162.3 million, an increase of 17.4 million, or 12 percent, from 2004 levels. Between 1994 and 2004 the labor force grew by 14.4 million, an 11.3 percent increase. However, by 2014 the labor force will have a somewhat different composition than it did in 2004—it will be more racially and ethnically diverse, more evenly split between men and women, and will be older.

Gender

The women's labor force is projected to increase by 10.9 percent between 2004 and 2014, which is lower than the growth of 13.6 percent between 1994 and 2004. However, women's labor force participation will increase faster than will men's. Consequently, women are projected to increase as a portion of the labor force from 46.4 percent in 2004 to 46.8 percent in 2014, while men's presence in the labor force will decrease, from 53.6 percent in 2004 to 53.2 percent in 2014.

Although the number of men in the labor force is projected to grow between 2004 and 2014, the growth rate will be slower than it was in the past. This reflects, in part, declining employment in good-paying production jobs in manufacturing and a continued shift in demand for workers from the goods-producing sector to the service-producing sector. Men with little education and training may find it increasingly difficult to find jobs that match their experience.

Age

The projected labor force growth will be affected by the aging of the baby-boom generation, people born between 1946 and 1964. By the end of the 2004

Adapted from articles in the Monthly Labor Review, vol. 128, no. 11, November 2005. These articles include "A Summary of BLS Projections to 2014," by Norman C. Saunders; "The U.S. Economy to 2014," by Betty W. Su; "Labor Force Projects to 2014: Retiring Boomers," by Mitra Toossi; "Industry Output and Employment Projections to 2014," by Jay M. Berman; "Occupational Employment Projections to 2014," by Daniel E. Hecker. All are available online at http://www.bls.gov/opub/mlr/2005/11/contents.htm.

Civilian Labor Force by Sex, Age, Race, and Hispanic Origin, 1984–2014*

Group	Number of Jobs (in thousands)				Percent Distribution				Annual Growth Rate (percent)		
	1984	1994	2004	2014*	1984	1994	2004	2014*	1984–1994	1994–2004	2004–2014*
Total, 16 years and older	113,544	131,056	147,401	162,100	100.0	100.0	100.0	100.0	1.4	1.2	1.0
Men	63,835	70,817	78,980	86,194	56.2	54.0	53.6	53.2	1.0	1.1	0.9
Women	49,709	60,239	68,421	75,906	43.8	46.0	46.4	46.8	1.9	1.3	1.0
White	98,492	111,082	121,086	129,936	86.7	84.8	82.1	80.2	1.2	0.9	0.7
Black	12,033	14,502	16,638	19,433	10.6	11.1	11.3	12.0	1.9	1.4	1.6
Asian	3,019	5,472	6,271	8,304	2.7	4.2	4.3	5.1	6.1	1.4	2.8
All other groups	—	—	3,406	4,427	—	—	2.3	2.7	—	—	2.7
Hispanic origin	7,451	11,975	19,272	25,760	6.6	9.1	13.1	15.9	4.9	4.9	2.9
Other than Hispanic origin	106,093	119,081	128,129	136,340	93.4	90.9	86.9	84.1	1.2	0.7	0.6
White non-Hispanic	91,296	100,462	103,202	106,373	80.4	76.7	70.0	65.6	1.0	0.3	0.3

*Projected

SOURCE: Bureau of Labor Statistics, *Monthly Labor Review*, November 2005.

to 2014 period, most of the baby boomers will have turned fifty-five. Consequently, the age fifty-five and older segment of the labor force is expected to grow most rapidly, increasing by 11.3 million, or 49.1 percent. Because of the aging of the American population, this segment of the labor force will increase at almost five times the rate of the overall labor force (10 percent). The numbers of those twenty-five to fifty-four years of age in the labor force will grow by only 3.4 percent, a significantly lower growth than in the previous decade (8.8 percent). The growth rate of the youth labor force, workers between the ages of sixteen and twenty-four, will actually decrease between 2004 and 2014 by 0.5 percent.

Race and Hispanic Origin

The federal government today recognizes four racial groups: white, black or African American, Asian, and all other groups (Native Americans, Pacific Islanders, and those reporting two or more races). Those groups may be further broken down into Hispanic and non-Hispanic groups. Although non-Hispanic whites will continue to hold the majority of jobs in 2014 (65.6 percent), the workplace will be more racially and ethnically diverse. Hispanic representation in the labor force is expected to increase by 33.7 percent between 2004 and 2014, Asian representation is expected to increase by 32.4 percent, and African American representation is expected to increase by 16.8 percent. In contrast, white, non-Hispanic representation in the labor force is expected to increase by only 3.1 percent between 2004 and 2014.

The number of African Americans in the American workforce is growing rapidly, but the number of Hispanic workers surpassed the number of African American workers by 2004 (19.3 million vs. 16.6 million). Hispanics will continue to increase their presence in the workforce between 2004 and 2014. The Hispanic population is now the largest minority in the U.S. population and is expected to grow faster than the African American population because of high

Employment by Major Industry Sector, 1994–2014*

Industry	Number of Jobs (in thousands)			Jobs Gained or Lost (in thousands)		Average Annual Rate of Change (percent)	
	1994	2004	2014*	1994–2004	2004–2014*	1994–2004	2000–2014*
Total	129,245.9	145,612.3	164,539.9	16,366.4	18,927.6	1.2	1.2
Nonagriculture wage and salary	114,983.8	132,191.7	150,876.9	17,207.9	18,685.2	1.4	1.3
Goods-producing, excluding agriculture	22,691.6	21,817.3	21,787.3	-874.3	-30.0	-0.4	0.0
Service-providing	92,292.2	110,374.4	129,089.6	18,082.2	18,715.2	1.8	1.6
Agriculture, forestry, fishing, and hunting	2,890.1	2,139.9	1,910.0	-750.2	-229.9	-3.0	-1.1
Nonagriculture self-employed and unpaid family workers	9,360.0	9,556.4	10,011.9	196.4	455.5	0.2	0.5

* Projected

SOURCE: Bureau of Labor Statistics, *Monthly Labor Review*, November 2005.

immigration and a higher-than-average birthrate among Hispanics. By 2014, Hispanics are expected to make up 15.9 percent of the workforce while African Americans are expected to make up 12 percent of the workforce.

The number of Asians in the workforce is also growing rapidly, but this group will remain the smallest racial/ethnic group in the labor force well beyond 2014. In 2004 Asians made up 4.3 percent of the workforce; by 2014 their share will increase to 5.1 percent.

INDUSTRY EMPLOYMENT

The total number of jobs over the 2004 to 2014 period is expected to increase by 13 percent, or 18.9 million, from 145.6 million in 2004 to 164.5 million in 2014. This growth rate is slightly higher than the previous ten-year period. Between 1994 and 2004, growth was 12.7 percent, and the economy gained 16.3 million additional jobs.

Of the 18.9 million new jobs projected for the period from 2004 to 2014, nearly all (91.7 percent) will be nonagriculture jobs earning wages or salaries. There will be 455,500 new nonagriculture, self-employed, and unpaid family worker jobs, an increase of 4.8 percent, a substantially larger increase than in the 1994 to 2004 period (2.1 percent). The agriculture, forestry, fishing, and hunting industry will lose 229,900 jobs, a decrease of 10.7 percent. While this is a substantial decrease, it is significantly less than the decrease in the previous decade, when the industry lost 26 percent of its jobs.

According to the BLS, the service-providing sector will account for most of the non-farm wage and salary job growth between 2004 and 2014. The goods-producing sector will lose thirty thousand jobs. In this sector, only construction will add a significant number of jobs, offsetting declines in mining and manufacturing.

Ten Industries with the Fastest Wage and Salary Employment Growth, 2004–2014*

Industry Description	Number of Jobs (in thousands)		Jobs Gained (in thousands)	Percent Increase
	2004	2014*	2004–2014*	2004–2014*
Home health care services	773.2	1,310.3	537.1	5.4
Software publishers	238.7	400.0	161.3	5.3
Management, scientific, and technical consulting services	779.0	1,250.2	471.2	4.8
Residential care facilities	1,239.6	1,840.3	600.7	4.0
Facilities support services	115.6	170.0	54.4	3.9
Employment services	3,470.3	5,050.2	1,579.9	3.8
Independent artists, writers, and performers	41.9	60.8	18.9	3.8
Office administrative services	319.4	449.9	130.5	3.5
Computer sysytems design and related services	1,147.4	1,600.3	452.9	3.4
Outpatient, laboratory, and other ambulatory care services	836.1	1,160.4	324.3	3.3

Projected

SOURCE: Bureau of Labor Statistics, *Monthly Labor Review*, November 2005.

Service-Producing Industries

The service-producing sector is very diverse, covering a wide array of services to individuals and businesses. Almost all of the total employment increases expected by 2014 are from industry divisions within this sector. Professional and business services, health care and social assistance, and educational services will see the highest rates of growth by 2014.

Professional and Business Services Professional and business services will add the most number of jobs to the economy between 2004 and 2014; 4.6 million new jobs will be created, for a projected annual employment growth rate of 2.5 percent. The demand for employment services, one of the fastest growing industries, will fuel this growth with a projected addition of 1.6 million jobs, a 45.5 percent increase between 2004 and 2014. Interest in the industry, which includes temporary staffing services, reflects the growing trend among U.S. businesses to hire workers on an as-needed basis. Temporary workers tend to have low wages, low job stability, and poor job benefits, although this may change as the industry becomes more important to the American way of doing business.

Health Care and Social Assistance Employment in the health care and social assistance industry will increase by 30.3 percent between 2004 and 2014, an annual growth rate of 2.8 percent. This sector will add 3.6 million jobs to the economy. Factors contributing to the overall growth of the health industry group include the aging population, which continues to require more medical services, and the increased use of innovative medical technology for diagnosis and treatment. In an effort to contain costs, patients are increasingly being moved out of hospitals and into outpatient facilities and nursing homes, leading for an increase in demand for staff for those facilities. The health industry group includes medical care at private hospitals, offices of health practitioners, and nursing and personal care facilities. Jobs in the home health care services industry, providing in-home health services like nursing and physical therapy, will increase at a huge 5.4 percent annual rate, the highest annual growth rate among the nation's employers.

Five of the ten fastest-growing occupations are in health services. Employment of medical assistants is expected to increase by 52 percent, of physician assistants by 50 percent, of physical therapist assistants by 44 percent, of dental hygienists by 43 percent, and of dental assistants by 43 percent. More than 400,000 new jobs will be created in these five occupations alone by 2014. In addition, 703,000 new jobs will be created for registered nurses, for an employment increase of 29 percent; 325,000 new jobs will be created for nursing aides, orderlies, and attendants, for an employment increase of 22 percent.

Employment in social services will also increase between 2004 and 2014. The expansion of services for older people, the sick and physically disabled, mentally ill individuals, substance abusers, and children is the driving force behind this industry's growth. Although the projected 3 percent annual growth rate is lower than the 4.4 percent annual growth rate of the 1994 to 2004 period, 740,000 new jobs are expected to be created by 2014. Employment in rehabilitation services will lead the subsector, expected to increase at a 2.9 percent annual rate, for a resulting 445,000 new jobs by 2014.

Educational Services Educational services will grow at the greatest annual rate (2.9 percent) between 2004 and 2014. These occupations will grow by almost a third (32.5 percent), although they will grow at a slower rate than during the 1994 to 2004 period, when these occupations increased by 46 percent. This sector includes private education at the primary through college levels. More than 50 percent of this sector's projected growth will be at postsecondary schools—private junior colleges, colleges, universities and professional schools—as children of the baby boomer generation reach college age. Private colleges, universities, and professional schools will add 503,000 new jobs by 2014. Other educational services, including computer training, technical and trade schools, tutoring services, and educational testing services, will grow at a sector-leading rate of 3.2 percent annually, adding an additional 175,000 jobs by 2014.

Other service-providing industries that will experience significant growth during the 2004 to 2014 period include leisure and hospitality, expected to add 2.2 million jobs (an increase of 17.7 percent); state and local government, expected to add 2.1 million jobs (an increase of 11.3 percent); the retail trade, expected to add 1.6 million new jobs (an increase of 11 percent); financial activities, expected to add 849,400 new jobs (an increase of 10.5 percent); transportation and warehousing, expected to add 505,900 new jobs (an increase of 11.9 percent); and information services, expected to add 363,800 new jobs (an increase of 11.6 percent).

Goods-Producing Industries

By 2014 the transformation of the U.S. economy from a goods-producing economy to a service-producing economy will be even more apparent. Nine of the ten industries projected to have the most rapidly declining employment between 2004 and 2014 are from the goods-producing (nonagriculture) sector. Although manufacturing output will remain strong, improved productivity (increasing output with fewer workers) will be a major factor in the loss of jobs in this sector. Construction is the only goods-producing industry sector expected to see an employment increase.

Mining A projected decline of 46,000 wage and salary jobs in the mining industry will continue a long-term trend. Employment in the coal mining industry, metal mining industry, and oil and gas extraction industry will all decline. Employment in metal ore mining will decline rapidly, from 27,300 jobs in 2004 to 19,300 jobs in 2014, an annual decline of 3.4 percent. Employment in coal mining will decrease from 71,700 in 2004 to 55,000 in 2014, a 2.6 percent annual rate of decline. International competition and global price pressures, combined with advances in technology, increased automation, and industry consolidation, account for the reduction in the number of metal ore mining and coal mining jobs. Employment in the oil and gas extraction industry will decline from 123,100 in 2004 to 107,000 in 2014 due to limited potential resources, foreign competition, and environmental regulations. The annual rate of decline, however, will fall from the average of 2.7 percent in the 1994 to 2004 period to an average of 1.4 percent from 2004 to 2014.

Manufacturing The long-term decline in manufacturing jobs is expected to slow during the 2004 to 2014 period. Most manufacturing industries will experience a pattern of strong output and growth in productivity, on the one hand, and employment declines on the other (though some will see an increase in employment). Overall, wage and salary employment in manufacturing is expected to decline from 14.3 million jobs in 2004 to 13.6 million jobs by 2014, for a net loss of 776,600 jobs, or a 5.4 percent decrease. In the previous ten-year period, employment fell by 2.7 million jobs, a decrease of 15.8 percent. Manufacturing's share of total employment will drop from 13.2 percent in 1994 to only 8.2 percent by 2014.

The transportation equipment manufacturing subsector, including motor vehicle, aerospace, railroad, and ship production, is the largest manufacturing employer. While this sector's production output will increase significantly, its employment will only moderately increase, from 1.8 million jobs in 2004 to 1.9 million jobs in 2014. The workers in this industry tend to be older than average, and as these workers retire from the workforce, they will need to be replaced.

Despite a continuing demand for personal and business computers, technological advances and productivity gains in the computer and electronic product

Ten Industries with the Most Rapidly Declining Wage and Salary Employment Growth, 2004–2014*

Industry Description	Number of Jobs (in thousands)		Jobs Lost (in thousands)	Percent Decrease
	2004	2014*	2004–2014*	2004–2014*
Cut and sew apparel manufacturing	219.9	80.0	-139.9	-9.6
Fiber, yarn, and thread mills	54.4	25.0	-29.4	-7.5
Apparel knitting mills	42.0	20.0	-22.0	-7.2
Textile and fabric finishing and fabric coating mills	68.5	35.0	-33.5	-6.5
Fabric mills	115.7	60.0	-55.7	-6.4
Tobacco manufacturing	29.4	16.6	-12.8	-5.6
Footwear manufacturing	19.4	12.5	-6.9	-4.3
Apparel accessories amd other apparel manufacturing	23.0	15.0	-8.0	-4.2
Basic chemical manufacturing	156.1	110.0	-46.1	-3.4
Metal ore mining	27.3	19.3	-8.0	-3.4

Projected

SOURCE: Bureau of Labor Statistics, *Monthly Labor Review*, November 2005.

manufacturing subsector will lead to a projected annual decrease in employment of 0.7 percent, from 1.3 million in 2004 to about 1.2 million in 2014. The first half of this decade has seen a saturation of the computer market, which may also affect future employment in the industry. Employment in the computer and peripheral equipment manufacturing subsector will also decrease about 1.9 percent annually, from 212,100 in 2004 to 175,000 in 2014. Employment in the communications equipment manufacturing subsector will decrease annually by about 1.1 percent, from 150,500 jobs in 2004 to 135,000 jobs in 2014.

Highly labor-intensive, nondurable goods industries, like the apparel and textile subsectors, will suffer from the largest numerical decline in employment. Employment in apparel manufacturing will decline by more than half, from 284,900 in 2004 to 115,000 in 2014, an annual decrease of about 8.7 percent. This is due in large part to changing trade regulations and increasing competition from imports. The slowdown in population growth during the projection period is also expected to decrease consumer demand for clothing. Employment in textile mills, as well, will decline by half, from 238,600 in 2004 to 120,000 in 2014, an annual rate of decline of 6.6 percent. Jobs assembling apparel will continue to be lost to offshore workers.

Construction The construction industry group is expected to gain about 792,400 jobs between 2004 and 2014. This is the only division of the goods-producing sector forecast to experience employment growth. The demand for new and remodeled nonresidential structures, including industrial plants, nursing homes, medical facilities, and schools, will fuel this growth.

OCCUPATIONAL EMPLOYMENT

The Bureau of Labor Statistics (BLS) projects that between 2004 and 2014, 18.9 million jobs will be added to the economy. This is about 2.6 million more jobs than were added between 1994 and 2004. Consequently, growth rates among major occupational groups will be different from those of the past, resulting in a change in the structure of employment between 2004 and 2014.

Employment Growth by Major Occupational Group, 2004–2014*

Occupational Group	Percent Increase in Number of Jobs
Management, business, and financial occupations	14.4
Professional and related occupations	21.2
Service occupations	19.0
Sales and related occupations	9.6
Office and administrative support occupations	5.8
Farming, fishing, and forestry occupations	−1.3
Construction and extraction occupations	12.0
Installation, maintenance, and repair occupations	11.4
Production occupations	−0.7
Transportation and material moving occupations	11.1

*Projected

SOURCE: Bureau of Labor Statistics, *Monthly Labor Review*, November 2005.

The BLS provides employment projections for ten major occupational groups: management, business, and financial occupations; professional and related occupations; service occupations; sales and related occupations; office and administrative support occupations; farming, fishing, and forestry occupations; construction and extraction occupations; installation, maintenance, and repair occupations; production occupations; and transportation and material moving occupations. This section highlights information on expected job growth for each occupational group for the period 2004 to 2014. It should be noted that an occupational group can be found in more than one industry group. For example, administrative support workers can be found in professional and business services, health care services, government, manufacturing, mining, and in almost all other industries.

Professional and Related Occupations

Employment in professional and related occupations is expected to grow the fastest and increase more—by six million workers—than any other major group during the 2004 to 2014 period. Almost 75 percent of all growth will occur in three of eight occupational subgroups: computer and mathematical occupations, health care practitioners and technical occupations, and education, training, and library occupations.

Computer and mathematical science occupations will add 967,000 jobs, growing fastest among the subgroups. Almost 30 percent of the jobs in this subgroup will be in computer systems design and related services, growing at a rate of more than three times the average for all occupations. Health care practitioner and technical occupations will add 1.8 million jobs, a 25.8 percent increase, nearly twice as fast as the average growth for all occupations. Registered nurses will account for 40 percent of the new jobs in the health care practitioner and technical occupations group. Education, training, and library occupations are projected to add 1.7 million jobs, a 20 percent increase between 2004 and 2014. Jobs for postsecondary teachers are projected to grow particularly rapidly in this group. Community and social services occupations; arts, design, entertainment, sports, and media occupations; architecture and engineering occupations; life, physical, and social science occupations; and legal occupations are all expected to grow as well, at a slower rate.

Service Occupations

Employment in service occupations is expected to show the second-fastest growth rate and the second-largest numerical gain in the number of jobs. Together, professional and related occupations and service occupations should provide about 60 percent of the total job growth from 2004 to 2014. In contrast to workers in professional and related occupations, however, service workers tend to be on the low end of educational attainment and earnings.

Service occupations expected to show the most substantial numbers of additional jobs include food preparation and food service occupations and health care support occupations. Food preparation and serving will add about 1.7 million jobs, growing about 16 percent. Health care support will add about 1.2 million jobs, an increase of about 33.3 percent, two and a half times the average increase for all occupations. Employment in personal care and service, building and grounds cleaning and maintenance, and protective service occupations will also show increases higher than the average for all occupations (21 percent, 17 percent, and 14 percent, respectively).

Management, Business, and Financial

The number of management, business, and financial workers is projected to increase by 2.2 million between 2004 and 2014, a 14.4 percent increase over the period. This represents the third-fastest growth rate among occupational groups. Nearly 25 percent of the new jobs will be in the professional, scientific, and technical services sector, including management, scientific, and technical consulting as well as accounting, tax preparation, bookkeeping, and payroll services. Self-employment among this group is expect to decline by 1.2 percent, especially among farmers and ranchers.

Sales and Related Occupations

Employment in sales and related occupations is projected to increase by 1.5 million workers between 2004 and 2014. This represents a 9.6 percent increase in growth, lower than average for all occupational groups. The relatively small job growth may be attributable, in part, to increased use of automated sales systems in wholesale and retail trade occupations. Sixty percent of the new jobs in this field will be in retail trade.

Installation, Maintenance, and Repairs Occupations

The number of installation, maintenance, and repairs occupations is projected to increase by 657,000 workers, or 11.4 percent, between 2004 and 2014. Roughly one in six new jobs are projected to come from retail trade, which includes motor vehicle and parts dealers. Automotive repair and maintenance and construction will also see increases, while jobs in the manufacturing sector are expected to decline by 17,000.

Office and Administrative Support Occupations

Office and administrative support occupations will employ a projected 25.3 million workers by 2014, making it the third largest occupational group. However, this group will experience a relatively slow rate of growth between 2004 and 2014, increasing by only 5.8 percent. This group includes thirteen of the thirty occupations with the largest expected employment declines, including word processors and typists, stock clerks and order fillers, and secretaries. This decrease will be due to continued office automation and the greater use of temporary workers. Most of the growth in this sector will be in the health care and social assistance sector, the professional, scientific, and technical services sector, and the rapidly growing employment services industry.

Construction and Extraction Occupations

The construction and extraction occupations group will add 931,000 jobs between 2004 and 2014, with 60 percent of those coming from the construction sector. The fastest growth is expected in the employment services industry, while a decline of 12,000 jobs is expected for the mining sector.

Production Occupations

The number of production jobs will increase by 354,000 by 2014. In 2004, 70 percent of these jobs were in manufacturing; the manufacturing sector is projected to decline by more than 500,000 by 2014. However, employment in this sector is projected to grow in the employment services industry and the wholesale and retail trade sector.

Transportation and Material Moving Occupations

Transportation and material moving occupations are expected to see an employment growth of 11.1 percent, or 1.1 million jobs, by 2014. Forty percent of these new jobs will be for truck drivers and driver/sales workers. While employment in railroad occupations will continue to decline and water transportation occupations will grow slowly, 30 percent of the new jobs should be in transportation and warehousing and 25 percent in employment services. Self-employment for these workers, particularly truck drivers, taxi drivers, and chauffeurs, will increase moderately.

Farming, Forestry, Fishing, and Related Occupations

Farming, forestry, fishing, and related occupations will remain the smallest of the major occupational groups through 2014. Employment in this group will decline by 13,000 to only slightly more than 1 million workers, a decline of 1.3 percent.

DETAILED OCCUPATIONS

The BLS projects employment growth for more than seven hundred specific occupations. It should be noted that rate of growth does not equal numerical size; that is, a fast-growing occupation could still have fewer job opportunities than a slow-growing occupation, depending on the size of the occupation's original employment base. For example, the employment of environmental engineers is projected to grow rapidly between 2004 and 2014 (by 30 percent), adding 23,000 jobs. In contrast, the employment of secondary school teachers is expected to grow by less than half that rate (14 percent), but 474,000 new jobs for secondary school teachers will be created during the period.

Fastest-Growing Occupations

Not surprisingly, the fastest-growing occupations are concentrated in rapidly growing industries. Of the thirty fastest-growing occupations, sixteen are health-related, six are related to computers, three are related to the environment, and two are educational occupations. The remaining three are forensic science technicians; employment, recruitment, and placement specialists; and paralegals.

Health-related occupations are growing quickly because of the aging population. As people age, they become more vulnerable to the chronic and debilitating conditions that require therapeutic services and personal and physical care. Another factor is increased use of new medical technologies that treat the kinds of life-threatening and disabling conditions requiring these services. Jobs for home health aides will increase by 56 percent, for medical assistants by 52.1 percent, for physician assistants by 49.6 percent, for physical therapist assistants by 44.2 percent, for dental hygienists by 43 percent, for dental assistants by 42.7 percent, and for personal and home care aides by 41 percent. Nine other health-related occupations will see growth of between 30 percent and 40 percent.

Rapid advances in computer technology and the continuing demand for new computer applications will also increase demand for some computer specialists between 2004 and 2014. Network, systems, and database administrators will see a job growth of 54.6 percent, computer software engineers, applications, will see a job growth of 48.4 percent, and computer software engineers, systems software will see a job growth of 43 percent. Network and computer systems administrators, database administrators, and computer systems analysts will all see job growth of between 30 percent and 40 percent.

Ten Fastest-Growing Occupations, 2004-2014*

Occupation	Number of Jobs (in thousands)		Jobs Gained (in thousands)	Percent Increase
	2004	2014	2004-2014*	2004-2014*
Home health aides	624	974	350	56.0
Network systems and data communications analysts	231	357	126	54.6
Medical assistants	387	589	202	52.1
Physician assistants	62	93	31	49.6
Computer software engineers, applications	460	682	222	48.4
Physical therapist assistants	59	85	26	44.2
Dental hygienists	158	226	68	43.3
Computer software engineers, systems software	340	486	146	43.0
Dental assistants	267	382	114	42.7
Personal and home care aides	701	968	287	41.0

*Projected

SOURCE: Bureau of Labor Statistics, *Monthly Labor Review*, November 2005.

Occupations with the Largest Increase in Number of Jobs

The thirty occupations that are projected to have the largest job growth between 2004 and 2014 will account for 8.8 million new jobs, or 47 percent of the total job growth during the period. Eleven of these occupations are service occupations, including health care support positions, food preparation and serving positions,

Ten Occupations with the Largest Increase in Number of Jobs, 2004-2014*

Occupation	Number of Jobs (in thousands)		Jobs Gained (in thousands)	Percent Increase
	2004	2014*	2004-2014*	2004-2014*
Retail salespersons	4,256	4,992	736	17.3
Registered nurses	2,394	3,096	703	29.4
Postsecondary teachers	1,628	2,153	524	32.2
Customer service representatives	2,063	2,534	471	22.8
Janitors and cleaners, except maids and housekeeping cleaners	2,374	2,813	440	18.5
Waiters and waitresses	2,252	2,627	376	16.7
Combined food preparation and serving workers, including fast food	2,150	2,516	367	17.1
Home health aides	624	974	350	56.0
Nursing aides, orderlies, and attendants	1,455	1,781	325	22.3
General and operations managers	1,807	2,115	308	17.0

*Projected

SOURCE: Bureau of Labor Statistics, *Monthly Labor Review*, November 2005.

building and grounds cleaning and maintenance positions, and personal care and service positions. Office and administrative support occupations, teaching, transportation and material moving occupations, and sales and related occupations also will experience large job growth. The five occupations with the largest projected job growth are retail salespersons (736,000 new jobs), registered nurses (703,000 new jobs), postsecondary teachers (524,000 new jobs), customer service representatives (471,000 new jobs), and janitors and cleaners, excluding maids (440,000 new jobs).

Occupations with the Largest Decrease in Number of Jobs

The BLS focuses on occupations with the largest decline in the number of jobs rather than on those with the fastest rates of decline, because many occupations with the fastest rates of decline are small with small numbers of jobs lost. Industry employment change is a major factor in reducing the number of jobs. For example, the shift from family-operated farms to corporate farms accounts for the decline in the number of farmers and ranchers, the occupation with the greatest projected decline in jobs (155,000 jobs lost).

Change in occupational staffing patterns, especially those resulting from technological advances, is another major factor affecting the number of jobs. For example, advances in computer technologies will result in the loss of jobs within many office and administrative support occupations. Over a hundred thousand jobs (115,000) for stock clerks and order fillers will be lost, 93,000 jobs for file clerks will be lost, and 63,000 jobs for order clerks will be lost. Mail clerks, computer operators, secretaries, word processors and typists, and office machine operators will all lose jobs during the period.

Total Job Openings

In addition to employment growth, the need to replace workers who leave their jobs to retire or to enter other occupations or who leave the labor force for other reasons creates a demand for workers. Thus, even jobs predicted to decline will have some job openings. Overall, between 2004 and 2014, almost twice as many job openings are expected to result from replacement needs (35.8 million) than from employment growth (18.9 million). The number of job openings due to replacement will exceed the number due to growth in occupation groups with low expected growth as well as in service occupations, a group that includes many occupations, like retail sales and food service, with high job turnover.

Education and Training Requirements

The BLS divides occupations into three education clusters: occupations requiring a high school diploma or less, those requiring some college, and those requiring a bachelor's degree or more. Between 2004 and 2014, 35.7 percent of the new jobs that arise are expected to require a college degree or higher, 27.7 percent are expected to require some college, and 36.6 percent are expected to require a high school diploma or less. However, because jobs requiring less education have a much higher turnover rate than those requiring a college degree, many more job openings are expected to arise in that group (24.5 million) than in the group that requires a bachelor's degree or higher (16 million). The economy will continue generating jobs for workers in all categories over the period 2004 to 2014.

Ten Occupations with the Largest Decrease in Number of Jobs, 2004–2014*

Occupation	Number of Jobs (in thousands)		Jobs Lost (in thousands)	Percent Decrease
	2004	2014*	2004–2014*	2004–2014*
Farmers and ranchers	1,065	910	155	-14.5
Stock clerks and order fillers	1,566	1,451	-115	-7.3
Sewing machine operators	256	163	-93	-36.5
File clerks	255	163	-93	-36.3
Order clerks	293	230	-63	-21.4
Mail clerks and mail machine operators, except postal service	160	101	-59	-37.1
Computer operators	149	101	-49	-32.6
Secretaries, except legal, medical, and executive	1,934	1,887	-48	-2.5
Cutting, punching, and press machine setters, operators, and tenders, metal and plastic	251	208	-43	-17.2
Telemarketers	415	373	-42	-10.0

*Projected

SOURCE: Bureau of Labor Statistics, *Monthly Labor Review*, November 2005.

New Trends and Developments in Employment Law

Melissa J. Doak

The employment policy of the United States over the course of the twentieth century and into the twenty-first evolved to emphasize greater inclusion of all people seeking employment. The American workforce has grown dramatically and has diversified to include more women and minorities. These changes began with the massive entry of women and African Americans into the workforce during World War II. The number of minorities in the labor force will continue to increase in the twenty-first century primarily because of immigration and also because of federal policies that encourage minority hiring and promotions. The number of older Americans in the workforce will also increase, due to the rising age of the American population and the erosion of retirement benefits. New employment laws place obligations and limits on employers and confer new rights on prospective and present employees. Because these developments affect all of us, we should be acquainted with these rights and obligations and be aware of the new problems that arise in a changing labor force.

BASIC FEDERAL RIGHTS

Congress has provided many rights for job applicants and employees to ensure that all Americans have an equal opportunity in securing employment and gaining advancement. Under some of the basic employment rights provided by Congress since 1963, it is unlawful for employers to:

1) discriminate in employment on the basis of race, color, religion, sex, or national origin, provided the employer has a workforce of at least fifteen persons (Title VII of the Civil Rights Act of 1964);

2) not pay male and female employees equally when they perform the same or substantially similar kinds of work (the Equal Pay Act of 1963);

3) use age as a determining factor in hiring, promoting, or discharging employees age forty and over, where the employer employs more than twenty employees (the Age Discrimination in Employment Act of 1967);

4) discriminate against persons with disabilities who are otherwise qualified, with or without reasonable accommodation, to perform the essential functions of a job (the Americans with Disabilities Act);

5) discriminate against Vietnam veterans if the employer is a contractor or subcontractor of the federal government and its contracts equal or exceed $10,000 (the Vietnam Era Veterans Readjustment Assistance Act);

6) discharge an employee for reporting health or safety violations on the employer's premises (the Occupational Safety and Health Act);

Melissa J. Doak is a freelance writer of reference books and educational materials.

7) require the employee to work in an unsafe or hazardous area without providing adequate safeguards (the Occupational Safety and Health Act);

8) deny most employees the right to take leave to provide care for a child, spouse, or other close relative in a medical emergency or related to the birth or adoption of a child (the Family and Medical Leave Act).

The Civil Rights Act of 1991 made it easier for employees to bring charges of discrimination in hiring, promoting, or firing against an employer. The responsibility for disproving a charge is now on the employer. And, if the court finds workplace discrimination, the employee is entitled to receive payment for damages and for jury trials. The court can also order the employer to rehire, promote, or reassign the employee to whatever job he or she lost because of the discrimination.

Most states also have placed limits on employer actions, enacting laws that address many of the same issues. For example, almost all states have statutes barring discrimination based on race, color, national origin, religion, and sex. Many states also prohibit other types of discrimination (for example, discrimination based on ancestry, marital status, or sexual or political orientation). In employment law, the federal statutes provide the minimum protections for employees, but many state laws provide employees with additional rights and place greater limitations on employers.

LIMITATIONS ON EMPLOYERS' RIGHTS

Discrimination

By law, an employer cannot discriminate against employees or prospective employees. An employer who asks, either on an employment application form or in an interview, about an applicant's race, color, sex, religion, national origin, age, marital status, childbearing plans, disability, military service record, or arrest record and then uses the information for an employment decision may be violating federal or state anti-discrimination employment laws. Any employer who advertises a preference for applicants who are members of certain groups (for example, white, female, or Christian) may be unlawfully discriminating against individuals who are not hired.

Employers may be found to be discriminating against employees in two ways. A court may find that an employer treats some people better than others because of their race, color, religion, sex, national origin, age, or some other characteristic. This is called "disparate treatment." For example, a court may investigate a company that has been known to pass over its African American employees for managerial positions, even though it does not have a written policy of not hiring blacks for management.

A court may also find that although an employer's employment practices look neutral in their treatment of different groups, they actually are harsher on one group or another. This is called "disparate impact." For example, a court would question a height and weight requirement used to exclude applicants for a job as a cook. Although a height and weight standard could be justified as a valid business reason if it were clearly related to the physical demands of a job, such as logging, there is no legitimate reason why a cook must be a certain height or weight. And although requiring a cook to meet a height and weight requirement may seem neutral—it wouldn't explicitly require a cook to be white or male—it would have a disproportionate impact on women and people of Asian descent, for example.

Sometimes an employer has a legitimate reason to reject an applicant because of a characteristic. For example, some courts have permitted state prisons to choose to employ only males to guard male prisoners (and female guards for female inmates) where matters of the personal privacy of the inmates are of concern.

Anti-discrimination law continues to evolve to meet new challenges in the twenty-first century. For example, to guard against the misuse of genetic information, which may include information from a genetic test as well as from family medical history, thirty-one states have enacted statutes specific to genetic discrimination in employment. In addition, genetic discrimination has been prohibited in federal employment by an Executive Order signed by the President in February 2000. Under the Executive Order, federal executive agencies cannot use genetic information or family medical history to make employment decisions. Congress also is moving to act in this area. On February 17, 2005, the Senate passed the Genetic Information Nondiscrimination Act of 2005 and moved the bill to the House of Representatives, where it remained in committee as of May 2006.

Another evolving area of anti-discrimination concerns workers' sexual orientation and gender identification. In thirty-four states, it is legal to fire someone based on their sexual orientation; in forty-four states, it is legal to fire someone based on gender identity. However, employers themselves are changing their policies to provide basic protection to gay, lesbian, bisexual, and transgender people in the workplace. Only one of the Fortune 50 companies—ExxonMobil—does not have a sexual-orientation anti-discrimination policy, and 420 of the Fortune 500 companies include sexual orientation in their anti-discrimination policies. The federal government is lagging behind in this area. The Employment Non-Discrimination Act (ENDA), first introduced in Congress in 1996, would expand the nondiscrimination requirement found in Title VII and other laws to include sexual orientation. However, as of May 2006, it had not been reintroduced to Congress for consideration.

Affirmative Action and "Reverse Discrimination"

Affirmative action plans are designed to increase the representation of minorities, females, Vietnam veterans, and disabled people in the workforce. The federal government has required these plans since 1965 for all government contractors and subcontractors whose contracts with the federal government exceed $10,000. Many levels of government, including the federal government, also have "set-aside" programs that award a certain percentage of contracts to minority- and women-owned businesses. These programs were developed to remedy the effects of past discrimination, and to address the difficulties these generally small firms faced in competing with larger, more established firms for government contracts.

Affirmative action plans that include goals and timetables (but not quotas) have gained wide acceptance in industry, but they have also been subject to a debate that sharpened during the 1990s and early 2000s. Some critics have charged that such plans are contrary to the ideal of true equality, at least where there is no proof that an employer directly discriminated in the past against individual employees who would now benefit from the plan. They further argue that such plans have resulted in reverse discrimination—in other words, discrimination against non-Hispanic white males. Others claim that such plans are crucial to ensure that employers do not engage in discriminatory employment practices. Still others urge that race-conscious numerical goals should be used to ensure the representation of minorities or other groups in particular workforces, regardless of whether there is actual discrimination against individuals.

Congress and the voters and legislatures in the states may decide whether affirmative action will continue to play a role in employment. In California and Washington, for example, voters supported referenda ending the use of affirmative action in state employment and the awarding of state contracts. In the U.S.

Congress, there have been several attempts to end affirmative action set-aside programs that allocate money to socially and economically disadvantaged businesses (primarily minority- and women-owned businesses). Court rulings have fueled this legislative movement. The U.S. Supreme Court has issued rulings that require courts to closely look at the use of racial classifications in awarding government contracts. In June 2000 a federal court decided in *Associated General Contractors of Ohio v. Sandra A. Drabnik*, that the Ohio state set-aside program was unconstitutional.

Americans with Disabilities Act

The Americans with Disabilities Act (ADA) defined a disabled individual as someone who had physical or, in some cases, mental impairment that substantially limited a major life activity, such as the ability to see, hear, breathe, speak, walk, learn, or work. The regulations further define "substantially limit" to mean that a person cannot perform a major life activity that an average person can perform or that the person's condition significantly restricts the manner or duration of that performance.

While polls indicate that most disabled individuals want to work, only a third are employed even part time because of various barriers to employment, including accessibility problems, technology deficits, and prejudice against people with disabilities. The ADA was meant to begin addressing these problems by requiring employers and other public facilities to be more accessible to people with disabilities. It is illegal for a company to fire or refuse to hire someone simply because that person has a disability. Employers are also prohibited from using pre-employment medical examinations before they offer an applicant a job; they may require a physical examination of an applicant, but only after making a contingent job offer. An employer may withdraw a contingent offer if the post-offer examination reveals that the applicant is unable to perform the essential functions of the position sought.

The ADA requires employers to provide worksite accommodation for people with disabilities. The ADA defines reasonable accommodation broadly and provides examples: making existing facilities used by employees readily accessible to and usable by individuals with disabilities; job restructuring; part-time or modified work schedules; reassignment to a vacant position; acquisition or modification of equipment or devices; appropriate adjustment or modification of examinations, training materials, or policies; the provision of qualified readers or interpreters and other similar accommodations for individuals with disabilities; and making non-work areas, such as break rooms, locker rooms, or rest rooms, accessible to all employees. Employers and people with disabilities are required to engage in an interactive process designed to determine whether the individual can perform a job or needs an accommodation. If the individual needs an accommodation, the guidelines state that the parties should work cooperatively to achieve a workable solution.

The law applies to people with mental illness and AIDS, as well as to those with physical disabilities including obesity. Some of the more vexing issues under the ADA involve an employer's obligation to accommodate people with mental disabilities. In a 1997 Enforcement Guidance, the Equal Employment Opportunity Commission (EEOC) noted that the ADA protected people with mental illnesses, including depression, anxiety disorders (which include panic disorder, obsessive–compulsive disorder, and post–traumatic stress disorder), schizophrenia, and personality disorders.

Acquired immunodeficiency syndrome (AIDS) is also a disability protected by the ADA. AIDS is caused by the human immunodeficiency virus (HIV). It is transmitted through bodily fluids. The disease undermines a person's immune system and leaves it powerless to battle certain cancers and other potentially fatal illnesses. There is currently no cure for the disease. For the employer, AIDS has created the fear of substantial liability if an employee infects a coworker. However, medical experts agree that the risk that someone will get the disease from normal workplace conduct (outside of hospitals, medical labs, or medical research facilities) is almost nonexistent. For this reason and based on a Supreme Court case that held that a person with a communicable disease (tuberculosis) was protected under federal law prohibiting discrimination against the disabled, employers may not discriminate against someone who has AIDS or HIV.

Age Discrimination

Discrimination in employment based on age will become an increasingly significant problem as the U.S. population ages. By 2020, most of the baby boomers will be senior citizens. At that time, more than 54.6 million Americans will be age sixty-five or older, up from 35.1 million in 2000.

At the same time, some of the safety nets for older Americans that had been in place since the mid-twentieth century may be eroding. The age at which Americans can receive full retirement benefits from Social Security is rising; those born in 1960 or later will not receive full benefits until age sixty-seven. Federal budget constraints also may reduce health benefits for the elderly under Medicare. Many older Americans will need to work to survive.

Employees age forty and older are protected by the Age Discrimination in Employment Act (ADEA) of 1967 from discriminatory employment practices with respect to hiring, promotion, or discharge. In 2005 the national EEOC office received 16,585 age discrimination complaints—obviously, age discrimination continues to represent a significant proportion of discrimination complaints filed with the EEOC.

It is still lawful, of course, not to hire or to discharge an employee who is unable to perform necessary job duties in a safe and efficient way. It is also lawful to discharge an employee who lacks the necessary technical knowledge to continue in the position. The deciding factor in whether not to hire or to discharge an employee must be not age but the employee's ability to perform the duties required by the position.

There are, however, some jobs in which age can be a ground for discrimination. Airline pilots, bus drivers, police officers, and state troopers have been subjected to age limitations by statute or regulation. Courts have upheld such employment practices because of the safety risks that would arise from sudden incapacitation, such as a stroke or heart attack. Such medical occurrences are associated with advancing years and cannot be readily predicted. Age, in this limited context, has been considered a genuine occupational qualification. Under federal law, age discrimination in these cases is "reasonably necessary to the normal operation of the particular business."

ADDITIONAL LEGAL EMPLOYMENT ISSUES

Sexual Harassment

Employees have gained protection not only from direct adverse actions from their employer but also from certain unjustified treatment while on the job. Awareness of sexual harassment has increased in recent years, in part because of complaints and class-action lawsuits against large corporations and in part because of high-profile accusations of sexual harassment against such public officials as President Bill Clinton and Supreme Court Justice Clarence Thomas.

The EEOC defines sexual harassment as unwelcome sexual advances, requests for sexual favors, and other verbal or physical conduct of a sexual nature that affects an individual's employment, interferes with an individual's work performance, or creates an intimidating, hostile, or offensive work environment. According to the EEOC, the commission received 12,679 charges of sexual harassment in fiscal year 2005, down from a high of 15,836 filed in 2000. The percentage of sexual harassment charges filed by men has increased substantially since 1992 (from 9.1 percent to 14.3 percent).

Meritor Savings Bank v. Vinson The U.S. Supreme Court, in the landmark case *Meritor Savings Bank v. Vinson* (477 U.S. 57, 1986), ruled that sexual harassment was a violation of Title VII of the Civil Rights Act of 1964, which prohibited sexual discrimination. Mechelle Vinson claimed that her supervisor harassed her at work and outside of work and raped her. A lower court ruled against her, finding that sexual favors had not been a condition of her employment. The Supreme Court reversed the decision, ruling that "Title VII affords employees the right to work in an environment free from discriminatory intimidation, ridicule, and insult."

The Employer's Responsibility In 1998 the Supreme Court ruled that (1) employers could be held liable when a supervisor threatened to demote or take other action against an employee who refused a supervisor's sexual demands, even when the threats were not carried out (*Burlington Industries v. Ellerth* [66 LW 4643]), and (2) that companies were liable for the misconduct of their employees even though the company was unaware of the behavior (*Faragher v. Boca Raton* [118 S. Ct. 2275, 1998]). The Court's majority decision (seven to two) stated that employers could generally avoid liability for sexual harassment by showing that they had strong anti-harassment programs, that the programs were communicated to all employees, and that systems were in place for submitting and reviewing complaints. Following these rulings, many companies reexamined their sexual harassment policies and revised them to meet the Court's tougher standards.

Equal Pay for Equal Work

In 1964 Congress made it unlawful for an employer to pay different wages to male and female employees "for equal work on jobs the performance of which requires equal skills, effort, and responsibility, and which are performed under similar working conditions." The concept of equal pay for equal work, although not controversial, is difficult to apply. Jobs need not be absolutely identical to be equal but must be substantially similar. In close cases, courts will refer to the skill, effort, responsibility, and working conditions under which the jobs are performed to determine whether they are substantially similar. Betty Dukes had been a cashier at Wal-Mart for nine years and had not been able to get promoted in that time; Stephanie Odle was being paid $10,000 less than a male coworker in the same position. These two women, along with ninety-eight others, filed a sex discrimination lawsuit against Wal-Mart that led to the largest class action in history. On June 21, 2004, a federal judge in San Francisco certified a class action against Wal-Mart involving 1.6 million women.

A new form of sexual discrimination involves the dilemmas of single mothers. One single mother living and working in New York City was a key player in her company's success. The result of her achievements was an increased demand on her time, making it virtually impossible for her to raise her daughter. When she said that she could not work the longer hours, she was fired. In Massachusetts and California, two women have taken similar cases to court, only to lose because at-will employees can be fired "for any reason or for no reason at all." Another case that may have an impact on this area is one in which twelve current and former female employees of Novartis Pharmaceuticals Corp. filed a $100 million sex discrimination lawsuit against the company in February 2005. Their attorneys maintain that the New Jersey firm's employment practices are unfair to working mothers.

Employee Benefits

Family Leave In 1993 Congress enacted the Family and Medical Leave Act. The act requires employers with fifty or more employees within a seventy-five-mile radius to provide up to twelve weeks of unpaid, job-protected leave to eligible employees for certain family and medical reasons. An employee is considered eligible if he or she has worked for the employer for at least one year and for more than 1,250 hours during the preceding twelve months. An employee may take this leave because of the birth of a child or the need to care for his or her child; the adoption of a child; the care of a seriously ill spouse, child, or parent; or the need to care for his or her own health impairment.

Although the statute requires the employer to provide the employee with unpaid leave, it also permits the employee to use whatever paid leave may be available. Employees must give an employer at least thirty days' advance notice of the request for leave, but this requirement may be waived in an emergency. The law also states that the employer must return the employee to the same position or to an equivalent position, with the same benefits, pay status, and other terms and conditions of employment.

Many employers, often at the insistence of labor unions, rely on some form of seniority system to determine which employees will get certain benefits. Seniority is often regarded by employees as the most valuable feature of their jobs, entitling them to such benefits as preferred shifts, desirable vacation time, opportunity to engage in or to avoid overtime, job security, and early recall rights. Systems that protect these interests are usually strenuously defended from challenge.

A number of the federal employment laws that make discriminatory employment practices unlawful explicitly permit employers to maintain seniority plans. Employers who use seniority systems are not engaging in discriminatory employment practices if the seniority system was not adopted to discriminate against employees. This is so even when the seniority system perpetuates the effect of past discriminatory employment practices. When a disabled worker at U.S. Airways requested reassignment to a vacant position and more senior workers had the right to bid for the job under the company's seniority system, U.S. Airways decided to allow seniority to trump the disabled employee. The disabled employee filed suit under the ADA but lost when the U.S. Supreme Court ruled in 2002 that seniority systems generally prevail over disabled workers' rights.

Drugs in the Workplace

Workplace drug testing began in the 1980s. The Reagan administration advocated such testing as part of its War on Drugs. As a result, a number of states have enacted statutes that regulate employer use of drug testing. Several statutes place severe limits on an employer's right to test applicants and employees, whereas other statutes are much more limited in focus. Various courts also have ruled that drug testing is intrusive and involves the protection against unreasonable searches and seizures contained in the Fourth Amendment of the U.S. Constitution. The Supreme Court has ruled, however, that in certain circumstances a drug-testing program does not constitute an unreasonable search and seizure where significant public interests are at stake. It gave the federal government broad discretion to impose drug-testing requirements on both private employees and government workers whose duties involve public safety or law enforcement. In 2006 a variety of legal challenges to drug testing policies were pending.

The law says that an employee may be tested on several occasions. The first is during an applicant's pre-placement physical. Medical personnel may request that applicants provide urine and blood samples for detection of illegal and prescription drugs. If an applicant tests positive for illegal substances, he or she usually will be denied employment. When the drug test is positive for a prescription medication such as Valium, the applicant may be asked to provide a letter from the prescribing physician explaining the purpose of the medication. If a prescription medication may adversely affect a person's ability to safely perform a job, the applicant may legally be barred from being hired.

An employee may be tested for drug use during an annual physical examination, randomly during the year, "for cause," or after an accident. Drug testing during the annual physical or done randomly may deter substance abuse, but such testing has legal implications. Employees who test positive are subject to disciplinary action or termination. They also may be referred to an EAP or for professional evaluation and recommended for individual or group counseling, outpatient care, or hospitalization. Those testing positive for illegal drugs after an accident may be denied unemployment, worker's compensation, or disability benefits.

One federal law requires that certain employers maintain drug-free workplaces and develop drug education and training programs. The Drug-Free Workplace Act of 1988 requires that government contractors and recipients of federal financial assistance maintain drug-free workplaces and develop drug education and training programs. Such policies, at a minimum, must inform employees that possession, distribution, or use of a controlled substance in the workplace is prohibited, and must indicate what actions the employer will take against employees who violate the policy. Employers also are required to develop "drug-free awareness" programs to educate employees about the dangers of drug abuse in the workplace, the employer's policy concerning drugs, the availability of counseling or employee assistance for employees in need of such help, and the penalties applicable for violations of the policy. Noncompliance with this law may result in the termination of the employer's contract or grant.

ENDING THE EMPLOYMENT RELATIONSHIP

Employment at Will and Its Exceptions

Courts have long recognized that when an employee is hired for an indefinite term, either the employer or the employee may terminate the employment relationship at any time. This is known as "employment at will." Since World War I, new laws and legal developments have limited the concept of employment at will. For example, both the Railway Labor Act of 1926 and the National Labor Relations Act of 1935 make it unlawful to fire or otherwise discriminate against employees because of their involvement in protected union activity. It is not that these laws make it illegal to fire an employee for no reason; rather, they make it illegal for an employer to fire an employee for the wrong reason.

The list of "wrong reasons" has grown rapidly. In addition to being illegal to fire an employee for union activity, it is now unlawful under federal law for an employer to discharge an employee for exercising rights in an employee benefit plan; having his or her wages garnisheed; performing jury service; declaring bankruptcy; participating in an investigation, proceeding, or hearing brought against the employer for discriminatory employment practices; or opposing the discriminatory practices of the employer.

Furthermore, federal law makes it unlawful to discharge an employee for "whistle-blowing," that is, for notifying the employer or an appropriate authority of violations of federal safety and environmental laws on the employer's premises. In addition, several states have passed laws protecting those who report violations of state law. In May 2002 Congress passed the Federal Antidiscrimination and Retaliation Act. This law requires that federal agencies be accountable for violations of antidiscrimination and whistleblower protection laws.

Court decisions have also limited employers' rights to terminate employment at will. If an employer has made a policy statement or has otherwise given assurances that the employee will not be fired without cause, courts may find implied contract rights in favor of the employee. For instance, in a case in which an employer's personnel manual contained statements of policy regarding termination of employment and did not contain a disclaimer protecting the employer's freedom of action, a court found an implied contract that the employee would not be discharged except for just cause. In addition, if a termination occurs in an unnecessarily humiliating manner or otherwise causes the employee severe emotional distress, without adequate justification, the employee may have an actionable claim against the employer.

Defamation

Defamation concerns strike at the heart of information collection and distribution about individuals, and are a significant cause of employer concern. Defamation is a legal term meaning any communication that causes someone to be shamed, ridiculed, or to suffer from a damaged reputation. Employers have limited rights to make negative statements about current or former employees, but this privilege may be lost if the information clearly is false or is shared with people who do not have a need to know. Because of the threat of lawsuit, employers have become hesitant to share information about employees with others and wary about keeping records necessary for use in employee assessment and personnel actions. However, if incomplete information is documented about an employee who is fired, an employer may face charges for wrongful discharge or discrimination.

Worker Adjustment and Retraining Notification Act

The Worker Adjustment and Retraining Notification Act (WARN) provides for mandatory notice of employer plant closing and mass layoff. WARN requires covered employers to provide their employees (or their employees' union representative, if any) and certain state and local government officials with written notice sixty days in advance of a plant closing or mass layoff. A company that fails to provide adequate notice can be liable for back pay, lost benefits, attorney's fees, and other civil penalties.

Although Congress had manufacturing industries in mind when passing what generally is thought of as a plant-closing bill, WARN is not limited to any particular business sector. It applies to all employers with one hundred or more full-time employees. WARN is also not limited to hourly workers but covers all employees.

Employment Opportunities at Home

Sandy Dutkowsky

James Mathison owns and operates his own landscaping business. Denise Lyons is a computer programmer who works at home four days a week and in the office one. Jeff Riley gives piano and voice lessons in the basement of his home. Chrystal Holumbo is a freelance writer and editor. After work and on weekends, Pamela Chang cleans several doctor and dentist offices.

What do all these people have in common? They are part of the growing number of Americans who work from home. Although their reasons for doing so are diverse, they are all enthusiastic about the benefits of home-based employment. For James Mathison, the most important advantage of owning his own business is he can be his own boss and set his own hours and goals. Working primarily at home allows Denise Lyons to reduce her commuting time from ten hours a week to just two. Jeff Riley is able to keep a flexible work schedule so he can care for his two young children and spend more time with his family. Chrystal Holumbo enjoys the convenience of working in her own home. Pamela Chang likes being able to earn extra income by "moonlighting" at her second job.

The many and varied advantages of working from home have helped it to become a rapidly growing trend. A study conducted in 2005 by the technology research firm Gartner, Inc., states that 82.5 million Americans currently work from home at least once a week. They predict that that number will increase to 100 million by 2008. Although home-based workers currently represent a minority of the nation's workforce, their numbers have been rising dramatically in recent years. It is estimated that 25 percent of U.S. households operate some type of home business. And nearly four out of ten (39 percent) of workers who do not telecommute say they would like to have the opportunity to do so in the future.

THE INFORMATION AGE

Why is working from home becoming so popular? The main reason is the drastic change in the type of work that people do. In the past, the average American earned money by working in agriculture or manufacturing. In today's Information Age, the majority of Americans are involved in work that creates, processes, and moves information. Historically, this work has been done in offices.

Over the past few decades, however, the traditional office has evolved. The standard company model has changed to maximize efficiency. Companies realize that in today's fast-paced environment, they no longer can afford to have a bulky chain of command and complicated bureaucratic structure. To remain competitive in the rapidly changing Information Age, many companies have found they must develop their information systems while simultaneously reducing red tape. By relying increasingly on computers, modems, fax machines, videoconferencing, and other innovative tools, companies are able to achieve their goals while saving time, money, and energy.

Sandy Dutkowsky is a freelance writer and educator.

The advent of this technology means it is no longer always necessary for all employees to work in centralized offices. The availability of inexpensive computers and other business equipment has enabled many workers to set up offices in their own homes. Through the use of high-speed Internet access, e-mail, and fax machines, home-based workers can communicate quickly and easily with coworkers and clients.

However, not all employees can work from home. The availability of home-based job opportunities is limited by the type of work a person does. Truck or bus drivers, retail sales clerks, and traditional factory production workers, for example, all have to be at their respective worksites in order to do their jobs. Therefore, these types of workers do not have a future in home-based employment.

TYPES OF HOME-BASED WORKERS

The employment situations of individuals who work from home vary greatly. Some are home-based corporate employees, called "telecommuters." Others hold down regular office jobs while moonlighting at home in their off hours to supplement their incomes. Still others are entrepreneurs embarking on their own business journeys. For some professionals, such as computer consultants, accountants, editors, writers, and graphic designers, creating a home office simply makes the most economic sense. Although these individuals have different educational backgrounds and possess a diverse range of skills, they share one important trait: they live in an age in which technology and the economic climate have made home-based employment both feasible and often more advantageous than working in a traditional office.

Telecommuters

Currently, the average American worker is a commuter who travels by car, bus, or train to get to work. As the nation's population has grown and people are living further outside of urban centers (where housing is less expensive), more and more people are using their cars, instead of public transportation, to commute to work. As a result, the country's roads have become increasingly congested. Exhaust from millions of vehicles also has had a negative effect on the air quality in many cities and towns. Most recently, the rising price of gasoline has made the average worker's commute very expensive.

Today's difficult economic picture is not only taking its toll on America's workers, it is also having an impact on the companies that employ them. Competition from foreign companies causes many companies to look for ways to cut costs and overhead without sacrificing worker productivity. Corporate America and government agencies have looked at all of these problems and decided that the answer lies, in part, with technology. Armed with a computer and an Internet connection, a commuter can transform easily into a telecommuter, working at home while maintaining contact with the office and cutting costs.

Telecommuting has benefits for government, companies, workers, and the environment. Seeking to cut down on pollution, the federal government passed the Clean Air Act in 1990. One amendment of this act requires large companies in many major cities to reduce the number of vehicle miles their employees travel each day. Allowing a portion of the workforce to telecommute helps employers meet these requirements.

Telecommuting also has relieved some of the financial burdens many corporations face. When some of its employees work at home, a company can spend less money on office space and related expenses. The average corporation has invested approximately 30 percent of its total worth in real estate and buildings to house its workers while they work. By allowing workers to stay at home, companies are reducing the amount of money they have to spend. This helps to significantly reduce overhead costs.

Additionally, according to the CIGNA Corporation, companies with employees who telecommute report one to two days fewer of missed work per employee. Telecommuters tend to call in sick less frequently, have fewer childcare emergencies, and miss fewer days for doctor's appointments than their colleagues who report to a work site. Therefore, telecommuting, by reducing the amount of time workers are absent from the job, increases productivity and profits for corporations.

Workers also benefit from telecommuting. A home-based work environment is often more comfortable, less stressful, and freer from distractions than a standard office. Because telecommuters do not have to contend with the frustrations of rush-hour traffic, they are able to start the work day fresh and focused. Telecommuters also do not have to spend as much money as commuters on parking fees, eating out, and buying work clothes. Also, since they do not have to spend time getting to and from work, telecommuters have more time to spend with family or on leisure activities, which makes them happier overall and more loyal to their employers.

Working at a home on a computer, a telecommuter can perform many tasks that previously had to be done at the office. In a matter of seconds, workers can transmit files using high-speed Internet connections, or they can send documents by fax. Workers can maintain close working relationships with individuals in their company offices through e-mail and telephone calls.

Although telecommuting makes sense on many levels, some companies have been slow to embrace this strategy as a viable option for their employees. Employers may fear that placing workers at home with limited supervision will lead to reduced productivity. However, recent studies have shown telecommuters actually are more productive than office-based workers because they are happier and more focused. In a survey of commuters conducted by Netilla Networks and Infosecurity Europe at New York's Penn Station and London's Liverpool Street Station ("Flexible Working Survey 2004"), and reported at CNN.com in March 2004, most respondents believed that setting up shop, that is, workspace, at "the kitchen table" would improve their lives by making work less stressful and allowing better relationships with loved ones. A survey conducted by Cornell University's International Workplace found that the workers' beliefs were true. People who work from home are between 10 percent and 30 percent more productive than those who work at a job site.

Some industry observers believe telecommuting will be the primary corporate model in the years ahead. In the late 1990s, the specialized staffing firm Robert Half International reported that 87 percent of 150 corporate executives polled anticipated an increase in telecommuting in the future. As technology becomes less costly, companies are able to furnish their employees with more advanced equipment, making it increasingly common for employees to "meet" and work together using video teleconferencing instead of meeting physically, face to face. According to *Business Week* ("There's No Workforce Like Home," May 3, 2006), more than 100,000 customer-service representatives are already working from their homes; estimates are that 300,000 will be doing this by 2010.

There are downsides to working from home as well, however. Due to the accessibility of communication tools, an estimated seventeen million Americans work from their homes at least once a month, in addition to putting in their required office or workplace hours, and most do not get additional pay for their at-home work hours. Many of these workers regularly bring their work home with them from the office at the end of the day and continue to work once they are home. The majority who do this say that it is the only way to keep up with their normal workload. According to the Bureau of Labor Statistics, 75 percent of employees who continue to work once they get home do not get paid for their efforts. Of the 10.2 million workers who bring work home with them, 22 percent report working more than eight hours per week at home; the average is seven hours per week.

Moonlighters

Home-based work is not the exclusive domain of telecommuters. A number of Americans are moonlighting, which means they work at one job all day, and then work at another one later in the day. The reasons that Americans moonlight vary. The majority do it because they find that their weekly paycheck, although it may be steady and reliable, just doesn't stretch as far as it did years ago. The rising costs of homes, cars, education, and living expenses often prove too much for today's families, even those with dual incomes. Therefore, moonlighting allows them to earn extra income and pay off debt. Others work two jobs because they are trying to gain new experiences in order to make a career change. Others simply enjoy working at their second jobs. According to the U.S. Department of Labor approximately eight million workers—or one in seventeen Americans—consider themselves moonlighters.

The Self-Employed

In the early years of the twenty-first century, many Americans are finding that a guaranteed paycheck, good benefits, and job security are things of the past. As companies downsize, outsource work to foreign countries, and look for other ways to cut costs, many workers, often those with years of experience, find themselves unemployed. Whereas many seek new jobs in traditional work settings, others see their newfound freedom as an opportunity to use their skills and experience to start their own businesses.

Of course, not all those embarking on self-employment are doing so as a result of losing their jobs. Many people simply see the possibility of being their own boss as a more direct and desirable road to success and prosperity. These individuals often use their skills and client contacts as a springboard to launch their own companies. A large number of people who are retiring and yet still want to remain productive afterwards are starting their own businesses. Whatever the reason for starting a business, those who do it in a thoughtful, organized manner will have the greatest chance for success.

There are many types of home-based self-employment, but in general they can be divided into two main categories: entrepreneurs, who run small businesses from home, and independent contractors, who do work on assignment at home for various companies and organizations.

ENTREPRENEURS

Many people find that starting and running their own home-based business is a very rewarding and profitable experience. It is not necessarily easy, however. Home-based workers often find that visitors, household chores, television, and Web surfing can easily distract them and therefore must be avoided during work hours. Entrepreneurs need to be determined, goal-oriented, and focused. They also must enjoy their chosen business and be willing to spend long hours working at it. Many successful entrepreneurs have turned a favorite hobby, something previously thought of as an activity done just for fun, into the inspiration for and basis of a home-based business. A famous example of a person taking a hobby and turning it into a hugely successful business is the Mrs. Fields cookie company. In 1977, Debbi Fields was a young mother who decided to turn her love of baking cookies at her home into a business. By 1990 the company began offering franchises of its Mrs. Fields flagship brand, and by 2006, there were nearly 390 locations in the United States, with more than eighty locations worldwide.

Types of Entrepreneurs

Entrepreneurs, like businesses, can be divided into two types: those who provide services and those who provide products.

Providing Services In today's fast-paced world, many people are willing to pay others for services that will save one of their most valuable resources: time. Many entrepreneurs find a niche providing services to busy professionals who have little free time in which to take care of daily or weekly tasks, such as dog walking or housecleaning. Other entrepreneurs offer services people may not have the qualifications or skills to do themselves, such as preparing tax returns or cutting hair. There are several ways to develop the skills needed for service-oriented businesses, including taking adult education classes, contacting trade associations, and practicing on friends and relatives. Almost any service can become the basis for a home-based business. For example, some entrepreneurs plan weddings, prepare resumes, or create Web sites.

Skilled workers, especially those who have been in their fields for a number of years, can go into business as consultants. They usually have expertise in one area, such as computers or advertising. As experts in their fields, these workers are hired to assist businesses and organizations in troubleshooting problems, developing solutions, and meeting goals. Experienced consultants can earn more than $100 an hour for their services, but building up a clientele willing to pay for their expertise can take a lot of time and energy.

Providing Products Other entrepreneurs choose to manufacture products, such as gourmet cookies or children's clothing. However, the cost to manufacture, package, and advertise products can be quite high. In addition, it may take years to break into some markets. People starting this type of home-based business should become familiar with the many federal and state regulations that govern such operations. For example, food manufacturers who work out of their homes must have a local food regulator inspect and certify their kitchens as clean and sanitary. In certain instances, small business owners work from home on a computer while their employees do much of the labor associated with their product in a factory setting elsewhere.

One popular type of product-oriented home-based business is making and selling craft items such as greeting cards or candles. Such a business generally is not expensive to launch because large numbers of craftspeople already possess their own tools. As a result, the production of the product can be done in the worker's home, by the worker. Many craftspeople who wish to begin a home-based business start out by moonlighting, producing products during evenings and on weekends while holding down full-time jobs. They often visit craft shows and shops to get a sense of the market and to determine trends, and then return to the shows as vendors selling their own wares. They also use the Internet as a venue for selling their products.

Another type of home-based business that is growing in popularity uses the Internet as a "store front." The most widely known example of this is the sale of items through online auction sites, such as eBay, Amazon.com, and Yahoo! Auctions. Entrepreneurs can buy and sell antiques, vehicles, jewelry, art, or clothing. In 2003 online retailing grew 51 percent to become a $114 billion industry, with a significant portion of this coming from online auction sites. To be successful in this form of home-based business, individuals must keep their prices competitive with the wider market and ship products to buyers quickly.

Becoming an Entrepreneur

For those who are interested in starting their own home-based businesses, there are many instructional books and articles online, at local libraries, or bookstores. The tips that follow can help a potential entrepreneur get started.

Research and Planning Research is an essential part of starting a successful home-based business. It is very important to thoroughly investigate competitors in the particular market. For information on the competition, as well as about the market, look in the local Yellow Pages, visit the library, search the Internet, and interview prospective clients.

Government and other nonprofit agencies, including the U.S. Small Business Association, can be contacted for advice. These agencies can point the way to small business loan programs. Government grants may be available for some types of ventures. Working at home has become a common topic of discussion on message boards and in chat rooms on the Internet. Such forums can serve as a helpful resource for new entrepreneurs as long as they do not consume too much time that should go into building the business.

An essential aspect of starting any new business is the creation of a business plan. According to the U.S. Small Business Association, the business plan, "precisely defines your business, identifies your goals, and serves as your firm's resume." A typical business plan should include a detailed picture of the company's aspirations, an outline of marketing strategies, and a close estimate of expenses and projected revenue for the first few years of operation. Once the business plan is in place, it can be used to decide whether or not the business is on track and what changes should be made to increase revenue.

Before starting any business, it is always important to explore its legal aspects. Many communities require business owners to obtain licenses. It is also important to determine whether the business is a sole proprietorship, corporation, or partnership because the tax liabilities will be different in each case. The Internal Revenue Service (IRS) frequently alters the regulations for self-employment deductions. Depending on which category a business falls into, it is possible to deduct a variety of business-related costs when filing taxes. These deductions could include such things as travel expenses, a portion of rent or mortgage, or the cost of additional telephone lines. An accountant can help the business adhere to the law as well as benefit from any allowable deductions. At all times, it is essential to maintain detailed records of expenses and to keep business expenses separate from personal expenses.

Figuring out how to pay for business and personal expenses as the business gets underway is also an important part of the start-up research process. Since it often takes a new business six months or more to get off the ground, entrepreneurs should plan to have enough savings set aside for living expenses during the start-up period.

Among the monthly expenses entrepreneurs may incur is the cost of health care insurance. According to the U.S. Census Bureau, 60 percent of Americans receive their health insurance coverage through their jobs. Persons who are self-employed do not enjoy the benefit of having an employer pay for their health insurance. Therefore, entrepreneurs have to find ways to provide their own health insurance coverage. As health care costs continue to rise, in order to avoid huge medical expenses, it is very important to have insurance that will cover basic visits to the doctor as well as expensive surgeries. Persons who are seeking health insurance coverage can buy it from private insurance providers. Additionally, some states offer health insurance programs to small business owners at a reduced rate. For example, New York State has a health insurance program called "Healthy New York," which sells quality health insurance packages to sole proprietors and small business owners at lower rates than if it was purchased through a private insurance company.

Equipment Each year, computers and other business tools become more powerful and less expensive. For some entrepreneurs, such as desktop publishers and Web site designers, a computer is necessary for producing their goods or services. For all entrepreneurs, a computer can aid in the promotion and maintenance of their business. For example, the computer can be used to help design and produce promotional brochures, keep track of income and expenses, and monitor inventory. The Internet provides the ability to send files instantly to clients located thousands of miles away. An up-to-date computer is essential for most entrepreneurs and can be a worthwhile investment.

Attitude People who want to start their own home business must be highly motivated. Many entrepreneurs find it helpful to establish a strict daily routine, including planning regular working hours and dressing as if they actually were going to a traditional place of work instead of simply to their home office. By creating mental boundaries between work and home, they lessen the chances of succumbing to distractions and help ensure greater productivity. Author Neal Zimmerman, in *American Way Magazine*, also recommends establishing an at-home workplace that is "an environment that you feel good about, that's a personal reflection of you. You'll spend a lot of time there earning the money that pays for everything else. You should not only be comfortable, but you should enjoy being there."

Marketing Just as successful job hunters do, entrepreneurs must network. Instead of looking for an employer, however, entrepreneurs are looking for potential clients. Networking involves talking about and promoting the business with everyone, including friends, relatives, associates, and strangers. Marketing tools may include brochures, business cards, or Web sites. Samples of work (or product) should be available for prospective clients to review. Depending on the target market to be reached, some inexpensive ways of promoting a new business include posting flyers on bulletin boards located inside grocery stores or on college campuses, advertising in weekly newspapers, or placing an announcement on an Internet bulletin board service such as http://www.craigslist.org, which offers local listings in all fifty states and more than thirty countries around the world.

INDEPENDENT CONTRACTORS

Independent contractors—also called "freelancers"—agree to work for a company or individual on a project-by-project basis. Many independent contractors work in the arts, including writers, photographers, and artists. Other freelancers include building contractors, computer consultants, and medical transcriptionists. Almost any kind of work can be done on a contract basis, if the worker has the tools and resources available.

Freelance work can be rewarding for several reasons. The pay can be lucrative and the work is very independent. Freelancers can pick and choose the jobs that interest them the most or pay the highest rates. Freelancing is ideal for people who cannot (or choose not to) work standard office hours. Freelancing does have drawbacks, however. The biggest one is that freelance work does not generally guarantee a steady income. Freelancers may have periods of little or no work, especially when beginning such a career. In addition, many companies have long billing cycles, and freelancers may not be paid for several months after submitting their invoices. Some freelancers supplement their income by taking odd jobs or working part time.

OTHER TYPES OF HOME-BASED WORKERS

Some kinds of home-based employment do not fall within the categories outlined above. Independent sales representatives, for example, sell a company's goods but are not salaried employees. They usually earn a commission on the products they sell. A famous example of this type of home-based business is Mary Kay Cosmetics. In 1963 Mary Kay Ash invested her life savings in starting a small cosmetics company that would organize women to sell makeup to their friends and associates. By 2005 Mary Kay Cosmetics had 1.6 million independent sales representatives selling Mary Kay brand products worth more than $2 billion. Some other well-known companies that offer opportunities to independent sales representatives include Avon and Tupperware. Although some sales representatives still sell their goods door to door, an increasing number also use e-mail, phones, and Web sites to reach potential customers.

Another type of home-based business is inn keeping. The business owner transforms a home, or part of a home, into a small inn, and provides visitors with a quaint, home-like setting and breakfast for the price of an overnight stay. This type of business venture can be very expensive, requiring the investment of a great deal of capital. There are also legal considerations, because these accommodations must conform to state and local regulations.

Many people who want to start a home-based business scour newspapers, magazines, and the Internet for business opportunities—but they should do so with caution. Whereas some listings are for valid business offers, others are fraudulent. Some promise high payment for stuffing envelopes or assembling items at home. Others promote seminars that promise to offer the secrets of making large sums of money by buying and selling real estate or doing medical billing from home. The key to identifying these fraudulent schemes is to look for advertisements that offer high returns for little work and that charge a fee to get in on their business secrets. Avoid these types of opportunities. It is wise to remember the old adage: if it seems too good to be true, it probably is.

THE DISADVANTAGES OF WORKING AT HOME

Although home-based employment offers many advantages, it also has some drawbacks. Telecommuters who are employed by a company may feel isolated from their coworkers and left out of day-to-day office functions. In a survey conducted in 2004 by Netilla Networks and Infosecurity Europe, eight out of ten respondents said that even if they worked at home, they would still enjoy going into the office for the social life. Working on a team also can be more challenging for home-based workers. When team members are working at different locations and not able to meet face to face, brainstorming and problem solving can be more difficult than if all participants were in the same physical location.

There are also financial drawbacks for home-based workers who are self-employed. In addition to not receiving health insurance, these workers do not receive other benefits such as paid vacations, sick days, and retirement plans. In addition, they pay substantially more in taxes than they would if they were employed by a company.

However, the biggest challenge faced by those who work at home is finding a way to balance their work lives and personal lives. At-home workers can find themselves working all the time due to the rigors of starting up a business, the insecurity of freelance work, the need to earn additional wages to cover the cost of benefits usually supplied by an employer, or simply the proximity of the office. Those who have chosen to work at home as a means to spend more time with their families may find that they are working so much that the opposite is true. In order to avoid this problem, many home-based workers attempt to work a fixed schedule with little or no overtime.

THE FUTURE OF HOME-BASED EMPLOYMENT

In the early decades of the twenty-first century, the boundaries between the workplace and the home will probably continue to blur. The number of home-based workers has increased steadily in recent years and will continue to do so. Although many people find working at home to be an ideal situation, it is not the right choice for everyone. Working at home, especially for small business owners, requires a great deal of determination, dedication, and perseverance. However, the potential rewards for this hard work, both personally and financially, can be well worth the effort.

Health in the Workplace

Albert A. Kowalski, M.D.

In the first years of the twenty-first century, the health of employees was a major concern for many companies due to the escalating costs of occupational (work-related) and non-occupational health care. In 2004 national health expenditures rose 7.9 percent over the previous year, more than three times the rate of inflation. In 2004 total spending on health expenditures was $1.9 trillion, or $6,280 per person in the United States. Health care expenditures in 2004 represented 16 percent of the gross domestic product (GNP).

Health care expenditures are projected to reach $4 trillion in 2015, or a 20 percent share of the GDP. This is up from only 8.8 percent in 1980. Such escalating costs reduce companies' profits and inflate the prices of goods and services.

Government regulations have also influenced health in the workplace. Since 1970 federal regulations have required companies to maintain accurate records of work-related illnesses and injuries, institute medical surveillance programs, provide safety equipment, and control the use of hazardous chemicals. As a result, the number of serious occupational injuries and illnesses has been greatly reduced. Companies must continue to monitor the health of their workers to keep insurance spending and premiums to a minimum.

This essay discusses the role of employee health services in a company, the types of programs often provided, and the federal regulations that pertain to health in the workplace. It also addresses current issues in employee health services, including AIDS in the workplace, employee assistance programs, drug testing, fitness programs, and health care trends.

ROLE OF EMPLOYEE HEALTH SERVICES

Today's occupational health care professional is not only responsible for the health of the employee but also may be involved with company medical policies and benefits, disability and workers' compensation evaluations, health promotion, wellness and fitness programs, industrial safety, and compliance with state and federal regulations. Employee health services vary widely from company to company. Employers may provide any or all of the programs outlined below to their employees.

Emergency Medical Care

Every company is responsible for establishing policies and procedures for providing first aid and emergency medical care to employees who become ill or injured at work. These services can be provided by appropriately trained personnel on-site or at local health care facilities. Many companies have organized voluntary first-aid squads from within the ranks of their employees. Some employers offer classes in first aid and cardiopulmonary resuscitation (CPR) certification.

Albert A. Kowalski, M.D., is a medical director in the Health Affairs Organization, AT&T Corporation, Basking Ridge, New Jersey.

Pre-placement Examinations

A pre-placement or pre-employment examination is a medical assessment provided by a company. The examination serves two functions: to determine an applicant's ability to perform a specific job, and to provide a baseline medical status against which to evaluate any occupational illnesses or injuries that might arise during employment. A physician who is employed or contracted by the company usually performs this examination. It may include a physical examination, vision test, hearing test, pulmonary function test, electrocardiogram, chest X-ray, blood tests, urinalysis, and drug testing.

The physician must determine if the applicant can perform necessary job functions despite any medical condition he or she may have. A company cannot, however, legally deny an applicant a job solely on the grounds of a diagnosis such as cancer or AIDS. In addition, federal, state, and local laws prevent discrimination against people with disabilities. The company can only deny the applicant employment if, in the opinion of the physician, the applicant is unable to perform the essential functions of the job.

The pre-placement examination also establishes a baseline medical profile for the protection of the company and the employee. It may help determine whether any illness or injury that occurs later is occupational, non-occupational, or the result of previous employment.

Medical Surveillance Examinations

Medical surveillance examinations are usually required by company policy or by government health standards for employees exposed to toxic chemicals or other substances that may pose a health risk in the work environment. The purpose of the examination is early detection of work-related medical illnesses so measures can be taken to prevent serious disability or death. The physician is responsible for notifying the employee and for arranging appropriate treatment and follow-up care of all work-related illnesses. The company in turn must take appropriate action to minimize the exposure of its employees to hazardous agents. This can be done by rotating jobs, installing special engineering devices, improving ventilation, using safer chemicals, or providing workers with protective equipment.

Periodic Health Examinations

Some companies offer regular health examinations for employees and executives who do not work in hazardous environments. These assessments, which are similar to the pre-placement examination, are preventive in nature and stress the early detection of disease or predisposing factors to disease. Employers are beginning to provide these examinations free of charge because early detection and treatment of illnesses reduce absenteeism, improve work productivity, and may prevent long-term disability.

Return-to-Work Programs

Return-to-work programs help injured or sick workers return to the workforce as early as they are able. They focus on easing the transition for employees returning to work. Companies that use return-to-work programs see benefits such as lower insurance costs, enhanced retention of skilled workers, and better employee relations.

A physician evaluating candidates for return to work programs must have a good understanding of the work employees perform and the types of restrictions an employer can accommodate. The physician must determine whether the employee can return to full-time or part-time work, to regular duty, or to modified duty. In modified-duty programs, injured workers return to jobs that are designed according to their interests and capabilities. Workers make a gradual transition back to their regular jobs while performing as many of their usual duties as possible. Modified duty should be discussed in detail with the employee and his or her supervisor. The employer should predetermine the duration of modified duty, adding responsibilities as the employee's condition improves. Collaboration between health services and management is essential for the program to be effective.

Disability Management

An estimated one out of five employees will use short-term disability during his or her working years. Many companies provide short-term disability programs for their employees. However, many employers neglect to control the length of absenteeism and the loss of productivity. Ideally, every disability case should be reviewed by a health care professional. The length of disability given by the personal physician should be compared with accepted standards for that disability. If the length of disability is excessive for a diagnosis, additional information should be obtained to affirm the reason. If the company's case manager or its disability insurance representative disagrees with the employee's personal physician about the length of disability, the company may request an independent medical examination (IME). A physician chosen either by the company or by its disability insurer performs the IME, which determines a return-to-work date and the length of time the employee will receive disability pay.

The type of work the employee performs also must be considered. Durations of disability are significantly shorter for clerical workers than for manual laborers.

Employee Health Management Programs

Some companies have employee health management programs that offer workers and their families convenient access to medical care. These companies have established large medical facilities off-site that offer medical care by a group of physicians and specialists, diagnostic testing, and pharmacy services.

Other companies have limited employee health management programs that offer medical care at the workplace for employees only. Employees are evaluated for non-occupational illnesses by the company physician and given the appropriate treatment. By providing workers with early diagnosis and treatment on-site, the employer benefits in reduced absence rates.

Employee Health Screening

Many employers offer special health-related screenings to their employees. These programs educate employees, detect illnesses, and increase employees' awareness of certain diseases. These screenings usually are very cost-effective, allowing early diagnosis, early treatment, and reduction of subsequent medical absences. The most common screening program is for hypertension. Blood pressure screening during lunch or before or after work is simple and often performed by a nurse. Employees with elevated blood pressure may be referred to employee health services or more often to their personal physician.

Mammography programs for early detection of breast cancer are becoming increasingly common. The most effective programs provide a mammography van or a portable unit at the workplace. Some smaller companies contract with a local mammography facility for services. Such programs usually are free to the employee or reimbursed by health insurance. Other common programs screen for cholesterol, glucose (diabetes), and skin cancer. Some companies also have screening programs for colon cancer, prostate cancer, and osteoporosis.

Wellness Programs

Many companies have introduced wellness programs or disease management programs to promote good health. Companies subsidize such programs, which can be implemented onsite or in the community, in order to reduce future health care costs and losses in productivity from workers' preventable illnesses. While these programs vary greatly from company to company, they usually include courses on smoking cessation, general nutrition, low-salt diets, cholesterol reduction, weight loss, hypertension, diabetes, asthma, prenatal care, stress management, and depression.

Smoking is the leading cause of preventable disease in the United States today. The Centers for Disease Control and Prevention estimates that cigarette smoking causes 440,000 deaths, or 20 percent of all deaths, each year. Adults who smoke will die, on average, thirteen or fourteen years earlier than nonsmokers. Cigarette smoking is a primary cause of many diseases, such as lung cancer, heart disease, emphysema, and chronic bronchitis. Because of these statistics, many companies have instituted smoking cessation programs, such as the American Cancer Society's Fresh Start program or Smokenders, to help employees stop smoking. In addition, most companies have established strict policies to create smoke-free workplaces.

Elevated cholesterol is also a significant risk factor in the development of heart disease, the leading cause of death in the United States today. Programs that educate employees about cholesterol and good nutrition are the most effective methods for long-term reduction of cholesterol.

Obesity can lead to many serious medical problems, and recent studies show it may soon match or even replace smoking as the leading cause of preventable deaths. Programs encouraging weight reduction are usually very popular with employees. The easiest and most effective weight-counseling programs are onsite, such as Weight Watchers. Such programs may be provided at the workplace on a weekly basis to educate employees and encourage weight loss. Some company cafeterias offer reduced-fat or low-calorie entrees in conjunction with these programs.

Some companies offer prenatal care courses for pregnant employees. These programs are especially valuable in companies where employees have a high incidence of complicated births. The March of Dimes offers an effective prenatal education program called Babies and You that has been adopted by many companies.

Wellness programs also may include company-published health literature. These publications may range from one-page newsletters to complete magazines. They help increase employee awareness of the importance of a healthy lifestyle by providing information about weight reduction, smoking, exercise, and early signs and symptoms of common diseases.

Through their medical insurance or another health care company, employers also may provide disease management programs. These companies identify employees with specific chronic diseases such as depression, diabetes, asthma, or hypertension. They provide the employees with educational information to better control their conditions and encourage employees to follow physician instructions. Some of these companies have health care professionals available by telephone to answer general medical questions employees may have.

Immunizations

Some companies offer workers immunizations through employee health services. The most commonly given immunizations protect against influenza, tetanus, and hepatitis B. For workers who travel outside the United States, immunizations may be provided against such diseases as cholera, typhus, yellow fever, hepatitis A, and polio.

Companies whose workers travel internationally may provide necessary medications and immunizations to their workers for free. Medication for the prevention of malaria is given for travel to certain parts of the world. Company health care professionals can access Travax, a travel immunization computer program updated weekly that incorporates information from the Centers for Disease Control and Prevention, the U.S. Department of States, and the World Health Organization, to stay on top of immunization recommendations for international travelers. They may also access travel immunization information directly via the Internet at the Centers for Disease Control and Prevention (CDC) or the World Health Organization (WHO) Web sites.

COMPLIANCE WITH STATE AND FEDERAL REGULATIONS

Occupational Safety and Health Administration

The most important legislation concerning health in the workplace is the Occupational Safety and Health Act of 1970. This act established the Occupational Safety and Health Administration (OSHA) under the direction of the U.S. Department of Labor to disseminate and enforce safety and health standards to protect employees at work. Over two hundred local OSHA offices exist throughout the nation in order to enforce protective standards and implement outreach programs to employers and employees. The OSHA standards described below affect a significant number of employers and employees in the United States.

Every employer with eleven or more employees must maintain records of work-related injuries and illnesses. The employer also is required to post an annual summary of the workers' injuries and illnesses. These records must be kept for five years and must be made available to employees and OSHA representatives on request. Major financial penalties can be levied against employers who fail to accurately document employee illnesses and injuries in the workplace.

Employers are responsible for identifying chemical, physical, biological, and ergonomic hazards in the workplace. For exposure to certain materials, medical surveillance is required under the Occupational Safety and Health Act. OSHA requires medical monitoring for exposure to asbestos, benzene, noise, lead, and other chemicals and hazards. This monitoring generally begins with a medical history and physical examination. In some cases it may include specific blood tests, pulmonary function tests, chest X-rays, or hearing tests.

OSHA also requires that employees be given certain protective equipment if there is a reasonable probability of an injury at the worksite. The most common pieces of equipment supplied to employees are safety glasses and shoes, helmets, respirators, and hearing protectors.

The hazard communication standard, enacted in 1983, is one of the most important regulations formulated by OSHA. Its goal is to ensure that employers and employees know about the substances with which they work and understand how to reduce illnesses and injuries associated with chemical materials by identifying the chemicals and including hazard warnings. Employers also must provide a Material Safety Data Sheet (MSDS) for a hazardous material. This is a technical bulletin describing the chemical, its characteristics, the health and safety hazards, and precautions for safe handling and use.

Workers' Compensation

State workers' compensation laws regulate work-related injuries and illnesses. These laws require that employers provide replacement incomes to employees who suffer work-related injuries or illnesses. States have different laws, but they follow similar principles under a "no-fault" system. This means the employee is entitled to receive benefits regardless of whether the employer has provided a safe workplace or the worker's own carelessness contributed to the injury or illness. Employers are required to pay a portion of the salary lost (usually about 70 percent), and many have a fee schedule for hospital and physician services. Employers pay for insurance to cover this cost, either through a state fund or through a private insurance company.

There usually is little doubt as to whether an injury or illness is work related. Basically, any injury that occurs in connection with work is covered unless it was intentionally self-inflicted or caused by substance abuse. An illness or disease is likely to be covered if it was the gradual result of working conditions. For example, lost time and health care costs caused by carpal tunnel syndrome, tendonitis, lung disease, and heart attacks often are covered by workers' compensation.

Many companies view the expense of employee health services as cost effective, since these services can have a major impact on a company's workers' compensation costs. Early onsite treatment is extremely cost-effective and reduces lost time. Appropriate referral by health services may expedite early medical treatment. In addition, health services can perform case management to aid the employee through the health care maze and avoid wasting time or undergoing unnecessary procedures.

Health services also may participate in safety programs and accident investigations. These activities prevent accidents, reduce their severity and the time lost from work, and lower medical costs.

CURRENT ISSUES IN EMPLOYEE HEALTH SERVICES

AIDS in the Workplace

AIDS is a viral disease that gradually destroys the body's immune system. As a result, unusual or opportunistic infections and certain cancers, such as Kaposi's sarcoma, may occur. It can be transmitted by sexual intercourse, the use of infected needles, the transfusion of infected blood, or the transfer of the virus from a mother to her infant before birth or while breast-feeding. There also have been reports of AIDS transmission to health care workers via accidental sticks from contaminated needles or contact with infected blood. This disease is not transmitted by casual contact or social association in the workplace. Unfortunately, much fear and misinformation still surrounds AIDS.

In 1986 zidovudine, the first antiviral drug used in preventing HIV replication, was approved by the U.S. Food and Drug Administration. Many more antiviral drugs, which attacked the HIV virus in different ways, were approved for use in the subsequent decade. Since 1997 these drugs have been used in combination—referred to as "highly active antiretroviral therapy," or HAART—to great effect. The development of these drugs and drug combinations does not represent a cure for AIDS, but they do significantly reduce the amount of virus present and significantly increase the life expectancy of AIDS patients.

In terms of company policy, AIDS should be treated like any other disease or disability and should not be the basis of discriminatory practices. If an employee with AIDS is able to perform the duties of the job, he or she should be allowed to work. If the employee is not able to work, he or she should be placed on short-term or long-term disability.

Employee Assistance Programs

Some employers offer employee assistance programs (EAPs) to help workers and their families with personal problems that may affect the employees' well-being and job performance. Alcoholism, drug abuse, and emotional, medical, legal, financial, work-related, or family problems are commonly treated. Early intervention, counseling, and appropriate referrals are the primary objectives of EAPs. The employee is given between three and eight EAP counseling sessions, usually at no cost. If further intervention is necessary, the costs usually are covered by the employee's medical benefits.

EAPs generally are not located at the workplace. An employee often uses a toll-free telephone number to make the initial contact. Employees can seek help on their own by calling the EAP directly—which is usually the case—or they can be referred by supervisors. Once the employee makes contact with the program, he or she is evaluated by either a social worker or a psychologist, depending on the problem. After the evaluation, the employee may continue with the social worker or psychologist or may be referred to an appropriate specialist or center. The information gathered about a particular employee and his or her problem is confidential, and the employer is not notified.

A referral to an EAP by a supervisor is usually made because of an employee's poor job performance or behavior at work that may reflect personal problems. In this case the employee is required to contact the EAP and to comply with the EAP's treatment or recommendations. Failure to do so may result in disciplinary action by the company.

In 2001 a survey found that about 60 percent of employees surveyed had access to an EAP. The overwhelming majority (86.3 percent) of employees working in large firms with more than five hundred employees had a company EAP. All federal agencies have EAPs. These programs are successful and cost-effective. They help increase productivity by reducing employee turnover, absenteeism, and accidents. The federal government estimates that for every $1 a company invests in an EAP, $1.50 to $15 is saved in lower absenteeism, turnover, and medical claims.

Drug Testing

Many companies have instituted substance abuse programs to deal with the problem of drug and alcohol abuse in the workplace. These programs take a firm stand against the use of substances that may affect safety or the performance of employees in the workplace.

During the administration of President Ronald Reagan (1981–89), the federal government began to aggressively pursue drug testing in the workplace. By the late 1980s new Department of Transportation regulations mandated extensive drug-testing programs in numerous fields including the aviation, maritime, mass transit, motor carrier, pipeline, and railroad industries. Despite periodic challenges to these regulations and specific company policies, the U.S. Supreme Court has upheld the federal government's right to impose drug-testing requirements on both private employees and government workers when their duties affect either law enforcement or general public safety. Various laws regulate drug-testing policies at the state level, as well. Legal challenges to drug-testing policies continue to be brought before the justice system at all levels.

An employee may be tested on several occasions. The first is during an applicant's pre-placement physical. Medical personnel may request that applicants provide urine and blood samples for testing purposes. It is important that the company follow a proper procedure called "chain of custody," which requires an applicant's signature and witness of the specimen's sealing with a special tape. This procedure guarantees it is the applicant's urine and prevents tampering. The specimen is sent to a laboratory for detection of illegal and prescription drugs. Some drugs, such as marijuana, may be positive in the urine for up to twenty-eight days, whereas other drugs may be detected for only three to four days. If the initial results are positive, a more sensitive testing method is used to confirm them. If an applicant tests positive for illegal substances, he or she usually will be denied employment. Even marijuana found in urine weeks after use can be a legal cause for denying employment. When the drug test is positive for a prescription medication such as Valium, the applicant may be asked to produce a letter from the prescribing physician stating the reason for the medication. This information is important and might prevent the applicant from being hired (for example, if the job includes operating heavy machinery).

An employee may be tested for drug use during an annual physical examination, randomly during the year, "for cause," or after an accident. Drug testing during the annual physical or done randomly may deter substance abuse, but such testing has legal implications. It is important for the company to have a clear drug policy covering this type of testing. Employees who test positive are subject to disciplinary action or termination. They also may be referred to an EAP or for professional evaluation and recommended for individual or group counseling, outpatient care, or hospitalization. Those testing positive for illegal drugs after an accident may be denied unemployment, workers' compensation, or disability benefits.

When an employee acts in an unusual manner, the supervisor may request drug and alcohol testing commonly referred to as "for cause" testing. It is important that the employee be examined by a medical doctor before testing to document the problem and to be sure the symptoms are not the result of a medical condition.

Fitness Programs

Many companies have instituted fitness or exercise programs to improve the health of their employees. When employees take advantage of these programs they can increase productivity, decrease absenteeism and turnover, reduce stress, and improve morale, in addition to reducing health care costs.

Surveys show that most large employers are active in promoting health. Employers may offer subsidized gym memberships or onsite fitness facilities. The simplest type of program reimburses the employee for participation in an exercise course at a local YMCA or health facility. Such a program is easy to initiate and manage. Disadvantages include low employee attendance and scheduling problems.

Some large corporations have taken this idea further. They have constructed complete onsite fitness centers that include exercise bicycles, elliptical trainers, treadmills, rowing machines, muscle-strengthening equipment, specially equipped aerobics rooms, running tracks, basketball courts, and full-size swimming pools. An exercise specialist evaluates the employees and designs individualized exercise regimens. This type of program is very popular because it provides a convenient facility and a customized exercise program.

Evidence suggests most companies experience a direct reduction of medical costs as a result of these programs. Companies also benefit from decreased absenteeism and increased productivity.

Health Care Trends in the United States

A serious health care crisis exists in the United States today. It is an economic crisis as well as a medical one. According to the National Coalition on Health Care, insurance premiums increased by 10 percent in 2005. This increase was nearly three times the rate of inflation. The annual family health plan premium averaged $10,800 in 2005, which is more than the earnings of a full-time, minimum wage worker.

National health expenditures are expected to continue to outpace inflation. Inflation, the aging of the population, and major technological innovations have contributed to the increase in the cost of health care. To make matters even worse, according to an April 2005 article in the *Hamden Journal*, the U.S. health care industry is losing $100 billion a year due to payment errors. This means even higher premiums for employers and employees.

In the past, many employees and their families had health benefits paid entirely by their companies. Employees were enrolled in indemnity programs, which provided the freedom to see any physician and go to any hospital. Rising health care costs have caused many companies to switch to managed care plans, which include health maintenance organizations (HMOs), preferred provider organizations (PPOs), and point-of-service (POS) plans. Under managed care, employees are limited to network physicians and hospitals and are required to get referrals to see specialists. In addition, employees may be asked to pay a larger percentage of their health insurance premiums while receiving less coverage and having higher deductibles. Coverage for new employees may not start for one to six months from the date of employment. This trend of rising costs and declining coverage is projected to continue.

Some companies have even tried to eliminate or reduce the medical benefits of retirees. With escalating costs for their medical benefits and longer life expectancies, many medical plans for retirees were underfunded. As a result, many companies are reducing and eliminating medical benefits for future retirees.

In 2004 45.5 million Americans under age sixty-five were uninsured. More than 80 percent of these uninsured people come from families with workers, and 70 percent of them from families with at least one full-time worker. Two-thirds of uninsured people come from low-income families. Uninsured people rarely receive primary care, generally waiting until their condition reaches the emergency stage before seeking medical attention. The results are higher costs and poorer prognoses (predictions of the probable course of a disease and the chances of recovery).

Companies have looked to insurers to better manage their health care costs. As a result, insurance companies developed physician networks, such as managed care systems and HMOs, to reduce health care costs. These networks of hospitals and doctors provide medical services at discounted fees. Companies did not, however, realize the savings they anticipated because they incurred increased administrative costs from the programs. Instead, companies have reduced costs primarily by shifting premium increases to employees for the same or less coverage than they had before. Unfortunately, this trend will continue as companies try to remain competitive in an increasingly changing business environment.

How to Get Your First Job

Melissa J. Doak

Looking for your first job—whether for a part-time job while you're in high school or college, or for a full-time job after graduation—can seem like an overwhelming task. Finding a job is hard to begin with—but if you haven't had any work experience, have never written a resume or been through an interview, and don't even know what kind of job you want or are qualified for—job hunting can seem impossible. Take heart—everyone has to search for, and land, their first job sometime. But how do you go about doing it?

PREPARING YOURSELF

Do Your Research

What do you want to do? Where would you like to work? What jobs might fit your skills, appeal to your interests, or possibly advance your career goals? These are important questions to ask yourself before you begin your job search.

Even if you are only searching for a part-time summer job while going to school, you should do some research into occupations that might interest you in the long term. Consider using even a part-time job to explore larger career goals. Why take a job as a stock clerk at your local department store if you think you might be interested in landscape architecture someday? Instead, you may look for a local landscaper who needs summer workers to help maintain the gardens of business clients, or you could approach the family-owned nursery about a part-time position in the greenhouse.

Take the time to explore your options. There are many books that list careers and jobs, including the books in the *Career Information Center* series. The Bureau of Labor Statistics maintains an up-to-date online career guide, the *Occupational Outlook Handbook*, at http://www.bls.gov/oco/home.htm. You might also talk with friends and family about what types of jobs are available where they work. Employment counselors or college or high school career counselors also may provide useful guidance.

Volunteering

A common problem for first-time job seekers is lack of experience. One way to address this problem before looking for your first job is to volunteer your time. Volunteering not only provides valuable experience, it also is a great way to contribute to your community while fostering your own personal growth. And you won't be alone—the Bureau of Labor Statistics found that between September 2004 and September 2005, 28.8 percent of Americans volunteered at least once; and those who did volunteer donated, on average, fifty hours of their time.

Melissa J. Doak is a freelance writer of reference books and educational materials.

Once again, you should consider your own personal career interests and goals as you choose an organization or company to approach about volunteering opportunities. For example, someone interested in a career in social work might want to volunteer at a homeless shelter, food bank, or senior citizens' center. Someone interested in a career in education might volunteer to help others learn to read or spend time helping in a local elementary school classroom. Those interested in health care might volunteer at a hospital or nursing home. Someone interested in forestry might look into volunteer programs at state and national parks. Aspiring politicians might offer to work on local political campaigns. Not only are the possibilities endless, but volunteering will help you explore your career interests and give you valuable experience to give your resume some punch.

Internships

Students planning their careers should investigate the possibility of an internship. An internship is a cooperative learning activity that provides students with professional experience outside of the classroom related to their career goals. While the focus is on the educational aspect, internships also provide real-world, practical experience. Typically, internships are unpaid but provide college credit. Internships are actually required in many fields—think of the ubiquitous student teachers in elementary school classrooms—but even in fields where they are not required, an internship is a good way to build experience and credentials for the job you want when you graduate. You might intern at a library or a bank, in a historical society or counseling center, at an advertising agency, a television or radio station, or a newspaper, in a variety of social service agencies, at a community theater, or in a political action group. You might explore career possibilities in education, medicine, public administration, or computer programming. As with volunteering, internship opportunities can be found almost anywhere.

Sometimes internships lead directly to job offers. At the very least they provide valuable experience by helping you to explore what types of work you may want to do, bolstering your confidence, and strengthening your resume. The *Occupational Outlook Quarterly Online*, published by the Bureau of Labor Statistics, asserts that employers look first to their interns when seeking to hire new college graduates. Internships also help you gain and practice crucial communication skills; employers responding to the Job Outlook 2006 survey conducted by the National Association of Colleges and Employers cited these as the most important "soft" skills or qualities possessed by job candidates. You should also emerge with a good letter of reference from your supervisor. And searching for an internship gives you good practice for many of the skills you will need when searching for your first job: researching and speaking with potential employers, completing applications, and writing resumes and cover letters.

Most colleges have formal internship programs, and some high schools are implementing them as well. For example, the Constitutional Rights Foundation in Los Angeles has helped nearly one thousand high school students find internships with law firms, non-profit organizations, and corporations since 1995. Check your course catalog for information on credit for internships. Visit your career information center or guidance counselor's office for guidance on where to begin looking for the internship that will best help you advance your career goals.

A Special Kind of Preparation for Your First Job: Apprenticeships

Apprenticeships are highly structured programs of on-the-job training combined with classroom instruction. Apprenticeships typically train people for highly skilled production or crafts jobs—although they are available for more than 850 occupations. Programs vary in length from one to six years. Searching for an apprenticeship is actually a lot like searching for a job. People accepted into apprenticeships typically learn on the job while being paid for their work, and, in addition, they receive classroom instruction in technical aspects of the job. Formal apprenticeship programs are registered with the Department of Labor, and graduates receive certificates of completion that are accepted by employers around the country.

Although the process of being accepted into an apprenticeship is generally competitive, many apprenticeship opportunities are available. There are nearly thirty thousand apprenticeship programs in the United States, including more than three thousand programs newly established in 2005. Common apprenticeship programs train people for jobs in the building trades and manufacturing industry. Apprenticeships are available for prospective firefighters, cooks, and telecommunications technicians. People can also apprentice in less common fields, training to be stage technicians and actors, designers, paralegals, environmental technicians, computer programmers, and landscapers. Many apprenticed occupations are expected to enjoy an exceptional job outlook over the coming decades—including cooks, auto mechanics, practical nurses, carpenters, electricians, and hairdressers. And apprentices pay nothing for their education (although they may have to pay for the tools of their trade); in fact, they are actually paid to learn.

If you think an apprenticeship program might be right for you, the first thing to do is to find an open program. Begin with your state Bureau of Apprenticeship or state office of the Department of Labor. Also try career counseling offices, trade unions, and professional associations. Some apprenticeship programs will also be publicly advertised in the newspaper, on job boards, or with state job services. Military recruits can also participate in apprenticeship programs. Local recruiters are the best source of information for these opportunities.

Once you find an apprenticeship program, the next step is getting in, and in some occupations, apprenticeships are highly competitive. You generally must be eighteen years old and possess a high school diploma or passing score on a high school equivalency exam. You must fill out required forms and take any required proficiency or aptitude tests. Common tests measure reading, math, and problem-solving skills, but specific programs may require other assessments as well. The application process will usually include an interview, after which qualified applicants are ranked and placed on a waiting list.

For your best chance at being accepted into an apprenticeship of your choice, prepare yourself with a solid high school background in the basics of English, math, and science. High school courses in drafting, mechanical drawing, and industrial arts can also provide an advantage for those interested in construction, production, or mechanical occupations. There may also be tutoring programs available to help applicants prepare for and pass the qualifying exams for particular apprenticeships.

SEEKING WORK

Creating a Resume and Cover Letter

For most jobs, putting together a resume is very important. Even if a particular position does not require one, having a resume will help show prospective employers that you have put some effort into the job search, and therefore will put some effort into the job. In addition, a well-done resume and cover letter will show employers that you have good written communication skills, which are crucial for many jobs in today's information-based economy.

First-time job seekers may believe they have little of value to place on a resume. That is untrue. Your goal is to answer the prospective employer's big question: How will this candidate add to the company or organization? To answer that question, consider your education, extracurricular activities, awards or recognition you have received, and unpaid work.

Here are some things you will want to include in your resume:

Schooling and Other Training Of course, list any degrees you have received. Include any coursework you have completed that is relevant to the position. List your GPA if it is over 3.0. Also list other training you have received. Think broadly. Your CPR certification might be very important if you are applying to work at a summer camp for kids, as will the babysitting class you took in ninth grade.

Extracurricular Activities Were you on the yearbook committee? That might be important if you are applying to work in the local photography shop. Did you play on the school's basketball team? After-school programs for youth will want to know that. Did you help organize your school prom? A catering business might be very interested in your organizational skills. Make sure you include your participation in extracurricular activities, especially if they relate to the position you are seeking.

Volunteer Work You may have already explored your career interests while volunteering at a local business or organization. Any work you have done, even unpaid work, counts as experience. Make sure to list it on your resume.

Awards or Special Recognition Did you get elected into the National Honor Society? Get special recognition at an athletic awards banquet for your leadership as captain of the football team? Win an essay contest? List this recognition on your resume. It will make you stand out from the pack and help a prospective employer evaluate what she stands to gain from hiring you.

Technical and Computer Skills You may take for granted your ability to design a Web site or use advanced functions in Microsoft Office, but your prospective employer won't. List these skills on your resume.

References You can choose to list your references and their contact information right on your resume, or to include the phrase, "References are available upon request." Make sure you can provide the names and contact information of at least three people who can vouch for your ability and responsible nature. Good choices include teachers, people you have helped in the past, and supervisors in any organizations for which you have volunteered.

Once you have compiled all of the information you want to use in your resume, you will need to focus on its design. You want the look of your resume to make the right impression on prospective employers. Go to the library or your school's career information center and study books on resumes. All books will provide examples. Choose the style that most appeals to you and that is most relevant to your information, and lay out your resume in that format. Make sure to include a header with your contact information, including your name, address, phone number, and e-mail address. Limit your resume to no more than one page.

Cover Letters When mailing a resume to a prospective employer, you should include a cover letter. In this letter, you are introducing yourself, stating what position you are applying for, and explaining your interest and qualifications. A good cover letter will have a three-paragraph format. In the first paragraph, explain why you are sending a resume and indicate where you heard about employment opportunities at the organization. Are you looking for a part-time summer job or a permanent position? Are you responding to an ad in the newspaper or following up on a suggestion from a worker at the organization?

Use your next paragraph to convince the reader to look at your resume. Summarize how your combination of skills and experience makes you perfect for the job. Be specific. Call attention to the parts of your resume that are most relevant to the position. Expand by using examples of your experience that are not listed on your resume. Make sure to emphasize personal qualities that are important for the position: your motivation, enthusiasm, responsibility, and communication skills, for example.

End by providing any information that was specifically requested in a job advertisement (for example, state that you have attached a writing sample, or indicate when you are available to begin work). Thank the prospective employer for his or her time and consideration, indicate what you will do to follow up (for example, "I will be in touch the week of June 15th if I have not heard from you"), and make note of how you can be reached.

Where to Search

So now you have your job hunting materials. But where do you look for job openings? You should use a variety of sources to search for advertised openings (for example, print and online advertisements, job banks, and career centers). But you should also target companies or organizations where you would like to work but which have not advertised any positions.

Advertised Openings How do you know what employers are hiring? You can look at a variety of sources. The help wanted ads in your local newspaper are a good place to start. Sometimes retail stores and restaurants have help wanted signs in their windows. Your school's career center should also have lists of job openings.

The Internet also has thousands of sites that list job advertisements. Some sites offer tens of thousands of job listings; others offer only a handful. Some are sponsored by professional trade associations, others are sponsored by local, state, or federal governments, and still others are for-profit ventures that charge job hunters for their services. Some offer the ability to post resumes online—but it is unclear how many employers bother to search these resumes, so it may not be worth the time. And some occupations are not very well represented in the job banks. So while online job sites are worth visiting, evaluate very carefully which ones are most worth your time and effort.

You should also locate the nearest provider of public employment services, either by visiting http://www.servicelocator.org or calling 1-877-USA-JOBS. These services generally include help planning your career, finding work, finding summer work, and getting skills and training. These centers often have a library with books on how to craft a good resume and cover letter. Take advantage of these free resources where they are available.

The Hidden Job Market Don't discount targeting employers you want to work for, even if they are not advertising in the help wanted pages. Experts generally agree that the number of unadvertised job openings exceeds the number of advertised ones. Therefore, if you only apply for advertised positions you will miss more than half the opportunities available to you. Although it takes more time and effort to search out these opportunities, job seekers probably face less competition for these vacancies. And seeking out these prospective employers gives you a chance to demonstrate your commitment and initiative.

To access this hidden market, a job seeker needs to do three things: research companies and organizations for which she would like to work, cold call for job leads, and network. First, job seekers need to use various methods—business directories, the Yellow Pages, word-of-mouth, and online searches—to identify companies that are likely to hire workers like them. Job seekers should put in a little extra time and research each identified company or organization to find out more about them and what they are like to work for. Newspaper articles, company Web sites, and informal questions of current workers are good places to look for this kind of information. This research will not only help job seekers determine which companies will likely be hiring and which companies are good to work for, but also may eventually help in the interview process.

Once prospective employers are identified and researched, job seekers must make contact with those organizations. Because job seekers are not responding to a help-wanted advertisement but instead making unsolicited contact with prospects, this contact is called "cold calling." Some job seekers telephone targeted companies to ask if there are any openings. Others may show up in person to inquire. Still others may send resumes and cover letters out to prospective employers, although this is a less successful method—after all, it is much easier to ignore a letter than it is a phone call or an in-person request for information. Without a compelling reason to do otherwise, making a telephone call or an in-person inquiry is generally your best strategy.

With luck, your cold calling will uncover unadvertised job opportunities. And since you have sought these opportunities out yourself, you face less competition than you would for an advertised position. And taking the initiative will impress the prospective employer as well as save him the work of reading through hundreds of cover letters and resumes that he might receive in response to an advertisement—both of which give you the advantage.

Job seekers looking for unadvertised positions should also network. Using the people you know, and the people they know, to discover job leads and other employment information is called networking. Make sure to use basic manners and common courtesy when making job-related inquiries of your network. Tell everyone you know that you are searching for a job, and what kinds of positions you are interested in. Make sure to follow up on any suggestions or leads you receive, as well as thank those who help you in your job hunt.

Temporary Staffing Services Another place you may want to look for your first job is with a temporary staffing services company like Kelly Services. Temporary staffing agencies provide employees to other organizations, on a contract basis and for a limited period, to supplement the client's workforce. Some employers are using contingent workers—workers who are employed on a temporary basis to meet an immediate need created by employee absences, temporary skill shortages, and varying seasonal workloads—to fill 30 to 80 percent of their jobs. More than two million people per day are employed by the temporary staffing industry, which is one of the fastest-growing in the country. According to the U.S. Bureau of Labor Statistics, the industry is expected to gain about 1.6 million new jobs between 2004 and 2014.

Temporary workers tend to be younger, with less experience, than other workers. The hiring process is more relaxed than it is for permanent positions, which is helpful for workers with no prior work experience. Usually temp workers are employed in clerical, service, or sales positions, although there are opportunities in production occupations, health care, and even professional positions in the temporary services industry. Temporary work will definitely bolster your resume. In addition, an assignment as a contingent worker within an organization will help you get on the inside to find out about permanent positions. In fact, as many as one in five organizations use temporary staffing services to screen employees for permanent jobs. Other advantages to this work include the opportunity for a short-term source of income while enjoying flexible schedules, an ability to take extended leaves of absences and the ability to explore various careers, and the opportunity to experience a variety of work settings and employers.

If you decide to register with temporary staffing services companies, make sure you are on the roster of several agencies, rather than just one, to enhance your opportunities for temp jobs. Make sure that you are clear with the company about what kind of work you want. The Web site of the American Staffing Association, http://www.americanstaffing.net, can provide you with more information about this quickly growing industry.

Interviews

The prospect of an interview can be very frightening, but there are ways to make it easier. The keys to a successful interview are to be prepared, present yourself professionally, and describe your qualifications for the position well.

Before the Interview One secret to a successful interview is to do some work ahead of time to learn all you can about the position you are interviewing for and the company itself. Search the Internet, ask your friends and family, and visit public libraries and career centers. Make sure you know what the company does, how big it is, if it has undergone any changes recently (or is preparing for any), and what the organization's goals and values are. Employers are impressed by well-informed job seekers.

Also practice describing yourself and explaining how hiring you would benefit the organization. Think about examples from your schooling, extracurricular activities, or volunteer work that illustrate important skills and characteristics. Your interviewer will probably ask you questions along the following lines: What are your strengths and weaknesses? Why do you want to work here? Why should we hire you? Preparing for and practicing the answers to these questions in advance will give you an advantage. Simple yes or no answers will not do; make sure you are able to draw on examples to give your answers some substance. Try to put everything in a positive light, including your weaknesses.

The Interview Itself On the day of the interview, dress appropriately. You want to look professional and well groomed, but you do not want what you wear to be the most memorable part of the interview. Be conservative with makeup and cologne, wear muted colors, and don't make bold fashion statements.

Make sure you arrive on time. Drive your route ahead of time, or take public transportation there the day before. This way, you can be certain you will not get lost and you will know how much time it takes to get there. Leave early anyway. If you arrive early, you can use the extra time to collect your thoughts.

When you meet your interviewer, greet her with a smile and a handshake and look her directly in the eye. The interview will probably begin with the interviewer describing the position or the organization in more detail, and then move into questions for you in order to evaluate how well you will fit into the organization. If you have prepared adequately, you can feel confident about describing yourself and your abilities and how they will contribute to the company or organization.

Most interviewers will end the interview by asking you if you have any questions. This gives you a chance to not only find out more about the organization and the position, but also to make a favorable impression. A thoughtful question will communicate as much to the interviewer about you as will your answers to his questions. Questions you might want to ask are: Are there opportunities for advancement? How do you train employees? What do you like about working for this organization? Use your research to come up with other questions that relate directly to the company. As you leave the interview, make sure you thank the interviewer and state again your interest in the position.

Following Up Sending a thank-you note after the interview is an important step that many job seekers omit. Be sure you send this note within two days. It should be printed on simple, white business paper, not a flowery thank-you card. Use standard business format for this letter. In the first paragraph, thank the interviewer for the meeting and express again your interest in and enthusiasm for the position. In your second paragraph, briefly restate the main skills that make you a good candidate for the position. If you forgot to mention anything important during the interview, this is the place to include it. In your third paragraph, thank the interviewer again, mention how you can be contacted, and tell the interviewer you look forward to speaking with him again. Proofread your letter carefully. Grammatical errors at this stage could cost you the job.

Remember that Rejection Is Part of the Process It is a highly unusual job hunter who lands the first job he applies for. Usually, job seekers are rejected several times, even dozens of times, before being hired, so you need to prepare yourself to hear "no." Remember, a business owner or a manager may not need to hire anyone right now, may have hired his aunt's cousin's son's sister-in-law to fill the advertised position, or you may just not be exactly what he is looking for. When you are told a position is filled, make sure you respond appropriately—you never know when another position will open. Show the manager or owner you are serious in your job hunt by being polite, leaving your resume, and inviting her to call if she needs anyone in the future.

Following the rules of the job hunt, knowing where to look for positions you are interested in, and persevering will pay off in the end, and you will land your first job.

Identifying Opportunities for Retraining

Judith Peacock

All of the following members of the American workforce have a common need. Can you tell what it is?

- Southeast Tool and Manufacturing is updating its equipment. Fred Warner, a floor worker at Southeast, must learn to use computer controls to operate massive steel casters and stamp presses. He risks being fired if he doesn't master the new system.

- Charlie Rucker lost his job when the noodle factory where he worked for twenty years shut down and moved to a different state to take advantage of cheaper labor. Now Charlie works as a janitor, at a much lower rate of pay and with fewer benefits.

- Despite earning $60,000 a year as a pipe fitter at Summit Metals, Bruce Blazek finds the work tedious and boring. He dreams of being a psychologist in the company's human resources department.

- Mollie Atterberry loves her job as an accountant with Andrew Fleming and Associates. She knows that if she wants to rise in the firm and make more money, she has to get a master's degree in business.

- Sue Fleming has a bachelor's degree in art, but she needs hands-on skills in computer graphics and process camera work to get the kinds of art and design jobs she wants.

- After spending nine years at home raising twins, LaFleur Greene wants to go back to work. Before staying home with her children, she worked as a telephone operator.

If you answered "retraining" to the above question, you would be absolutely right. All these workers could benefit from updating their job skills or learning new ones.

Retraining occurs for a variety of reasons: the need to keep pace with new technology, company reorganization or relocation, job obsolescence, and the desire for more challenging work, more money, or advancement. Even those who are perfectly satisfied with their jobs will find periodic retraining will be essential. Old jobs and old ways of working are rapidly disappearing, while new jobs and new ways of working are being created. Technological advances and economic developments have wrought workplace change on a scale and at a pace that was previously unimagined.

Even as many people feel threatened by this epidemic of workplace change, however, there is hope on the horizon. People can take charge, educate them-

Judith Peacock is a former educator who has worked in publishing for more than twenty years.

selves, and retool their skills to meet the needs of tomorrow's workplace. In his High Growth Job Training Initiative, President George W. Bush vowed to increase the number of workers in training programs from 200,000 to 400,000 a year and give states more flexibility in using federal job training and employment grants. Employers also provide worker training. Local community colleges are partnering with businesses and opening their doors to people who want to be retrained. Educational opportunities are available through trade associations and for-profit businesses and vocational schools. No matter how and why one goes about changing or increasing workplace skills, however, it is necessary to think about the broader context of social change and how such change affects the workplace.

TRENDS IN THE WORKPLACE

Whether you are entering the workplace for the first time or have already worked for a number of years, many changes are already having a profound effect on you, your work, and your relationship to the workplace.

The Heightened Pace of Change

Change is everywhere, but nowhere is it more evident than in offices and factories. As leadership scrambles to maintain or improve the business bottom line, some workers find themselves in the midst of frequent reorganizations, technological changes, physical moves, or new "programs for improvement." Learning how to feel comfortable with change should be one of the prime tools in every worker's new toolkit.

The End of the Lifetime Contract

The concept of working forever for the same employer—a product of the post–World War II ethos—began to erode almost as soon as it came into being. In fact, by the late 1960s most workers were changing jobs two or three times during their lives. It is estimated that those coming to their first job today will change employers up to a dozen times before retirement, while the median number of years that workers had been with their current employer was four in January 2004. The average person in the United States holds around nine jobs from age eighteen to age thirty-four, according to the Bureau of Labor Statistics. In many places the "lifetime contract" has given way to the "life of the project contract" or the "contract employee." Many workers actually view this as a positive development. They look forward to the challenge of continuing to learn as they take their skills and talents from employer to employer. These new "hands for hire" are themselves changing the shape of today's workplace.

Fewer Management Layers

If the recent workplace has had a slogan, it could well be "Do More with Less." The positive impact of technology and computers on the bottom line has, in many workplaces, meant having one secretary do the work that once took three and eliminating layers of middle management. Now managers crunch their own numbers on computerized spreadsheet programs and receive support from a secretary with three other bosses. However, with faster computers and new software, twenty-four-hour voice mail, global e-mail, and fax machines and other equipment, most companies have maintained—or even enhanced—productivity. Doing more with less has become an accepted way of corporate life.

New Ways of Working

In the 1980s the North American workplace raised its collective head, somewhat tired and battered from the beating it was taking from imports, and wondered if there were lessons to be learned. It was discovered that our international competition had taken quite seriously the workplace methodologies learned from (of all places) the United States, most notably lessons on quality from W. Edwards Deming, whose early work on quality has been the virtual bible of Japanese industry. These new ways of working—teamwork, quality circles (employees who meet regularly to discuss quality or productivity solutions to problems), and benchmarking—were quickly imported back to the United States, where they continue to enjoy success because they help create better products, help newly empowered workers derive more job satisfaction, and often establish a better workplace.

New Managers and Coworkers

The workplace is becoming more diverse. Women are now assuming managerial positions that were once the sole domain of men, and most people work for at least one woman at some time during their careers. According to the Bureau of Labor Statistics, the number of women in the labor force is expected to increase by 10.9 percent between 2004 and 2014, while the number of men is expected to increase by only 9.1 percent over that decade. Most people work for and with individuals whose culture and background are very different from theirs. Minority groups in the workplace are expected to grow significantly; by 2004 Hispanics, for the first time, made up a greater share of the labor force than did African Americans, and their numbers are expected to grow by 2.9 percent annually, compared to an annual growth rate of 1.6 percent for African Americans and 0.7 percent for non-Hispanic whites. Many people work for businesses whose headquarters are overseas and whose corporate culture is different from the North American business culture. To adapt to these changes, people need to be more aware, more flexible, and more tolerant than ever before.

New Kinds of Jobs

The meshing of the global economy and technology is creating new kinds of jobs even as others are being eliminated. Within five years there are likely to be jobs requiring new skills that are unimaginable now.

Most of the 18.9 million new jobs expected to develop between 2004 and 2014 will be in service-producing—rather than goods-producing—industries. Service jobs can be divided into two categories: traditional, low-paying jobs (including jobs at retail stores, restaurants, and hotels) and business services.

Service jobs—even some of those in the traditional, low-wage category—are changing to meet the needs of a new kind of consumer environment. More and more consumer-focused businesses employ salespeople and other workers who are technically trained and who understand what they are selling. For possessing these skills, the workers are well paid.

Even jobs that were traditionally labeled as "menial," such as garage mechanic, demand increasing technical competency. If you raise the hood of a modern car, you will find sophisticated electronic equipment and microcomputers. Today's garage mechanics must go through a great deal of training, and they receive substantial wages for their efforts. Similarly, in today's factories robots and computers may work the actual machines, but people are needed to control the robots and computers as well as to program and service them.

The business services category covers a broad spectrum of jobs. According to former labor secretary Robert Reich in *CQ Researcher*, "The business service job is everything from technical sales support, lab technicians, and paralegals to systems analysts. These are good jobs, the new middle-class jobs, replacing the factory work of twenty or thirty years ago as the gateway to the middle class." Service jobs in this category demand relatively high levels of training or retraining.

The New Workplace

"Too Few Engineers!" screamed the headlines. Consequently, many college freshmen, looking for a solid career, became engineering majors. Five years later, however, the headlines painted quite a different picture: "Engineering Glut! 'Too Many,' Say Experts!" What's a job seeker to do?

Forecasting the employment market has never been an exact science. The range of available jobs has always been subject to forces beyond the control of any one individual. For many people, deciding on a career has always been a bit like playing the lottery. They train for a specific career, but by the time they're ready for that job, there may be thousands of qualified workers ahead of them. Moreover, in today's climate another scenario is all too possible: the job may become obsolete before the training is even completed.

Never before in our history has there been a more compelling argument for training, retraining, and continuing education. Now, as never before, is the time to continue the education process that makes employees so valuable in the rapidly changing workplace. Even workers who have the desire or are fortunate enough to stay with the same company will find that the company is going to change. Today's companies acquire other companies or are acquired themselves; they refocus on the existing marketplace or focus on a new and emerging market segment; and they may want to do things differently to reverse a decline and become profitable or to increase profitability. These and other changes will most likely have a direct and immediate impact on company employees and their work.

For example, a company may suddenly eliminate its office space and move to the concept of "hoteling" or the "virtual office," in which—with a notebook computer and access to a telephone—your office becomes any place where you are. Or employees may find themselves in the midst of "teaming" and "quality circles," suddenly poised for leadership roles that demand new communication skills. Whatever the changes, the configuration of many jobs will be radically redefined. It pays to be prepared.

Skills and Tools to Fit New Needs

For the individual employee, the key word is flexibility. Everyone needs to be able to adapt quickly to different circumstances. Being flexible and adaptable means having tools at hand that will be helpful, whether in the context of a first job, a promotion within a particular company, or a sudden re-entry to the job market, in search of new employment. The following basic tools will always be useful.

The Written Word Being able to write clearly and concisely has never been more important. A great deal of information is being communicated in many words. The ability to synthesize information into a concise and well-written document is valuable to just about any part of any business organization. Taking a course in business writing (or even just plain writing) can be a sound investment.

Speaking Well You're at a staff meeting and your boss says, "Tell us what you think of the latest marketing strategy." In a job interview, you're asked, "What's your biggest weakness?" You have been given the opportunity to explain a new manufacturing procedure to your colleagues. In all these situations your response can be very important. Public speaking doesn't necessarily mean giving a speech in front of a large crowd. Being able to speak well in front of two, ten, or twenty people is a valuable asset. A course in public speaking can help anyone prepare for key career moments.

Computer Literacy Computer technology has been integrated into every business and industry, from trash hauling to aerospace engineering. Virtually every worker will need to know how to store information within a computerized network, access information within that network, perform computer analyses related to your job, and communicate with other computers in the network. In an article for *Career World,* Deborah O'Donnell Vasenda, a computer literacy teacher, said, "Computer skills will help [your] employment prospects.... Basic computer skills help a person to become more employable and give a person who receives on-the-job training a head start." Computer literacy involves more than knowing how to use a word processing program and a printer. It will be important to have some knowledge of programming and databases. Everyone will also need to know how the Internet operates and how to access information online.

Project Management Skills Understanding different models of how to move work from point A to point B, learning how to deal with problems, and knowing how to set and meet deadlines can all prove invaluable in the workplace.

People Skills If people are working in new ways with one another—in process teams or value circles, as empowered employees or frontline managers—they need to hone the skills that help them interact. They need to know how to become better listeners, coaches, and moderators; how to deal with men and women as colleagues; and how to understand and work with people from different backgrounds.

Job-Seeking Skills Not only will most people change jobs several times during their careers; many people will even change careers. Some of the best tools to have are skills that will be useful in seeking a new job or starting a new career. It is important to know how to market oneself through a resumé that works, letters that sell, and a structured process of job seeking. It is equally important to learn and relearn the process of self-presentation during interviews. Finally, it is a good idea to become adept at the negotiating skills needed to obtain optimal job conditions and a competitive compensation package.

SOURCES FOR RETRAINING

Some people look for retraining while they are still employed. For many, however, the prospect of changing from one field to another—and the retraining that such change would require—presents itself only when they have been made the subject of a reduction in force by being rightsized, downsized, or just plain "pink-slipped." In any case, several sources for retraining are available.

Federal and State Government

The federal government offers some retraining programs, mostly for workers whose job loss can be attributed to government policies or who are economically disadvantaged. For example, the Economic Dislocation and Worker Adjustment Assistance Act (EDWAA) offers retraining to workers who have been laid off and who will probably not be able to get jobs in their previous industries. Trade Adjustment Assistance (TAA) helps those workers who have been laid off because of federal policies that allow increased foreign trade. Federal employment and training programs largely function through state and local governments. As a result of welfare reform in the mid-1990s, state governments now face the challenge of providing job training services and employment for the unemployed, including homeless people and those suffering from mental illness and drug and alcohol addiction.

Government programs have undoubtedly been of help to millions of workers who lose their jobs each year and should be investigated as a possible source of retraining. At the same time, debate continues as to the scope and extent to which the government should be involved in employment services. Critics say that current government programs are too fragmented and short-lived, and that they fail to provide training that matches real jobs or jobs that pay a living wage. As an example, critics point to the failure of TAA to help thousands of workers in Texas displaced by the North American Free Trade Agreement (NAFTA). The Bush Administration has sought to rectify some of these issues. In March 2005, the House of Representatives passed the Job Training Improvement Act, a bill designed to simplify the job training system. The act includes a provision to allow states and local entities to create pilot programs that offer unemployed Americans personal reemployment accounts of up to $3,000. As of 2006, the Senate had not voted on the bill. If passed by the Senate, the Act would build on the High Growth Job Training Initiative of 2002, which invests in training programs for selected industries such as automotive, biotechnology, and health care, and the Workforce Investment Act enacted in 1998.

Company Retraining

U.S. companies spend more than $60 billion a year on programs to train new employees, improve employee performance, or prepare employees for new jobs. The training may be conducted in-house by a company trainer or outsourced to a private consulting firm, a professional association, or a college or university. As a way of recruiting and maintaining employees, many companies offer to pay the tuition for employees who want to take college courses. For example, McDonald's restaurants in Alabama cover the costs for employees who want to take computer courses at the University of Alabama.

In *T+D Magazine*, Chris Taylor described four companies that survived a difficult economic period in the early 2000s. These companies—Southwest Airlines, Viacom, Dell, and Guardsmark—place a high value on employee training. Southwest Airlines, which has an excellent training program, refrained from cutting its training budget after 9/11, despite a drop in business. In fact, Southwest actually increased its training budget during that time. Similarly, Viacom did not cut training after advertising revenue shrank during recession years. That company has also added training in the past few years. Dell added a new priority for their leadership, which was to create a winning culture. Dell provides training sessions that inform employees on financial education and on all aspects of Dell. The thinking is that employees who understand the larger picture of the company's performance can suggest practical ways to save time and money. Dell also customized some of their training and eliminated generic training courses.

In recent years, more and more companies have turned to local community colleges and technical schools for help in retraining their employees. As reported in *Business Week,* many companies in the Rockford, Illinois, area send workers back to school at local Rock Valley Community College to take courses in teamwork and problem solving, among other subjects. Other companies have developed other models. Hewlett-Packard (HP), for example, has worked with the College of San Mateo (in California) to develop computer-based, interactive training in electronics for HP technicians and production workers. In addition, the school has established computer centers at several HP plants. Corporate-sponsored retraining programs through community colleges are usually administered by individual companies. However, a group of corporations, including Xerox, Kodak, Motorola, and Texas Instruments, have joined together to form the Consortium for Supplier Training. The consortium chooses various community colleges nationwide to teach courses in proven quality methods to the suppliers of consortium members.

The Hartford Life Insurance Company provides a twist to company-sponsored retraining. Similar examples can be found elsewhere in the private sector. In contrast to offering job training to company employees, Hartford offers to help its policyholders who have a disability return to the workforce. The company pays the costs of schooling so that clients can retrain for positions that accommodate their disabilities. It also pays for tools, books, uniforms, and other items that will enable policyholders with a disability to switch to different lines of work. Hartford's program, while boosting the earning power of its clients, has benefits for the company, too. Paying for retraining is more cost-effective in the long run than paying a lifetime of disability benefits.

Community Colleges

Traditionally, two-year community colleges have served young people who were not yet ready for a four-year college. Whereas community colleges continue to serve this population, their educational outreach has greatly expanded in the last few years. Many people with advanced degrees are enrolling in community colleges. These "reverse transfer" students find that community colleges offer the specific skills they need to move ahead in their jobs, keep abreast of their professions, or change careers. As noted above, community colleges are reaching out to industry workers through corporate contracts to provide training. Community colleges are also helping to educate welfare recipients. In Oregon, for example, the state's Adult and Family Services agency and community colleges work together to help people get off welfare and into the workforce.

Community colleges are enjoying a new role in the academic world because they can provide exactly the kind of education or training that many workplaces require. For those who are unemployed or are planning to change careers, the message is clear: investigate the courses offered at a nearby community college as a means of improving or updating current skills or learning new ones.

Colleges and Universities

Colleges and universities continue to provide traditional four-year and graduate degree programs in various subject fields to young adults. Whereas corporations have recently pursued college graduates with business degrees, more and more employers are also seeking graduates with bachelor's degrees. A good liberal arts program can produce the kind of workers companies need—generalists who can think creatively, solve problems, communicate effectively, and adapt to change. People seeking to advance in corporate careers would do well to mix business courses with liberal arts courses.

During the past decade, colleges and universities have adjusted to declining enrollments in their undergraduate programs by offering nontraditional, occupation-related courses and programs. They have also been gearing courses toward older adults who may be seeking a graduate or an undergraduate degree. The newer programs take into account the fact that most adult students are full-time workers by scheduling classes in the evenings, on Saturdays, or even online. In many colleges and universities, continuing education programs are bursting at the seams.

Postsecondary Vocational Schools

Postsecondary vocational schools are for people who have left high school and who are not pursuing a four-year college degree. They focus on training or upgrading of skills for people in the labor force (blue-collar workers) as opposed to people in management (white-collar workers). They may provide some academic training, but they generally train an individual in one occupation (for example, mechanic, nurse's aide, home health worker, electrician). Public postsecondary vocational schools generally offer a variety of programs. The majority of private postsecondary vocational schools specialize in one area, such as cosmetology and barbering, arts and design, or broadcasting.

Labor Unions and Professional Associations

At some companies, workers have found that when their union joins in partnership with management, the potential for new job development actually increases. For example, when Ford Motor Company was faced with a major layoff in the early 1980s, the company met with the United Auto Workers (its major union) to form a plan of action. They worked together to establish a joint employee retraining program. The main goal of the program was to get the laid-off workers back in the workforce quickly.

Ford established reeducation centers where employees received training in skills that potential employers were looking for: high school equivalency, fluency in the English language, and a variety of technical skills, including basic computer programming. The company even allowed potential employers to interview Ford employees at the worksite. The results were extraordinary: within two years, 80 percent of the laid-off workers who had taken part in the program had found new jobs.

A developing trend in company and labor union cooperation is pre-crisis training. Rather than waiting until employees have been laid off, retraining occurs on an ongoing basis, with an eye toward possible workforce changes.

Apprenticeship Training

One of the oldest forms of training in the United States, and around the world, is apprenticeship. A clear advantage of this type of training is that it almost guarantees the participant a job when the training is completed. In fact, because on-the-job training is an integral part of an apprenticeship program, most graduates already have a job and have been receiving a salary while in the training program. "The apprenticeship-trained worker is more likely to earn more money, work more hours per year, and rise to a supervisory status than are workers who have learned the trade through other methods," according to *Monthly Labor Review*.

Hundreds of occupations in the United States can be learned through apprenticeship. Some of the jobs have highly structured requirements for entry; others are less structured. Close to five hundred thousand people participate in apprenticeship programs each year. Although most programs are in the manufacturing and construction fields, apprenticeships are being developed in service fields, including programs to train health care workers, child care providers, jewelers, medical technologists, and audio-video repairers.

Apprenticeship differs from other types of training in that the job must be learned in a hands-on, practical way. A minimum of two thousand hours of on-the-job experience, as well as instruction, is usually required. Most programs require a high school diploma or general equivalency diploma (GED) to enter. Other requirements depend on the nature of the job. For example, an apprentice electrician might be required to have a background in algebra or electronics courses.

Armed Forces

The armed forces are the largest employer in the United States, with more than 1.5 million people on the payroll. Since the end of the draft in 1973, the government has had to find ways to attract able men and women into the military. A key ingredient in its recruiting program has been the prospect for those who enlist of receiving extensive training. Many service people receive college credit for the technical training they receive on duty and, in addition to off-duty courses, it can lead to an associate's degree through a community college program, such as the Community College of the Air Force.

Training is indeed a considerable benefit to joining the armed forces. There are about two thousand basic and advanced occupations in the service, and most of them have civilian counterparts. Therefore, training received in the military can often be transferred to the civilian workplace. In addition to jobs with direct applicability to combat duty, jobs exist in such diverse areas as welding, plumbing, video editing, photography, and engineering.

Nonprofit Organizations

Job retraining is also available through nonprofit organizations across the country. These organizations receive funding through federal, state, and/or private sources. The Corporation for Business, Work, and Learning in Massachusetts sends rapid-response teams into industrial companies facing job cuts. The teams teach employees skills they need to have to compete in more consumer-oriented fields. Lifetrack Resources, Inc., in Minnesota, offers job training and retraining to people with mental and physical disabilities, people who are disadvantaged, and people experiencing transitions in their careers and personal lives. In addition to providing classroom training, Lifetrack Resources arranges with local businesses to provide on-the-job training.

Home Study

Each year five million Americans enroll in correspondence school programs. These include televised courses offered by colleges and universities for academic credit. Home study courses offer a convenient, inexpensive way to acquire new skills and knowledge. The *Directory of Accredited Institutions*, available in most libraries, assesses the quality and reputation of specific correspondence courses.

A JOB SEEKER'S MARKET

It is obvious that opportunities for retraining abound. A major impetus for seeking retraining today is that the job market for skilled workers is growing. The Department of Labor projects the education and health service industry sectors will have the fastest employment growth between 2004 and 2014. In most parts of the United States, workers with the right training can not only find jobs but also negotiate salaries, benefits, and working conditions.

THE NEXT STEP

There is no question that major economic and sociological forces are at work today, creating an uneasy sense that the future is out of our control. People can, however, reclaim some control by making retraining a high priority on their personal agendas. The skills that will make them valuable employees are not exotic, mysterious, or necessarily highly technical. Many are general skills, valuable precisely because they can be applied in a broad variety of workplace circumstances.

Trends in Employee Benefits

Fred Wish

Everyone has his or her own reasons for working, and pay usually is among the most important. Not surprisingly, though, many workers list other factors that are almost equally strong motivations. These can range from opportunities to grow or learn new skills to a sense of community and purpose to more tangible benefits, such as health insurance, flexible work schedules, and provisions for retirement.

BEYOND THE FRINGE

What were once popularly referred to as "fringe benefits" came into prominence during World War II. In the face of federal wage controls to curb inflation, employers began to offer benefits to attract, motivate, and retain employees. Eventually, these various benefits programs, instead of being on the fringe of a worker's compensation, became an expected and valuable part of a complete employment package.

Today the formal benefits programs offered to employees generally make up roughly one third of the average worker's total compensation, depending on the size, profitability, and philosophy of a given employer. When these programs are properly planned and promoted, they yield attractive advantages for both employees and employers.

Advantages to Employees

Most workers prefer receiving benefits as part of their overall compensation because certain benefits programs offer economic advantages that salary alone cannot. A pension plan, for example, guarantees income after retirement. Various insurance plans provide security for workers and their families in case of disability or death.

Programs such as these have the added feature of lower cost; negotiated group rates for insurance, for example, are almost always less expensive than individually purchased premiums. This feature is even more attractive if the employer picks up all or a portion of the premium.

Subject to certain limitations, many benefits such as employer-paid health insurance, life insurance, and child care do not count as taxable income to the employee. Still other benefits, such as money that an employer contributes toward a pension plan, are tax deferred. Because an employee does not pay income tax on the money until he or she receives it after retirement, the income likely will be taxed at a lower rate.

Fred Wish is a human resources consultant with more than twenty years of corporate experience in the financial services, health care, and publishing industries.

Advantages to Employers

Most employers understand that well-designed benefits programs that address the needs of employees can have a measurable effect on productivity. Moreover, an attractive benefits package, for the reasons outlined above, is a powerful recruiting tool for employers looking to hire and keep talented workers. Finally, benefits tend to reduce the pressure to raise salaries. Enhancing an existing program or adding a new benefit can accomplish the same business goals as increasing pay rates, but at a fraction of the cost to the employer.

Just as employees enjoy significant tax advantages from their participation in certain benefits plans, benefits offer tax breaks to employers as well. Subject to a number of conditions and limits, employers can claim a deduction for what they spend on employee health insurance, life insurance, certain retirement plans, and other benefits.

BENEFITS PLANS FOR TODAY'S WORKFORCE

Although the basic shape and intent of benefits programs have remained the same for the past twenty-five years or so, new developments and revisions to existing programs have occurred because of changes in the general business environment. Among the factors affecting benefits offerings are shifts in workforce demographics, new legislation, and the rising cost of medical care.

In the five decades from the early 1950s to the first years of the twenty-first century, the number of women in the workforce increased dramatically, leading to increased programs designed to help working mothers. In the early 1950s fewer than 30 percent of women worked outside the home. In 2004 nearly half of U.S. workers (46.8 percent) were women. Almost two thirds (62.2 percent) of women with children under six years of age were in the civilian labor force in 2004, a significant increase from 18 percent in the mid-1950s. This change has resulted in greater emphasis on day care, flexible work schedules, and leaves of absence to care for children.

Longer life spans and the number of baby boomers (people born in the years immediately following the end of World War II) approaching retirement age also will lead to changes in worker benefits. Employee pension plans will take on greater importance. Younger employees also will need a source—presumably through their employers—of affordable elder care and time off to care for aging parents.

Legislation passed during the 1990s, such as the Americans with Disabilities Act, the Family and Medical Leave Act, and the Health Insurance Portability and Accountability Act, placed additional pressure on benefits programs; some states also have passed similar legislation. Other statutory benefits programs provide a basic level of protection for nearly all American workers.

Mandatory Benefits

Social Security Social Security is a federal program funded by employer contributions and payroll deductions. Its intent is to provide a fixed monthly benefit for retirees age sixty-five and older, although benefits can begin earlier under certain circumstances, such as disability. The level of payment depends on the length of time the individual has worked.

Unfortunately, Social Security cannot be considered an adequate source of retirement income, and it was never intended to be. If people do not have other means of generating income, they will struggle in later years to make ends meet.

The larger number of people drawing money from the Social Security system due to increased longevity and the large baby boom population will continue to place pressure on the availability of Social Security funding. In 2006, the social security board of trustees projected that by 2017 the Social Security system will be paying out more than it is taking in and that social security trust funds will be exhausted by 2040. To help ease this strain on the system, in 1983 Congress ruled that the age at which retirees begin receiving full Social Security benefits would begin to rise in 2003. The required age was increased incrementally depending on year of birth; those who turned sixty-five in 2003 or 2004 had to wait only a few extra months past their birthday before beginning to collect full benefits. However, those born between 1943 and 1954 must wait until they are sixty-six, and those born in 1960 or later must wait until they are sixty-seven.

Congress is exploring other possible solutions to this dilemma, including paying benefits based on need, further increasing the age at which full benefits begin, and instituting voluntary programs that can provide for larger individual contributions.

Unemployment Compensation All states have an unemployment program. Unemployment compensation provides a minimal level of income for people who lose their jobs involuntarily. The benefit is paid for a limited time, generally twenty-six weeks, to those who have worked for a specified period. Although eligibility requirements vary from state to state, people generally must be available for work and able to demonstrate that they are actively seeking employment. In addition, many states offer continued benefits to recipients while they participate in job retraining programs.

During periods of high unemployment, states offer thirteen to twenty weeks of extended benefits. However, some workers who qualify for regular benefits are not eligible for the extended program. Length of benefits and terms of eligibility vary by state.

Workers' Compensation The rules and levels of benefits regarding workers' compensation programs also vary by state, but they usually contain these common features: full payment of medical and rehabilitation costs for covered conditions, disability payments, and death benefits. These programs face the same economic pressures as others that have health care provisions, with costs threatening to outpace the ability to fund them.

Medical and Health Benefits

Medical insurance is what most people think of when they hear the word "benefits." It is such a common and expected part of a total employment package that many small businesses as well as large corporations offer it. Coverage under most employer-sponsored medical plans is available to the employee and his or her family. These plans traditionally cover most medical, hospital, and surgical expenses.

Types of Coverage Most employers still offer conventional health care coverage through commercial insurance companies or not-for-profit agencies such as Blue Cross and Blue Shield. Conventional health insurance plans usually have two parts: basic medical coverage and major medical coverage. Basic coverage pays for most medical visits and other services up to a certain dollar limit. Major medical plans, designed to protect against large bills or catastrophic illness, take over when basic insurance runs out. They cover all medical costs, usually up to a certain lifetime amount.

Some employers offer complete, or "first dollar," coverage; others offer less generous plans. The most common plans offer no reimbursement unless an employee's medical costs exceed a set annual deductible ($200 to $300 is fairly typical), which comes out of the employee's pocket. Other plans, known as "coinsurance plans," pay a certain percentage (most commonly, 80 percent) of the employee's medical expenses, leaving the employee responsible for the rest. Many insurance plans incorporate a combination of deductible and coinsurance plans.

The costs of traditional plans are prohibitive for many employers. The 1990s saw the rise of health maintenance organizations (HMOs). HMOs provide comprehensive health care coverage to employers at a fixed rate, which make them a popular alternative to the traditional, or indemnity, plans. While HMOs are cost-effective for employers, employee reaction to them has been mixed. Employee costs are generally less than with a traditional plan, but the restrictions on choices of physicians and hospitals is a source of dissatisfaction for some. In recent years there has been a decline in HMO enrollment. According to a report published in 2001, in the years between 1996 and 2001 HMO enrollment fell from 31 percent of employees to 23 percent. Many employers offered a variety of managed care arrangements to allow their employees a greater degree of flexibility in choosing coverage; during that same time period, enrollment in point of service (POS) and preferred provider organization (PPO) plans showed marked increases.

Some employers contract with HMOs or other organizations to provide preventive programs. These "wellness programs," as they are known, typically consist of health screenings such as cholesterol and blood pressure tests, weight loss or smoking cessation courses, and fitness training. Some large companies offer on-site exercise facilities. Companies are finding that a small investment in preventive health programs can reduce health insurance costs and costs associated with absenteeism.

Flexible Spending Accounts A large number of employers also offer a way for their employees to afford medical expenses that are not covered by their health insurance plans. These flexible spending accounts allow employees to have deductions made on a pre-tax basis from their paychecks. While the IRS puts no limit on the deduction amount, most companies set the limit somewhere between $2,500 and $5,000. During the year, as employees incur non-reimbursable medical expenses such as deductibles, charges for elective surgery, mileage, and the like, they can draw on the flexible spending account. The tax advantages of arrangements such as these can be significant. The major drawback to the plan has been that tax rules dictate that any funds left in the account at the end of the year are forfeited, which requires advanced planning and realistic anticipation of expenses on the employee's part.

However, a new type of plan approved by the IRS in 2002, health reimbursement arrangements (HRAs), offered an attractive alternative to flexible spending accounts. In an HRA an employer funds an account for the employee's medical expenses. Any funds not used in the account may be rolled over from year to year. If the funds in the account are exhausted, the employee generally must pay for medical expenses until a deductible is met, after which time the employer covers the majority of medical costs, generally 80 percent or 90 percent.

Adjusting to Higher Health Care Costs The difficult economy has created a challenge for employers, who face balancing the need to provide competitive health care coverage with the need to contain costs. In addition to instituting alternatives such as PPO or POS plans, some employers concerned with watching costs encourage employees to seek less costly forms of health care. Some require mandatory second opinions, shorter hospitalizations, and a greater reliance on outpatient surgery in order to provide an attractive level of coverage that still meets budgetary requirements. Overall, rising health care costs have translated to higher contributions for employees. According to the National Coalition on Health Care, insurance premiums increased by 10 percent in 2005. This increase was nearly three times the rate of inflation. The annual family health plan premium averaged $10,800.

Federal Health Care Legislation In the past, Americans who lost their jobs and their insurance had little choice: They could either buy prohibitively expensive private insurance, if eligible, or they could cross their fingers and hope that neither they nor their families became ill or injured. Existing medical problems of employees or family members often were not covered under a new employer's plan.

Two major pieces of federal legislation were enacted to lessen the economic effect of these problems. In 1985 the Consolidated Omnibus Budget Reconciliation Act (COBRA) required employers to continue an employee's existing level of health care coverage for up to eighteen months (three years in some cases) after the employment relationship ended. Under COBRA, employers may charge their former employees 102 percent of the total premium, but in most situations that group rate is cheaper than individual coverage. However, only 7 percent of the unemployed can afford to pay for COBRA health insurance, since premiums average almost $700 a month for family coverage. The Health Insurance Portability and Accountability Act (HIPAA) of 1996 guarantees workers with existing health insurance uninterrupted coverage when they change jobs. It also sets a limit on how long employers can exclude coverage for preexisting conditions. Unfortunately for employers and employees alike, federal regulations pertaining to HIPAA have been slow to materialize, and there is still much guesswork involved when it comes to applying HIPAA provisions in a practical manner.

Individual states have passed their own laws pertaining to health insurance for lower wage earners, and the Federal Balanced Budget Act of 1997, along with supporting legislation, contains health care provisions that extend beyond the workplace.

Disability and Life Insurance

After health insurance, the two most common types of insurance that employers offer are disability and life insurance. To provide interim income when an employee becomes ill or injured, many employers offer disability insurance, which may be employer-paid, employee-paid, or shared. Disability coverage is private insurance, as distinguished from Social Security disability or workers' compensation coverage. A typical disability plan, when combined with any statutory insurance such as Social Security disability or workers' compensation for which the employee qualifies, pays about 60 percent to 65 percent of base salary until the employee is medically able to return to work. For extended disability periods of six months or more, employers may also offer long-term coverage, either as an extension of the basic plan or as an added option.

Life insurance is generally offered as either a free or low-cost coverage. Under a standard arrangement, the designated beneficiary receives one or two times the employee's annual salary upon the latter's death. Popular variations include optional coverage for dependents and the ability to purchase additional levels of coverage. At these levels, employees may be responsible for paying tax on a portion of the life insurance premium. One innovative approach is for employers to purchase insurance for their workers and maintain rights to a portion of the death benefit. These company-owned insurance policies are offered on a voluntary basis and can help provide an extra level of protection at no cost to the employee.

Pension Plans

Although the rules for pension plans vary widely from employer to employer, the intent is the same: to give an incentive to employees who make a long-term commitment to their workplace by providing them with a post-retirement income. Most pension plans require that employees work a certain number of years (generally five) before they are entitled to a pension. At this point the worker is considered vested in his or her pension, which means he or she has irrevocable ownership in the eventual benefit. Because the tenure of an employee in U.S. business is a median four years, a great number of workers never reach a point where they qualify for a pension.

Employers do not have to offer pension plans. However, the Employee Retirement Income Security Act of 1976 (ERISA) regulates pension plans to ensure that they are managed appropriately and that their members receive adequate information about how the funds are run. It also sets limits on annual contributions to both types of plans available: "defined benefit plans" and "defined contribution plans."

Defined Benefit Plans Defined benefit plans specify the amount of money an employee will receive at retirement. For most plans, this amount is based on the employee's years of service and average salary before retirement, although there are several combinations of rules that an employer may institute to calculate the benefit. One popular variation is the coordination of benefits with Social Security, which helps reduce the amount the employer contributes to the pension plan while still meeting the obligation to employees.

Defined Contribution Plans With defined contribution plans, there is no fixed amount of money the employee receives as a retirement benefit. Instead, the employee, and often the employer, contributes money to a fund that is used for investments in stocks or other securities. The eventual payout for employees depends on how well the investments have done. As the economy went into high gear in the mid-1990s, these plans became increasingly popular. While participation in defined benefit plans declined, the percentage of workers in defined contribution plans grew from 42 percent in 1999 to 50 percent in 2004.

Among the more common types of defined contribution plans is the "money purchase plan." In this plan, the employer contributes a fixed amount to the fund, and employees may add their own contributions.

In "thrift" and 401(k) plans, the employee makes the fixed contribution, and the employer may match it in whole or in part. A 401(k) plan (or 403(b) plan, a similar option many nonprofit organizations offer their employees) is also known as a salary deferral plan because employee contributions are made on a pretax basis, with distribution and tax liability normally deferred until the employee reaches $59\frac{1}{2}$ years of age.

As an addendum to, or in lieu of, these plans, a large number of employers offer plans in which the contribution is tied to the financial performance of the company. The most popular forms of this arrangement are the profit sharing plan and the employee stock ownership plan.

Despite the range and flexibility of these programs, employees should keep in mind that such plans and available Social Security benefits will provide only a portion of the income needed for a comfortable retirement. To form a complete retirement package, an employee should make an effort to supplement these benefits with individual savings and investments.

Other Financial Benefits

Many companies offer performance-based incentives to employees. These benefits are more commonly in the form of cash, but travel or automobiles at the high end or more modest enticements, such as electronic equipment, artwork, or sports gear, have also been used. Instead of merely recognizing an individual's contribution, a trend that developed in the 1990s among employers was to reward team effort with bonuses in one form or another for a group of workers.

Some of these rewards were based on a formal agreement regarding the achievement of some specific goal, whereas others are discretionary in nature—the occasional "pat on the back" for a job well done.

Many employers use signing bonuses to attract employees. The *College Journal* reported that in 2005, the average signing for a recent MBA was $17,428. This recruiting tool was once limited to upper-level managers and executives; however, during the tight labor market of the mid- to late-1990s bonuses were offered to employees in other positions as well. The practice of offering signing bonuses is becoming less common, however. A recent study found only 13 percent of management-level employees received signing bonuses in 2005.

Tuition reimbursement programs are meant to encourage employees to continue their educations. These programs were common among large private employers in the late 1990s, but in recent years many companies were forced to reduce or suspend them for economic reasons. Tuition assistance is often included in collective bargaining agreements for public-sector employees, particularly contracts that cover teachers.

Child Care

Although child care—and particularly employer-sponsored day care centers—is a much sought after benefit, all but the largest employers find it prohibitively expensive to offer a comprehensive program. As a more affordable alternative, some employers offer flexible spending accounts for child care. These programs cost the employer very little; the employee pays regular amounts into the account and then draws on it as needed to meet child care expenses.

Programs such as these aid the parent-employee in several ways. Because the payments are made via payroll deduction, they provide a "painless" way of budgeting for child care expenses. In addition, almost all such programs offer significant tax advantages because the contribution is taken on a pre-tax basis, which reduces gross income and, as a result, the amount of income tax owed. The same caution applies to these plans as to the flexible spending accounts for nonreimbursable funds left in the account at the end of the year are forfeited.

Employee Counseling and Professional Services

Employee assistance programs (EAPs) came into prominence in the 1980s and offer confidential counseling by referring employees with personal or work-related problems to mental health professionals. Although most people think of EAPs as dealing primarily with alcohol or drug dependencies, they also assist with counseling on financial or legal difficulties that interfere with on-the-job performance. These services may be offered through an in-house health department or contracted to an outside professional organization. Employers view counseling as a relatively inexpensive way to prevent health and work-related problems. Well-run EAPs can result in increased productivity, fewer legal bills, and higher morale.

Some employers also offer other professional services to employees at little or no cost. These may include services such as tax consulting or investment and pre-retirement counseling.

Time Off

Most employees are accustomed to receiving a number of paid holidays and some vacation or personal days. In addition, most employees are entitled to a certain amount of paid sick leave.

Companies with fifty or more employees within a certain geographic radius are subject to the Family and Medical Leave Act (FMLA), signed into law in 1993. The FMLA requires employers to allow workers to take up to twelve weeks of unpaid leave during any twelve-month period to care for their families. This leave may be used for caring for a newborn, a child who has just been adopted, or any close relative who is suffering from a serious health condition. Employees may also use it to receive treatment for serious medical conditions that prevent them from performing their jobs. Under FMLA, workers must be reinstated in their jobs or equivalent positions (with equal benefits and pay) when they return to work. Several states have enacted similar legislation that acts in concert with FMLA to provide additional protection for employees.

Alternate Work Schedules

Flexible work schedules, often called "flextime," have become an increasingly popular benefit, especially in two-career families. Under a flextime policy, employees work a set number of hours, but they may do so on a schedule other than the standard nine-to-five workday. They may, for example, come in early and leave early, work four ten-hour days, or work weekends in order to add days to their vacation.

Telecommuting has become another popular, low-cost benefit that can work to the advantage of employer and employee. With the availability of computers and fax machines, along with easy access to the Internet, jobs that do not require an employee to be physically present in the office are on the rise.

Despite the advantages, employers must apply their telecommuting policies carefully. Telecommuting employees may feel alienated from the rest of the workforce. Those who find it difficult to work without supervision may see their productivity suffer. In addition, the technical proficiency required to be a successful telecommuter may mean additional training for the employee (and additional expense for the employer).

"Cafeteria" Plans

In many families, both the husband and the wife have full-time jobs that offer health insurance plans, life insurance plans, and other benefits for themselves and their children. Rather than getting some of the same benefits from both employers, many couples prefer to choose which benefits they will receive. Employers, who benefit from the favorable tax treatment afforded these "cafeteria" plans, or flexible benefit plans, have responded to this need.

Originally, cafeteria plans offered only limited choices in health coverage. However, today's plans have evolved into comprehensive programs. For example, under some plans, employees can trade vacation days for disability insurance or prepaid legal services. They may choose to forgo all benefits and take cash payments instead. Congress has given cafeteria plans favorable tax status to encourage their use and development.

Adjusting to Changing Times

The American workplace has seen sweeping economic changes over the past two decades. The period from 1991 to 2001 was the longest period of growth in United States history. The economic downturn that followed hit Americans hard—by June 2003 the unemployment rate was 6.4 percent, the highest since the early 1990s. The jobless percentage then began a slow but steady decline, however, and was down to 4.7 percent by April 2006.

Rising health care costs have been another area of increasing concern. In 2004 national health expenditures rose 7.9 percent over the previous year, more than three times the rate of inflation. In 2004 the total spending on health expenditures was $1.9 trillion, or $6,280 per person in the United States.

To a degree, new legislation and negotiated collective bargaining agreements mandated some changes in benefits programs in the past decade. For the most part, however, changes have arisen out of business necessities. The economic climate has forced employers to institute unpopular changes, such as increasing medical premiums and eliminating or reducing "non-essential" benefits. Ultimately, all employers will face the challenge of finding ways to develop, and to pay for, new benefits that meet workers' needs.

Trends in Training and Development

Sandy Dutkowsky

The American workplace is rapidly changing. In the past, workers went to their jobs to perform a task. Now, the workplace is changing into a place where workers both work and learn, as companies transform themselves into learning organizations. Companies are joining high schools, trade and technical schools, colleges, and universities in assuming responsibility for the education of the American workforce. As learning organizations, companies provide ongoing work-related training to all levels of employees, offer a variety of information and resources, encourage the exchange of ideas, and reward employees who acquire new skills.

Companies have to invest significant resources in order to provide educational services to their employees. What motivates a company to spend time and money training and developing its workers? The answer lies in understanding the new economy that is emerging in the United States.

THE NEW ECONOMY

Technology, and the rapid pace at which it develops, is a major factor contributing to the development of the new economy. Advances in the speed and memory of microprocessors have opened up new worlds in technological development. Procedures that used to take hours or weeks to complete can now be performed in minutes or even seconds on high-powered desktop or notebook computers.

Technology has also improved telecommunications systems. It is now possible for companies all across the globe to quickly communicate with one another. Such rapid communication has made the international marketplace a reality. American companies are no longer just competing with each other for business; they are now competing with companies worldwide.

In order to remain competitive in this rapidly changing environment, companies are rethinking how they do business as a means to improve productivity and the quality of their products. There are many ways that companies try to change the way they do business, including redefining corporate structures and revising policy and procedures. In addition they can train their employees to understand the most effective ways to interact with customers and to be aware of the best practices of the most successful companies in the field. By doing this, corporations are attempting to increase productivity by rethinking processes.

How the New Economy Affects Workers

The new economy has a profound effect on the American worker. In the new economy, jobs can be performed more cheaply and efficiently through the use of technology than through human labor. By relying on technology instead of human beings, companies can increase their productivity and be more compet-

---

Sandy Dutkowsky is a freelance writer and educator.

itive in the global marketplace. However, this increased productivity through technology also renders some skills and jobs obsolete. For example, it is now possible to build automobiles and other large pieces of machinery and equipment primarily through the use of computerized robots. As a result, there is less and less demand for the traditional American factory worker. Therefore, workers need to be able to adapt to new workplace realities. The person who used to build objects directly with his or her hands will now need to learn to run the computer that will build the object. As quickly as jobs are made obsolete, new jobs will emerge. With training, workers doing these new jobs will become important players in the new economy.

Advancing technology also has its effects on employees in non-technical positions, such as managers and marketing personnel. They must learn enough about the technological aspects of their field to intelligently converse with employees and customers. All employees, in order to be successful in the new workplace, will have to have the ability to adapt and to learn as required. Those who have "learned to learn" will become most valuable in the new economy. Therefore, the role of education and training is becoming more and more important in the American workplace. Employees are recognizing the need to improve and broaden their skills to remain employable.

The Corporate View

Companies have found that investment in human capital in the form of training and development yields high returns. The ones that recognize the value of their employees and place a new emphasis on education and training are becoming more competitive, successful, and profitable as a result. According to a study conducted in 2002 by Knowledge Assessment Management, companies in the top 20 percent of those who spend money on training receive higher returns in the stock market. Is it possible that knowledge is equal to profit?

According to an article by Chris Taylor in *T + D Magazine* ("Recession Survivors: Training to the Rescue," October 2003), a knowledgeable workforce may ensure a company's survival. The article profiles four companies that survived the economic impact of September 11, 2001, and a business climate marked by recession and corporate scandals. These companies—Southwest Airlines, Viacom, Dell, and Guardsmark—all consider employee training an investment in company growth and stability. Rather than cutting back their training budgets during hard times, these companies chose to invest in the development of new skills and knowledge within their workforce. In doing so, these companies showed a commitment to their workers and gave them the educational background necessary to increase productivity and effectiveness in their respective markets. The workers, in turn, supported these companies and ensured their survival through a difficult chapter of American business history.

TRAINING IN U.S. COMPANIES

Some training and development programs teach new hires to perform a specific job, while others update the skills and knowledge of established employees. According to the U.S. Department of Labor, the majority of middle- and large-sized companies provide formalized training to their workforces, and it costs them billions of dollars.

Some of the money is spent to provide technology-related training that teaches employees to operate, maintain, or repair equipment used in the workplace. Technology training is needed for workers in industries as diverse as construction, manufacturing, health, and transportation. Technical professionals include scientists, architects, engineers, and health professionals. Blue-collar technical workers include mechanics, repair people, and those in precision production jobs. Technology is constantly changing and therefore job responsibilities are constantly changing, requiring many workers to update their skills on a regular basis.

Training in electronics, for example, can vary widely. Electronics jobs may require less than a year of training, done primarily on the job, or they can require an advanced college degree. However, regardless of whether an electronics technician is fixing television sets and DVD players or designing a new computer network, the need for training is paramount. The field is changing constantly, with new equipment being introduced almost daily.

While learning to work with technology is extremely important, companies provide many other kinds of training to their employees. For example, employers that emphasize teamwork and encourage employee problem solving may offer courses in effective communication and group work. Systems training helps illustrate to employees their role within, and their effect upon, the entire corporation. As the price of health insurance has increased dramatically, many companies have begun providing their workers with information about how to become healthier by, for example, quitting smoking or developing an effective exercise plan. Another growing trend in American corporations is to provide training sessions on issues that affect employee relations. The topics of such training sessions might include affirmative action, workplace diversity, the Americans with Disabilities Act, and sexual harassment.

Between 2000 and 2003, more than four million immigrants entered the United States, many of whom are not English speakers. Additionally, according to an estimate by the U.S. Department of Education, in 2004, over forty million Americans were unable to read effectively. Many of these people are employed in the American workforce. In order for these workers to be successful, companies are providing literacy programs to meet their needs. This includes teaching the non-English speaker the basics of the language. Training programs could also provide workers with basic writing and math skills. These programs are conducted in ways that are sensitive to the workers' cultural differences. For example, training programs for non-English-speaking workers might be conducted in a bilingual fashion, to assist them in making the transition to English from another language. American corporations are making a commitment to these workers because in addition to playing an important role as employees, they also play a role in the larger American economy as consumers of goods and services.

Cross Training or "Multiskilling"

As companies looked for ways to respond quickly to changing markets and personnel needs, the concept of cross training began to emerge. Whereas in the past employees were trained to perform only one job, the companies of today are recognizing the value of cross training employees to perform multiple tasks. In this model, employees are trained in a wide range of skills. If an employee's job becomes obsolete or if there is an overwhelming need somewhere in the corporation, the employee can easily transfer to another position and immediately begin to work productively.

According to an article in the *London Financial Times* (October 5, 2005), a flexible workforce—including a multiskilled one—can help a company expand its business capabilities while not necessarily expanding its staff. In small and medium-sized companies, multiskilling is particularly important. Rebecca Clake, resourcing adviser at the Chartered Institute of Personnel and Development, advises these companies to "recruit staff with broad skill sets [and] organize training to expand their capabilities." Multiskilling can not only make work more satisfying for employees but also help enhance employee performance.

For example, cross training is part of what makes the Japanese automaker Toyota so successful. The company avoided the massive layoffs that U.S. automakers were forced to make in the early twenty-first century. As Ron Harbour, head of Harbour Consulting, publishers of an annual industry productivity report, said in an article in the *Washington Post*, "Toyota is the Tiger Woods of flexibility and efficiency; they've got everybody a few strokes behind." Among other flexible working practices, the company cross-trains workers to build multiple car models on the same assembly lines. These practices help lead to the company's success. Multiskilling will become more important in the competitive market of the twenty-first century.

Just-in-Time Training

Another type of training within American corporations is known as just-in-time training, or "just-what's-needed" training. As the name implies, this short-term training fills a specific need or responds to a particular problem. For example, the Human Resources Department at California State University Fresno offers workshops to its employees on demand. These on-site training sessions are between twenty minutes and two hours in length, and they include programs related to contract issues, hiring guidelines, and diversity. Just-in-time training is cost-effective and saves time. Additionally, since the training ties in immediately with actual work and employees study only the skills they need, the content is less likely to be forgotten.

WHO DOES THE TRAINING IN CORPORATIONS?

When much of the training required within a company is specific to that particular organization's products and goals, it is usually done in house. As training areas become more general, such as in public speaking or supervisory skills, many companies will contract with a private vendor to provide the program. For computer training, representatives of the company from which the equipment is purchased often are contracted to provide employee training. Many times a training course combines prepackaged programs with in-house goals to create a customized training opportunity.

Corporate Education and Training Centers

Larger companies tend to do much of their training in house, and some have designed and built elaborate employee education centers known as corporate universities. Such facilities range from Disney University in Florida to the University of Toyota in Los Angeles. Many of these centers contain state-of-the-art classrooms and laboratories with expensive equipment for teleconferencing and video feedback. They may also offer housing accommodations, recreational facilities, restaurants, and libraries. In addition to the facilities and equipment, companies will also provide all necessary training materials including books, courseware, films, and video programs. Many companies have found that the development and utilization of their own corporate university is an effective way to pass valuable skills (which translate to profit) on to their employees. In fact, a survey conducted in 2005, with results published in *Fortune*, found that 55 percent of companies with corporate universities reported the program has increased the performance of their businesses (Anne Field, "Corporate America's Learning Curve," *Fortune Special Sections: Corporate*, http://www.timeinc.net/fortune/services/sections/fortune/corp/2004_01corporate.html).

McDonald's Hamburger University is a good example of a successful corporate university. In 1961 McDonald's started Hamburger University in the basement of one of its restaurants. In 1983 the company invested $40 million in the creation of its 130,000 square foot training facility on eighty acres in Oakbrook, Illinois. Since its inception, Hamburger University has graduated more than eighty thousand employees and currently graduates about five thousand restaurant managers, mid-level managers, and franchise owners each year. The curriculum, which focuses on Quality, Service, Cleanliness, and Value, is consistently recognized for its excellence. In addition to the main campus in Oakbrook, McDonald's has expanded Hamburger University worldwide with satellite campuses in Sydney, Munich, London, Tokyo, Hong Kong, and Brazil.

Colleges and universities recognize the high level of training that is going on within corporate classrooms around the country. In fact, they are awarding college-level credit to many of the training participants. Through the Center for Adult Learning and Educational Credentials, a special program administered by the American Council on Education (ACE), a company can have training courses evaluated. Once the course content is approved by ACE, a student can receive college credit at more than 1,200 colleges and universities across the country upon the successful completion of the course.

Small and Mid-sized Businesses

In small and mid-sized businesses (those with fewer than five hundred employees), the training department typically consists of one person. Usually this person does not run training programs themselves. Instead, this individual functions as a broker of training services. This means that he or she is responsible for finding outside consultants who can provide training to meet the company's needs at a time and place convenient to employees, and at a reasonable cost. In order to maximize training efforts, the company trainer may work with production line managers and supervisors on developing and conducting their own on-the-job training sessions. Small companies with limited funds may send their employees to other companies for training, or they may ask their major suppliers to help with the costs.

Federal Government

The federal government allocates funds for training programs around the country. The government's employee training programs are as varied as its own departments and agencies. For example, The United States Fire Administration houses the National Fire Academy. The goal of this program is to train firefighters to deal more effectively with fire emergencies that are related to, for example, terrorism or arson. The United States Department of State supports the Foreign Service Institute. Employees who attend this program's offerings learn how to adapt to living and working in foreign countries by learning their languages and customs. The United States Department of Agriculture provides farmers and other food producers a variety of training programs covering food inspection, safety, and environmentally conscious farming practices.

Among the many other types of training available to employees of the federal government are foreign language training, computer training, and equal employment opportunity education. Such training can be conducted either by bringing in an external specialist (if the number of people receiving instruction makes that cost-effective) or by sending individuals to an outside agency.

As in many corporate classrooms, much of the training that is conducted by and for the federal government is at the college level. Therefore, participants can receive college credit for courses that have been evaluated by the American Council on Education.

Colleges and Universities

Business organizations and higher education often form partnerships in training and development. Many colleges have started separate departments to meet the needs of business and industry. They offer a wide range of collegiate services, often tailored to fit a company's specific educational requirements. In some cases the company calls on the college to identify its training needs; in others the company's training department has identified the instruction it wants to offer and is looking for someone to provide it.

One example is Boston University's Corporate Education Center (BUCEC). People who attend this program through Boston University can obtain training in business and management, information technology, or corporate training. The training programs are offered in a variety of ways to meet the needs of those in attendance. Classes are available at the BUCEC training center or at a client's workplace, and services can be provided through online sessions, as well.

Other Postsecondary Institutions

America's two-year colleges also work with local businesses to meet the need for more highly trained employees. Kent Phillippe, senior research associate at the American Association of Community Colleges, estimates that 95 percent of the nation's approximately 1,600 community colleges provide employee training through direct contracts with businesses.

Training programs provided by the community colleges are designed with the specific needs of the corporations' employees in mind. A current trend in business training offered by community colleges is to provide measurable skills to employees, which can result in higher company profits. Tulsa Community College (TCC) in Oklahoma offers training in areas such as effective customer communication, listening skills, and basic word processing skills. TCC designs primarily half day programs so that employees are away from the office for only part of the day. Additionally, many programs offered by community colleges are developed specifically for the needs of the corporation who hires them. For example, Tacoma Community College in Washington conducts a needs assessment of the corporation's training needs before it develops a training program. This way, the corporation is assured that their employees are learning exactly what they need to know to be more effective at their jobs.

Private Vendors

A growing number of companies are in the business of training employees of other corporations. These vendors offer services as diverse as public speaking courses, writing classes, team development seminars, and computer training. One of the best known is Dale Carnegie Training, which has been used by hundreds of major companies, including AFLAC Insurance, Burger King, and AT&T, to provide specific, measurable skills to employees. These training programs are also available to individuals who are interested in developing their skills in public speaking, sales, human relations, and executive leadership. One of the ways both corporations and individuals can access this information is through widely available software programs and DVDs that are developed and sold by private training organizations. Companies and individuals can purchase these training programs and utilize them when it is most convenient.

TRAINING METHODS AND EVALUATION

Delivery systems for training include traditional classroom instruction, on-the-job instruction, and instruction via technology. Technology-based instruction includes computer-based training (CBT), multimedia CBT, televised distance learning, video training, and use of the Internet. Much of this technology falls under the term e-learning, which also includes virtual classrooms, Web-based courses, "Webinars," and digital collaboration.

Technology-Based Learning

TraCorp is a company that develops specific technology-based training programs for large corporations. TraCorp develops their products by utilizing the talents of software engineers, animators, and artists. Therefore, their training programs are interesting and fun to work with. TraCorp was hired by Procter and Gamble to create a program to educate veterinarians about their product, Iams pet food. This training program was highly successful due to its interesting and interactive content. The veterinarians also liked it because it was flexible to use and they could view and work with the content as they were able to find time in their busy schedules. As a result of the success of this product, TraCorp was hired by Procter and Gamble to create new programs that could teach veterinarians worldwide. TraCorp has designed and produced education programs for a number of other large organizations including the United States Air Force, Motorola, and Corning, Inc.

As e-learning technology continues to grow and develop, more corporations are finding that it is a cost-effective and efficient way to provide training to their employees. Studies show that individuals who participate in e-learning learn faster and retain more information than those who learned in a traditional classroom setting. Although this type of training may be cost-effective, it is not without its challenges. For example, some employees may resist e-learning because they are unfamiliar or uncomfortable with technology. The potential also exists that some employees are not motivated enough to progress through online training programs if there is no one around to keep them motivated. Additionally, a study conducted by economy professors Carl Liedholm and Byron Brown ("Can Web Courses Replace the Classroom in Principles of Microeconomics," *American Economic Review*, May 2002) found that online courses can teach basic concepts, but not complex analytical skills. Therefore the scope of what e-learning can do is limited. Regardless, it is clear that e-learning is here to stay, and it will continue to grow and change as technology and the needs of the learners change.

What Is the Most Effective Way for Employees to Learn?

Should employee training be conducted through technology or in person? This is a difficult question to answer because not everyone learns in the same way. For example, some people may learn the most through reading while others may do better listening to a lecture. Others may need to gather information and then talk about it in order to understand the material. Also, not all classes can be taught as effectively in an online environment as in person. For example, while it is possible to learn how to read Spanish online, speaking the language with other people is invaluable in the development of conversational skills.

Therefore, in order to address the best way to teach employees, some companies have decided to combine the two methods to meet the learning needs of a wider range of employees. For example, the city of Palm Beach, Florida, provides online computer instruction to all of its employees and provides learning labs that are run by instructors. In this learning environment employees have access to learning in the way that suits them best.

How Are the Programs Evaluated?

Given the expense involved in conducting training programs, many corporations are very interested in measuring their concrete outcomes. In the past, the success of a program was measured by how many classes were held and the number of employees trained. If the numbers were high, then the training was considered successful. In the current workplace, companies want to know to what degree the training assisted in the transfer of new skills to the job and to what extent individual and group performance improves. In fact, the movement toward outcome-based training is so strong in some companies, the professionals who provide such training refer to themselves as "performance improvement specialists."

CONCLUSION

Many of today's most successful companies realize that their employees are their greatest asset. Therefore, corporations are increasingly investing in educating their employees so that they can grow and change within the company and make it more profitable. The range of training opportunities varies considerably from company to company so, when researching potential employers, it is important for job seekers who care about this to investigate the level and type of training provided to employees.

Vocational Training

Melissa J. Doak

WHAT IS VOCATIONAL TRAINING?

Vocational training is training for a specific career or trade, excluding the professions. Vocational training focuses on practical applications of skills learned, and is generally unconcerned with theory or traditional academic skills. A large part of the education in vocational schools is hands-on training. Vocational training thus provides a link between education and the working world. It is usually provided either at the high school level or in a postsecondary trade school.

Why is Vocational Training Worth Considering?

Vocational training offers training for specific jobs. Since vocational training often begins in high school, students can graduate prepared to take a high-paying, skilled job immediately. Graduates of trade or vocational schools have an advantage over informally trained job-seekers because an independent organization certifies that they have the skills needed to successfully perform a specific, skilled occupation.

Traditional Venues for Vocational Training

Secondary School Most high schools offer some form of vocational training program, increasingly called career and technical education. The expanded concept of career and technical education provides for a planned program of courses and learning experiences that allow students to explore career options, develop academic skills, achieve high academic standards, and prepare for industry-defined work or advanced education. For example, the Tech Center at Yorktown, New York, offers twenty-nine vocational specialties, not only to prepare students for the construction and manufacturing industries (traditional specialties of vocational education), but also for jobs in business, human services, health services, and natural and agricultural science. Specialties are as diverse as advertising art and design, television production, computer graphics, cosmetology, business and computer technology, auto mechanics, carpentry, masonry, small engine technology, practical nursing, floral design, and urban forestry.

Public schools in some states have separate vocational schools where students attend part time, either as part of the school day or in the evening, for specialized programs in addition to academic courses. These programs usually include a sequence of courses as well as work-based learning experiences. Large communities and cities often have separate public schools that students attend full time that provide both academic instruction and vocational training to high school students. These schools commonly use the cooperative training technique, in which students work part time in the job for which they are preparing. The traditional focus of these schools is changing; no longer do students simply train for a vocation, but they are also required to work toward a high school diploma

---

Melissa J. Doak is a freelance writer of reference books and educational materials.

or a GED. Additionally, students are encouraged to consider going on to some form of postsecondary education.

The 2004 National Assessment of Vocational Education, published by the U.S. Department of Education, reports that nearly one-half of all high school students in that year were involved in some form of vocational training, even if just one course. The report found that vocational training at the high school level had positive effects on short- and medium-range earnings. It also found that high school students who participated in vocational programs also increased their academic course taking and achievement, as well.

Despite these positive findings, however, career and technical education in secondary schools is on the decline in the twenty-first century. One reason is that traditional vocational training prepared students for manufacturing jobs, such as mechanics and repair and precision production, but the manufacturing industry in the United States is in decline. Instead, the economy is becoming more service- and information-based. The National Center for Education Statistics notes that this change is partly responsible for a trend toward a greater emphasis on academics in vocational training, as workers in a service- and information-based economy have a greater need for critical thinking and social skills. The greater academic emphasis also results from toughening requirements for graduation from high school nationwide. The focus on academics has led to fewer high school graduates taking any specific labor market preparation courses, and an even bigger decrease in the number of students concentrating in the vocational curriculum.

Another reason vocational training at the secondary school level is declining is that low-achieving students were often "dumped" into the programs, undermining program quality and rigor. Traditionally, high school students in vocational programs have not been expected to go to college. While considerable federal effort and funds have been allocated to change that, there is evidence that those who participate in vocational programs at the high school level are more likely to get an associate's degree or postsecondary certificate than they are to go on to and complete a four-year college degree. Public high schools implemented some vocational education–related reforms in the late 1990s, including greater integration of academic and vocational education and less "block scheduling" of vocational courses. However, these reforms have not yet produced increased achievement or college attendance for those who select vocational training.

The administration of President George W. Bush proposed to eliminate all federal funding for high school vocational education in fiscal year 2006. While some funds would still be available through a new program known as the High School Intervention Initiative, wide local discretion on how those funds might be used, coupled with an expansion of required high school assessments, would lead many local educational agencies to pursue interventions other than vocational education. It seems probable that vocational education options available to high school students will be significantly reduced during the next decade.

Tech Prep Education The Carl D. Perkins Vocational and Technical Education Act of 1998, in addition to providing funds to postsecondary institutions, provided funding to programs known as Tech Prep programs. Tech Prep programs are based on a collaboration between secondary schools and postsecondary institutions to help prepare students for high tech careers in areas such as engineering, technology, applied science, health, and applied economics, and to improve the academic success of vocational students. Tech Prep is a sequenced program of study that combines at least two years of secondary and two years of postsecondary education. It is designed to help students gain both academic knowledge and technical skills. These programs typically lead to either a certificate or an associate's degree in a specific career field. Almost one half of the country's high schools offer some type of Tech Prep program. In fiscal year 2005 $106 million was appropriated for the program, although because of proposed budget cuts, its future is uncertain.

The effectiveness of Tech Prep programs is up for debate. Evaluations in Texas and New York found evidence that students enrolled in these programs were less likely to drop out of high school or have a chronic absenteeism problem and were more likely to enroll in postsecondary school. However, academic achievement and labor market outcomes were not demonstrably improved. This may be because Tech Prep programs are not always implemented as envisioned in the legislation, but instead are often implemented piecemeal or with a focus on improving only academics.

Postsecondary Trade School The 2004 National Assessment of Vocational Education reported that about one-third of college students were involved in vocational programs as a major part of their studies. Postsecondary vocational schools, also called trade schools, provide an educational option other than community colleges and four-year colleges. They also help older students who want to advance or change their careers. Often these schools cater to the needs of working adults by offering classes at night or online.

Trade schools offer both degree programs and vocational certificates. There are many occupations that require a trade school education, including hairdressing, massage therapy, auto mechanics, plumbing, and carpentry. Trade schools also teach students technological, culinary, and health care skills. Some trade schools offer apprenticeships as well.

Recognizing the need for more skilled workers in the information-based economy, the Carl D. Perkins Vocational and Technical Education Act of 1998 granted money to postsecondary schools to develop and enhance vocational programs. The Act focused federal investment in high quality vocational and technical educational programs that integrate academic and vocational education, promote student attainment of high vocational and technical standards, provide students with strong experience and understanding of an industry, and develop, improve, and expand the use of technology. Postsecondary institutions that receive the funds have the flexibility to design services to meet the needs of their students.

School guidance offices have information on trade schools. Two comprehensive online resources, http://www.trade-schools.net and http://www.trade-school.org, also list trade schools and the courses they offer. Institutions listed include mechanical and automotive schools, business schools, culinary schools, art and design schools, diving schools, cosmetology schools, education programs, health care schools, legal and criminal justice schools, schools focusing on occupations in the media, real estate schools, technology schools, and travel and tourism schools. These trade schools offer diplomas or certificates that employers nationwide will accept. They also provide their students with assistance in meeting necessary licensing requirements.

OTHER OPPORTUNITIES FOR VOCATIONAL TRAINING

Vocational programs at both the secondary and postsecondary levels vary in their quality and effectiveness. While graduation from a good vocational program or trade school can greatly improve one's employment outlook, there are other ways to get specific occupational training. Apprenticeships, military service, community colleges, and distance learning courses all provide opportunities to improve job skills and employment possibilities.

Apprenticeships

Completing an apprenticeship is an alternative to traditional vocational training. Apprenticeships are most common for highly skilled manufacturing or construction jobs, but are available for more than 850 occupations in many industries. Common programs train people to be boilermakers, bricklayers, carpenters, electricians, firefighters, machinists, millwrights, plumbers, roofers, telecommunications technicians, and tool and die makers. Less common programs train people to be stage technicians and actors, cooks, designers, paralegals, environmental technicians, computer programmers, and landscapers.

Apprenticeships combine on-the-job training with classroom instruction. Apprentices are paid while on the job. Apprenticeships typically take four to six years to complete, although some can be completed in as little as one year. Because apprenticeships are paid programs, competition for available slots is often fierce.

About twenty-nine thousand apprenticeship programs exist nationwide. These apprenticeship programs are registered with the Department of Labor, and graduates receive certificates of completion that are accepted by employers around the country. In 2005 more than 150,000 people began apprenticeships, while almost 57,000 graduated from their apprenticeship programs, becoming journey workers.

One reason apprenticeships provide a good alternative to traditional vocational training is that apprentices pay nothing for their education, and are actually paid for the hours they spend learning on the job. In addition, apprentices typically command relatively high salaries when they become journey workers. Among the commonly apprenticed occupations with the highest median annual earnings are power distributor and dispatcher ($48,570), ship engineer ($47,530), power plant operator ($46,090), and electrical power-line installer and repairer ($45,780). The Bureau of Labor Statistics projects that other apprenticed occupations are expected to have an exceptional job outlook between 2004 and 2013, including cooks, auto mechanics, practical nurses, carpenters, electricians, and hairdressers.

The first step in entering an apprenticeship program is to find an open program. Good resources include the state Bureau of Apprenticeship, the state office of the Department of Labor, and school career counseling offices. Trade union offices and professional associations frequently sponsor apprenticeships; contacting those offices may uncover openings. Some apprenticeship programs will advertise available openings in the newspaper, on job boards, or with state job services.

In some occupations, apprenticeship programs are highly competitive. Applicants typically must be eighteen years old and must possess a high school diploma or a GED. The application process will sometimes require a passing score on a proficiency or aptitude test, which varies by the program. Tutoring programs can help applicants pass proficiency exams in some fields. Once an application is complete and the applicant has met all qualifications, an interview is usually required. Applicants are then ranked and placed on a waiting list.

A little planning ahead can help hopeful apprentices shorten the waiting period. Successfully completing basic classes in English, math, and science is considered important for all applicants to apprenticeship programs, so a solid high school record in these subjects will help an individual qualify for an apprenticeship. In addition, special interest classes may provide early skill development and improve a student's standing in the application process. For example, classes in industrial mechanics, shop, or mechanical drawing will help those interested in apprenticing in an industrial or construction occupation.

Military Training

Military service also offers ways for enlisted people to pursue vocational and technical licensing and certification, called Vo-Tech programs. These programs either document past training and experience or offer new opportunities to take courses and exams to get the certifications necessary to make a successful transition to occupations outside of the military.

USMAP The United Services Military Apprenticeship Program, or USMAP, documents the training and skills learned by military personnel in the Navy, Marine Corps, and Coast Guard in order to allow them to earn national certification from the U.S. Department of Labor as journey workers in occupational fields. In fact, USMAP is the largest apprenticeship program sponsor registered with the Department of Labor, and nearly twenty thousand enlisted marines and sailors have completed the program. Of the three hundred enlisted Military Occupational Specialties, 257 are available for apprenticeship. The on-the-job training that military personnel receive is combined with technical instruction, as in a traditional apprenticeship program. The length of USMAP varies from one to four years, or two thousand to eight thousand hours of on-the-job training, as well as including 144 hours of apprenticeship-related classroom training per two thousand hours of on-the-job training. The apprenticeships are broken down into skill areas; each skill area requires a set number of hours. Those who complete the program have enhanced job skills that can further a military career or provide an advantage in getting better civilian jobs after the period of enlistment.

Qualifications for the USMAP program are as follows. Participants must:

1) be on active duty in the Coast Guard, Marine Corps, or Navy;

2) be designated in a job specialty that is an approved apprenticeable trade;

3) have sufficient time left in an enlistment to complete the program while on active duty;

4) have a high school diploma or GED; and

5) have been promoted to a certain grade level, depending on the branch of service and the trade.

Enlisted military personnel usually can choose their training or duty assignment either when they enlist or when they complete basic training. However, that duty assignment will severely limit their choice of apprenticeship. For example, an enlisted person who prepares food as her job cannot become a computer-peripheral-equipment operator, because it has nothing to do with the work she normally does—but she can become an apprentice cook or baker. However, unlike in civilian apprenticeships, acceptance into the USMAP program is a formality, rather than requiring a lengthy evaluation, ranking, and waiting period. Apprenticeships available in the military are diverse and cover the gamut from manufacturing to clerical work to professional occupations. For example, available apprenticeships include aircraft mechanic, carpenter, dental assistant, graphic designer, machinist, nurse assistant, paralegal, photographer, post-office clerk, purchasing agent, weather observer, and X-ray equipment tester.

Army COOL Program The Credentialing Opportunities On-Line (COOL) program helps Army Soldiers meet civilian certification and license requirements related to their occupational specialty in the military. COOL provides information on civilian jobs that are equivalent to a military occupational specialty. It also provides information on national certifications available in that occupation, and if state licensure is required. The Costs and Resources section helps

Army enlisted personnel see what resources are available to help pay for needed licenses and certificates.

An enlisted soldier transitioning to the civilian workforce may find that his military occupational specialty does not require a license or certificate in the civilian workforce. Or she may find that her military training and experience provides all the necessary credentials. COOL can help soldiers qualified by education, training, and experience to become licensed or certified in the civilian workforce, by helping them locate and navigate the appropriate administrative process (an application, documentation of training and experience, and/or an examination). COOL can also help those who do not yet meet licensing and certification requirements by providing information about resources available from the Army to help them get the supplementary training they need.

The Air Force The Community College of the Air Force (CCAF) offers sixty-seven fields of study directly related to Air Force specialties. These fields of study tend to be highly technical in nature; graduates are awarded an associate's degree. Enrollment is free to enlisted people in the Air Force. CCAF courses are recognized by organizations that issue certifications for specific occupations as well as by governmental organizations that issue licenses.

The Air Force Institute for Advanced Distributed Learning provides more than four hundred career development courses and other specialized training courses to enlisted people in the Air Force. These distance-learning courses are provided in correspondence and Web-based forms.

Community Colleges

Community colleges provide another way to train for a specific occupation. Community colleges have typically been a low-cost alternative for the first two years on the way to a four-year degree. Community colleges still serve this population of students who intend to transfer to four-year colleges, but they have expanded to serve people who want to expand their skills for a variety of reasons—to advance or get promoted, to learn new skills needed in the marketplace, or to change careers. Contracts with corporations also enable community colleges to provide training of various kinds to corporate workers.

About one-third of all students in postsecondary education are in vocational programs, including those enrolled in community colleges. They enroll with a variety of goals, from earning a certificate, to enhancing job skills, to earning an associate's degree. Most students in vocational programs in community colleges never earn a degree or other credential. However, the 2004 National Assessment of Vocational Education found that for the vast majority of participants in community college vocational programs, the vocational training had positive effects on their earning potential. The benefits were higher for those who completed more coursework, but even students who did not complete certificates or degrees derived some earnings benefit from the training they received.

Some occupations expected to grow most quickly in the near future require a two-year associate's degree, which is what community colleges specialize in. According to the Bureau of Labor Statistics, the top thirty fastest-growing occupations between 2004 and 2014 will increase job opportunities for physical therapy assistants, dental hygienists, forensic science technicians, veterinary technologists and technicians, diagnostic medical sonographers, occupational therapist assistants, cardiovascular technologists and technicians, and paralegals and legal assistants. Registered nursing, which also requires an associate's degree, is the occupation expected to have the second-largest job growth between 2004 and 2014. Community colleges offer cost-effective, affordable education and training options in these and many other vocational fields.

Employer-Provided Training

Another avenue for occupation-specific training is through an employer. Many employers provide the basic training needed to perform particular jobs. Others provide training that allows employees to advance in the company. Companies may also provide employees with general employment skills assistance such as computer skills training, human resources training, or training on how to work in a team. These are valuable to workers in their current jobs, as well as in future employment.

U.S. companies spend more than $60 billion a year on training programs—either to train new employees, provide employees with additional skills needed in their jobs, or to help employees prepare for new jobs. Large corporations may maintain a training staff in house, but medium- and small-sized companies usually hire a consulting firm or a professional association, or contract their training to a college or university. Sometimes training is provided by vendors; for example, a software company may provide training to customer service employees of a company that adopts new customer service software, either free of charge or for a small fee. Some companies also offer partial or full reimbursement of college tuition for their employees.

On-the-Job Training Employees learn on the job in many occupations. On-the-job training is particularly used in manufacturing. In textile mills, for example, extensive on-the-job training is generally provided. Training is offered to beginning workers as well as more experienced workers, to enable them to advance to more skilled jobs. This training often takes the form of being paired with a more experienced worker on the floor. Classroom instruction may also be used. As companies develop a greater emphasis on teamwork, many firms have developed training courses that encourage employee self-direction and responsibility as well as the development of interpersonal skills. In manufacturing sectors such as motor vehicle and parts manufacturing and machinery manufacturing, employers frequently offer formal apprenticeship programs that combine on-the-job training with technical classroom instruction.

Distance Learning Courses

Another option for obtaining job skills is to enroll in distance education programs that provide career training. Distance learning programs allow a student to learn at his or her own pace and complete work in his or her own time. They provide the same course materials that would be found in a typical classroom setting, but those materials are delivered outside of a classroom setting—typically either through the mail (a correspondence course) or online. In some distance learning programs a student must be online with a teacher or other students at a specific time, and assignments must be completed according to a rigid schedule. Other courses are designed for students to complete at their own pace. And these courses are diverse: one can develop skills and knowledge in bookkeeping, carpentry, home remodeling and repair, computer programming, Web site design, dressmaking, pet grooming, photography, day care management, motorcycle or small engine repair, court reporting, and many other fields.

Distance learning has many advantages. It can allow students the flexibility to choose when and where they will do their course work. Students may study at any time, read materials at their own pace, focus their efforts on topics that they aren't already familiar with, and also interact with teachers and other students from around the world. There are disadvantages to pursuing a distance education certificate or degree as well. Students must have a high degree of motivation as well as good time management skills in order to be successful. Some students struggle with a sense of isolation, since they can't meet the teachers or other students in person. Still, distance education provides another option for obtaining necessary or desirable job skills.

When looking into distance learning, it is important to find legitimate, quality schools. The key to a successful distance learning experience is having adequately researched and evaluated the program. The school should be accredited. Usually a school will put this information on the homepage of their Web site. The accrediting association should be recognized by the Department of Education. The U.S. Department of Education maintains a database of accredited schools at http://ope.ed.gov/accreditation/. The best schools are regionally accredited. Some schools may have Distance Education Training Council (DETC) accreditation, but caution is recommended when exploring these schools. While DETC is recognized by the Department of Education, less than half of regionally accredited colleges recognize the validity of DETC degrees. Some employers will not accept DETC degrees either. Unaccredited schools should be avoided.

Also investigate the quality of the faculty. Are the teachers and staff of the program listed on the Web page? If not, be suspicious. If the faculty members are listed, research their backgrounds. Do they hold advanced degrees from many different schools? Is there a good student-faculty ratio? Ten faculty members serving ten thousand students would be a poor ratio, for instance.

Finally, consider student service. All distance learning programs should provide several ways for students to get in touch with faculty or administrators—e-mail, mail, phone, fax, or online forms. Legitimate schools will do this. Phone calls to the school during regular business hours should result in contact with a school representative, not just an answering service or a generic voice mail message.

CONCLUSION

There are many options available for obtaining occupational skills. Traditional vocational education, offered in high schools and postsecondary trade skills, is still a good choice. Other excellent alternatives include apprenticeships, community college programs, the education and training offered by the military services, and distance learning courses.

New Trends in Employment:

Women, Minorities and Immigrants, Older Employees, and the Physically Challenged

Bonnie Williamson

The economy of the United States went through dramatic changes in the 1990s. A recession at the beginning of the decade was followed by a robust business environment. The beginning of the twenty-first century has seen a slowdown in the economic growth rate of the late 1990s. American businesses face challenges as the composition of the American workforce continues to change. Businesses must adapt to those changes in the new century. Women, despite their growing numbers in the workforce, have yet to make significant strides in the area of corporate leadership. Battle lines are forming between minorities and immigrants over available jobs. Our workforce continues to age. People want to work longer, but some in the corporate world still don't recognize the hidden resource in older employees. In addition, a majority of physically challenged people in our country are still not employed. These challenges exist when times are economically rosy or bad. They will not go away. They cannot be ignored.

WOMEN

One of the most significant social and economic trends in modern U.S. history was the increase in the proportion of women who were working or looking for work during the latter decades of the twentieth century. By April 2006, women made up approximately 46.2 percent and men made up 53.8 percent of the labor force. In the same month, 59.1 percent of women age sixteen and older participated in the labor force; 56.4 percent were employed. Women are projected to make up 46.8 percent of the labor force by the year 2014.

Women are the primary wage earners in 17.4 million U.S. families, more than double the number thirty years ago. Families with two working parents have become the majority. In 2005 husbands were the sole workers in only 20.2 percent of married couple families; in 6.5 percent of married couple families only the wife worked. The proportion of married couple families in which both the husband and wife were employed was 51.3 percent. In 61.3 percent of married couple families with children both parents worked. In 2005 70.5 percent of all mothers with children under eighteen were in the labor force, up from 47.4 percent in 1975, although the proportion of mothers in the labor force has been declining since 2000, when it was 72.3 percent. Among mothers with children younger than a year old, over half (53.8 percent) were in the labor force.

During the United States' involvement in World War II (1941–44), women entered the workforce in large numbers to support their families as well as to

Bonnie Williamson has worked in publishing for more than twenty years. She was speech writer for the former commissioner of the New Jersey Department of Transportation and served as public information officer with the New Jersey Senate for five years.

support the war effort, filling jobs left by men who joined the military service. After the war's end, the number of women working for pay dropped significantly. By the 1950s, married women who had jobs usually remained in the workforce only until the birth of their first child. They then left their jobs and stayed at home, at least until their last child was in school. When they reentered the workforce, they found themselves far behind men in terms of pay and seniority, who had been continually working their way up the employment ladder. Times have changed. Most of today's mothers with infants were already well established in the marketplace before they had their newest child. Many retained their jobs by taking only a brief period of maternity leave.

The changes our society has experienced over the past few decades encourage, if not require, women to work. Birthrates are lower, but there are more single mothers. Many women are delaying first marriages and childbearing. One out of two marriages ends in divorce. More people are living together without getting married. Levels of education are now identical for women and men, with about 30 percent of both men and women in the labor force holding college degrees, Higher levels of education mean a higher potential for earned income.

In 2002, 10.1 million, or 46 percent, of U.S. businesses were owned by women, according to the Center for Women's Business Research (http://www.cfwbr.org/nationalnumbers.html). As of 2004, that number had grown to an estimated 10.6 million women-owned firms in the country. This accounts for nearly half of all privately held firms in the country. These women-owned businesses employ more than 19.1 million people. The estimated growth rate in the number of women-owned firms (17 percent) was nearly twice that of all firms (9 percent).

Women's earnings over the past twenty years show a mixed picture of progress. In 2004 about three-fifths (59.2 percent) of women sixteen years of age and older were in the labor force. Their median weekly earnings were $573. However, as economist Mary Bowler has observed, women's earnings did not keep pace with men's in all demographic groups. The gender gap was largest for white workers, middle-aged and older workers, and those with only high school diplomas. Women's inflation-adjusted earnings increased by 27 percent during the same period, while men's real earnings increased by only 1 percent. Still, while women's earnings improved relative to men's, the income of full-time working women in 2004 was only 78.6 percent of the income of men. The good news is that women with college degrees have seen their earnings shoot up 34.4 percent since 1979. For women with a college degree, the median weekly income was $832 in 2003, and $860 in 2004. Yet the income disparity between men and women is even more pronounced at higher education levels. Women with professional degrees make even less relative to men with professional degrees (64.8 percent) than women with high school degrees make relative to men with high school degrees (75.7 percent).

On the whole, women are beginning to make themselves known in formerly male-dominated fields. The proportion of women physicians and surgeons in the United States grew from 7.6 percent in 1970 to 29.4 percent in 2004. In addition, 30.4 percent of workers in production occupations, 1.8 percent of carpenters, 3.2 percent of construction laborers, and 12.4 percent of construction and building inspectors are women. A larger proportion of employed men than women belong to (and enjoy the benefits of) unions. Only about 11.1 percent of employed women belong to unions, down from 14.6 percent in 1983; 13.8 percent of employed men belong to labor unions, down from 24.7 percent in 1983.

Women doubled their managerial positions from 20 percent to 36.7 percent from 1972 to 2004; in 2004 women held half of all management, professional, and related occupations, earning a median income of $799 per week. This is due, in part, to women's increased educational opportunities. In 2004 nearly 33 percent of women age twenty-five to sixty-four held college degrees, compared to approximately 11 percent in 1970. Women still, however, remain highly overrepresented in lower-paying clerical and service positions. For example, 93 percent of registered nurses are women while only 29.4 percent of physicians and surgeons are women. About one-half of women work in sales, service, and administrative support, compared with about one-fifth of male workers.

Women in Leadership Roles

Despite all of their past accomplishments in the working world, women still have a long way to go in breaking the barriers that keep them from becoming corporate leaders. In 1986 an article in the *Wall Street Journal* popularized the term "glass ceiling" to describe the invisible barriers that women confront as they approach the top of the corporate ladder. The Federal Glass Ceiling Commission was created by the Civil Rights Act of 1991. The commission's mandate was to identify barriers that have blocked the advancement of women and minorities, as well as the successful practices and policies that have led to the promotion of these populations into decision-making positions in the private sector. The commission's survey of senior-level managers in Fortune 1000 and Fortune 500 service industries showed that women comprised less than 2.5 percent of total employment in the top jobs in the private sector. Only two women were CEOs (chief executive officers) in Fortune 1000 companies.

By February 2005, that number had grown. But when Carly Fiorina resigned as CEO of Hewlett-Packard Co. that month, she left only seven female CEOs at the nation's Fortune 500 companies. The percentage of female corporate officers at Fortune 500 companies had risen to 15.7 percent in 2002, up from 12.5 percent in 2000, according to a survey by Catalyst, a nonprofit women's research group in New York. By 2006 that number had declined to 14.7 percent. The number of Fortune 500 companies that had 25 percent or more women board directors increased almost six times over, from eleven in 1995 to sixty-four in 2005. Catalyst's studies also reveal that more new women are being recruited into the boardroom each year. Despite these heartening numbers, however, a press release from early 2006 announced that at the current growth rate, parity between women and men on corporate boards might not be reached for another seventy years.

Some industries had much higher concentrations of female officers than others. The two industries with the highest percentage of women were diversified financial companies, with 31 percent, and the apparel industry, with 28 percent. The textiles industries and what Catalyst classified as "mining/crude oil production" companies had no female corporate officers. In 2002, although women held 15.7 percent of the corporate officer positions in the Fortune 500, fewer than one-third of women held positions that had responsibility for profit and loss operations. Even fewer, 7.9 percent, held titles in the highest ranks of the company, executive vice president and above. Studies show that in 2005, food and grocery wholesalers, petroleum refining, and telecommunications held the highest percentage of women directors.

In 2003 only 5 percent of women earned $1,500 or more per week, compared with 12 percent of men. A ten-year study of Stanford University's 1982 class of MBA graduates found that men were more likely than women to work in the upper echelons of business. Sixteen percent of the men were CEOs compared with 2 percent of the women; 23 percent of the men and 10 percent of the women were corporate vice presidents; and 15 percent of the men and 8 percent of the women were directors.

How can companies be encouraged to promote women into executive positions? The Glass Ceiling Commission's study revealed that if corporations realize it's good for business, promotions will accelerate. A rating of the performance of five hundred companies based on factors relating to the advancement of women and minorities demonstrates that it's definitely good for business. Companies that rated in the bottom one hundred earned an average of 7.9 percent return on investment, compared to an average return of 18.3 percent for the top one hundred. Lower employee turnover costs are also a motivating factor. A report published by Ortho Pharmaceuticals said that a yearly savings of $500,000 was made mainly from the lower turnover among women. The commission found that women appear to be advancing fastest in industries with relatively high growth, those undergoing change with regard to regulation, and those highly competitive and dependent on marketing and flexibility.

Women and Child Care

Child care remains a thorny issue for women. Despite the fact that more women now work full time, family still remains, for the most part, their responsibility. Increasing numbers of the nation's six million companies are providing day care facilities for their employees' children. The government also provides aid to low-income families. In fiscal year 2005, the federal Child Care and Development Fund, part of the U.S. Department of Health and Human Services Administration for Children and Families, made available $4.8 billion to states to help low-income families, families receiving temporary public assistance, and families transitioning from public assistance to obtain child care so family members could work or attend training or education programs to help them in the workforce. Nationally, more than 1.8 million children receive subsidized childcare funded through the Child Care and Development Fund each month. However, past data suggest that federal efforts fail to meet current demands.

Many employers are moving away from the traditional nine-to-five workday and are responding more to the needs of their employees, especially those with families. Hundreds of companies have adopted the concept of flextime, letting employees begin and end the workday earlier or later than the norm. Allowing employees to telecommute—work at home with personal computers—is also becoming an option for many companies. The Bureau of Labor Statistics found that in 2004, 26.7 percent of women and 28.1 percent of men who worked full time had flexible schedules, although only about one in ten were enrolled in formal flextime programs. In addition, the technology research firm Gartner, Inc., reports that 82.5 million Americans worked from home at least once a week in 2005. That number is expected to increase to 100 million by 2008. Flextime and telecommuting are two options that employers can use to better respond to the needs of workers with children.

MINORITIES AND IMMIGRANTS

Disturbing trends are developing for minorities and immigrants in our country. High immigration quotas have created what writer Norman Matloff calls a caste system among U.S. minorities, with Asian immigrants at the top, African Americans on the bottom, and Hispanic immigrants in the middle.

Despite the current growth in our country's economy, there still are not enough jobs. One Harvard University study found that a 10 percent increase in immigrant populations reduces immigrant wages by 10 percent. Another problem is language. Many immigrants who had professional jobs in their homelands are forced to take low-skilled jobs in the United States because of poor English skills. This increases the number of workers looking for such jobs and subsequently lowers wages. An increasing number of low-skilled immigrants are competing among themselves and with native workers in the United States for low-skilled jobs, a sector that has not grown in the last thirty years, according to George Vernez of the RAND Corporation. A study by the Urban Institute found that despite an ability to get jobs, immigrants entering the United States have a lower average income and use more welfare per capita than U.S. natives.

In regions where there are high numbers of immigrants, low-skilled jobs in hotels, restaurants, and airports that were once held by African Americans are increasingly filled by immigrants who are willing to work for a lower wage. A study by the U.S. General Accounting Office found that starting in the mid-1970s, employers in the Los Angeles area deliberately and systematically fired unionized black janitors and replaced them with lower-paid immigrants.

Affirmative Action

African Americans and other minorities may find life in the working world more difficult for yet another reason: challenges to affirmative action. In 1965 President Lyndon Johnson issued Executive Order 11246 prohibiting federal agencies from contracting with firms that were not committed to equal opportunity "affirmative action," that is, conscious and deliberate efforts to bring qualified people of color and women into jobs and educational opportunities from which they had been traditionally excluded.

From this affirmative action concept, programs have developed at many levels of government, including the federal government, that are known as "set-aside" programs. These award a certain percentage of contracts to minority- and women-owned businesses. These programs were developed to remedy the effects of past discrimination, and to address the difficulties these firms faced in competing with larger, more established firms for government contracts. Minority businesses are often newer and smaller and have difficulty competing with older, larger businesses that know the process and can afford to make lower bids. Acquiring government contracts can be a very complex and confusing endeavor for businesses unfamiliar with the process. Government agencies, especially those of the federal government, are often slow to pay their bills, so businesses frequently have to borrow money to bridge the gap between the delivery of goods and services that must be paid for and the time it takes the government to pay them.

While the U.S. Supreme Court has not yet declared the use of racial classifications unconstitutional, it has ruled them suspect and subject to strict judicial scrutiny. As a result, set-aside programs came under increasing attack in the 1990s and early 2000s.

In the 1989 decision *City of Richmond v. Croson Co.* (488 US 469), the U.S. Supreme Court struck down a Richmond, Virginia, city ordinance that reserved 30 percent of city-financed construction contracts for minority-owned businesses. The Court ruled that the ordinance violated equal protection because there was no "specific" and "identified" evidence of past discrimination, "public or private," against the Richmond Minority Business Enterprise in city contracting. The majority opinion, written by Justice Sandra Day O'Connor, also noted that the city had failed to "narrowly tailor" the remedy to accomplish any objective other than "outright racial balancing." The opinion further stated that it was a "completely unrealistic" assumption that a 30 percent assignment to minority business enterprises in a particular trade would be a fair representation of the community.

In a similar case, a white-owned company, Adarand Constructors, sued the government claiming the company's failure to receive a government contract because of racial preferences had violated the owner's right to equal protection under the Fifth Amendment. In 1989 the U.S. Department of Transportation awarded a contract for a federal highway project to a construction firm, which in turn subcontracted the job to a Disadvantaged Business Enterprise in compliance with the Subcontractor Compensation Clause. In 1995 the U.S. Supreme Court, in *Adarand Constructors, Inc. v. Peña* (515 US 200), expressed doubt in the validity of the affirmative action programs, based on the Surface Transportation and Uniform Relocation Assistance Act of 1987 (PL 100-17) that channeled $10 billion per year in construction contracts to women- and minority-owned businesses. The court, citing the need for stricter and narrower standards in determining racial preferences when awarding contracts, returned the case to the district court for review.

These Supreme Court decisions have brought many set-aside programs under scrutiny. In June 2000 a federal court, in *Associated General Contractors of Ohio v. Sandra A. Drabnik*, decided that the Ohio state program to set aside 5 percent of state construction projects for minority-owned businesses was unconstitutional. Even though that court had upheld the state's program in 1983, subsequent U.S. Supreme Court decisions required the federal court to apply a more stringent standard of judicial review, no longer allowing legislatures to use "implicit fact finding of discrimination" to justify racial preferences and affirmative action programs like set-asides.

Shifting Population Diversity

The full effects of the current anti-affirmative action trend have not yet been felt, but some patterns are emerging. California's Proposition 209 (passed by referendum in 1996) is a sweeping ban on affirmative action. Since then, affirmative action policies in higher education admissions and for minority and women-owned businesses have been challenged (though ultimately upheld) by the Supreme Court, and affirmative action for minority businesses continues to face bureaucratic as well as political opposition. While current law sets a goal of 5 percent of all contracts awarded to minority businesses, the federal government has failed as a whole to meet these numbers. Part of the situation can be attributed to the way the federal government is doing business. Federal agencies generally bundle contracts into huge deals that are too large for small minority firms to handle.

Regardless of the current travails facing America's minorities and immigrants, one fact is clear: the Census Bureau projects that by the year 2050, half of the population of the United States will be made up of non-Hispanic whites and half will be made up of people of color. In the twenty-year period between 2000 and 2020, the United States nation will grow from 282 million to 336 million people, and most of that growth will come from immigration. Most immigrants will be arriving from South and Central America and South and East Asia. Our country's population will be increasingly diverse in the future, and corporations must deal effectively with America's changing face if they are to survive.

It pays for businesses to meet the needs of immigrants and minorities. In the United States, Asians, blacks, and Hispanics collectively represent more than $500 billion a year in consumer spending. Recognizing cultural differences within the market can put more money in a business's pocket. By targeting advertising, hiring bilingual sales people, and holding special events, a Miami Toyota dealer gained more than 50 percent of the local Hispanic market and its sales increased 400 percent over a six-year period. On the West Coast, a San Francisco Volkswagen dealership credited improved sales to Asian and Pacific Islanders for a fivefold increase in overall sales per month. Salespeople learned through cultural sensitivity training that among Chinese Americans, family elders are often the ultimate decision makers for major purchases. Taking steps such as learning about different cultures and initiating mentor programs to help immigrant and minority employees succeed in corporate cultures ultimately makes good business sense.

Education Concerns

With technology developing at such a rapid pace, we must have a well-trained and well-educated workforce to compete in global markets. Unfortunately, some minority groups are underrepresented in both higher education and in occupations that require the most training and pay the best salaries. In 2003, while 66.2 percent of white, non-Hispanic recent high school completers enrolled in college, only 58.6 percent of Hispanics and 57.5 percent of African Americans did. College completion rates were even more divergent. In 2003, 34.2 percent of non-Hispanic white twenty-five- to twenty-nine-year-olds had completed a bachelor's degree; however, only 17.5 percent of African Americans and 10 percent of Hispanics had done so.

Minorities are also underrepresented in occupations that require post-secondary education. While 34.7 percent of all workers are in management, professional, and related occupations, only 26 percent of African Americans and only 17 percent of all Hispanics are in this relatively well-paid occupational group. While 20.3 percent of all workers are in professional specialty occupations, only 16.5 percent of African Americans and 9.9 percent of Hispanics are in those occupations.

The United States is experiencing a severe shortage of trained scientists and engineers. Steps are being taken to encourage minorities and immigrants to enter science and engineering fields. One of the leading programs is the National Action Council for Minorities in Engineering (NACME). This program was devised by fifty-five science and engineering schools and sixty-five corporations and research labs, and since 1980 has supported more than seventeen thousand minority students. The organization offers scholarships to minority students seeking master's degrees in engineering and fellowships to those seeking doctoral degrees in engineering and science. NACME awarded scholarships to 746 students in the 2004–05 academic year, a 41 percent increase over the previous year. Other organizations that help in this effort include the Society of Hispanic Professional Engineers, the National Society of Black Engineers, and the American Indian Science and Engineering Society. Companies seeking minorities for technical positions have included TRW; General Dynamics Corporation; Hercules Aerospace, Inc.; and Ball Aerospace Systems.

OLDER EMPLOYEES

By 2020, most of the baby boomers will be over sixty-five, once considered the benchmark age for retirement. More than 54.6 million Americans will be classified as senior citizens, up from 35.1 million in 2000. Many of those people will still want to work and need to work to survive economically.

According to the Bureau of Labor Statistics, in 2004, 15.6 percent of the labor force was aged fifty-five and older; that percentage is projected to increase to 21.2 percent by 2014. Three-fourths of workers ages fifty-one to sixty-one say they would like to continue working beyond the traditional retirement age of sixty-five, according to the Health and Retirement Survey sponsored by the National Institute of Aging. Studies have also found that people with more years of schooling are most likely to continue working after age sixty-five.

Federal regulations implemented over time will raise the normal retirement age for full Social Security collection from sixty-five to sixty-seven. The growth in Social Security benefits over the past thirty years has made early retirement more affordable, but federal budget deficits may prohibit such growth from continuing. A tight budget environment may also affect Medicare, the health insurance program for the elderly. All of these elements may compel older workers to delay retirement, even if they don't wish to do so. As the life expectancy of the average American approaches eighty years, more and more people will live fifteen, twenty, or twenty-five years after they retire.

Long-term care insurance could become a frequently requested benefit. So-called old-age diseases will require adequate insurance coverage for vision care, hearing loss, arthritis, and cancer. During the recent downsizing by many businesses, midlevel and senior management positions were the first to go. The longer-tenured employees had the highest salaries. In the future, employers may consider linking pay with performance rather than seniority. Employers currently find that employees in their forties and fifties are more expensive to keep than hiring new employees in their twenties and thirties. However, as the baby boom generation begins to retire, employers may find themselves keeping older workers instead of considering them a liability.

There is no question that in the coming decades, millions of older skilled and experienced workers will exit the workforce. Many employers will find it necessary to alter their employment practices and pension plans to induce some of those who would otherwise retire completely to remain on the job, perhaps on a part-time or part-year schedule. This is referred to as phased retirement. Employers want Congress to amend the tax code to allow them greater flexibility in designing phased retirement programs for their employees. One proposed amendment would permit pension in-service distributions to employees who have not reached the pension plan's normal retirement age. Employers say this would allow them to offer older employees the chance to cut back their work schedules to part time while supplementing their reduced salaries with pension income.

In many industries, computers have reduced the physical demands of holding a job, so it makes sense for older workers to keep their skills current. Many older workers have what are called "bridge jobs." They don't leap from full-time employment into total retirement. For instance, many act as consultants to their employers after they retire from full-time employment.

Job banks are offered through states and corporations for those fifty-five and older. Temporary agencies actively seek older workers. Temporary jobs can range from office work to helping other elderly people. The National Older Worker Employment Partnership is a national advocacy organization for older workers. A unit of the National Council on the Aging, it provides technical assistance, information exchange, training, and a forum for discussion of issues for older workers.

There are many myths about older employees that lead employers to believe that older employees will retire early. However, older Americans will make up a significant percentage of the population in the coming decades. Because the number of workers twenty-five to fifty-four years old is expected to increase by only 3.4 percent between 2004 and 2014, while the number of older workers is expected to increase by 49.1 percent, an older workforce will be in demand.

Recruiting and Retraining Older Workers

Employers might want to consider adopting a strategy to recruit older workers. Traditional benefits and enticements may not be appropriate. One good plan is to offer accommodations for older workers. Amplified telephones, large-print documents, orthopedic and ergonomic furniture, and wellness programs would help older workers perform their jobs well. Age issues should be included in diversity training programs for employees. This would help reduce intergenerational conflicts. The key is to provide a wide range of options to both employers and older employees. Properly managing older workers is just another way for industry to master the growing diversity of the labor force. Older workers can be utilized as mentors to pass on their knowledge and skills to other employees.

Some employers have the perception that older employees cannot adapt to new technologies. However, Sun Life Assurance Company of Canada reports that there is no difference in the ability of old and young workers to adapt to new technology, and that limited training essentially levels the playing field for workers of all ages. According to the American Association of Retired Persons, half of what workers need to know today to do their jobs will probably be obsolete in ten or twenty years. To be effective, employers should conduct training programs in a nonthreatening, noncompetitive environment so that employees can learn at their own pace. One operator of several hotel chains offers a three-week training course for seniors. The $1.5 billion hotel company routinely turns to older applicants when it needs new hires for its 4,000-employee reservations system. About 10 percent of its sales agents who work out of eight centers across the United States and Canada are at least fifty-five years old, and another one-fourth are between forty and fifty-four. The company finds that older workers are dependable, loyal, and punctual and that they possess a strong work ethic. Chicago-based McDonald's Corporation also has special recruitment programs for older workers.

However, age discrimination is still a problem that older workers face. The Age Discrimination in Employment Act (ADEA) was enacted by Congress in 1968 "to promote employment of older persons based on their ability rather than age; to prohibit arbitrary age discrimination in employment; to help employers and workers find ways of meeting problems arising from the impact of age on employment." The act originally protected workers between the ages of forty and sixty-five. Later amendments first prohibited mandatory retirement before age seventy and then outlawed it altogether. A 1991 amendment dropped a two-year statute of limitations on age discrimination lawsuits, allowing broad recourse to virtually all middle-aged and elderly workers. In 1993 tenured college professors and police officers, who had once been exempted, were given protection. The Equal Employment Opportunity Commission (EEOC) office in Washington received 16,585 age discrimination complaints in fiscal year 2005. Age discrimination continues to represent a significant proportion of complaints filed with the EEOC.

THE PHYSICALLY CHALLENGED

There are over thirty-three million Americans with disabilities who are between the ages of sixteen and sixty-four. Of those, eleven million have a type of physical disability. Twenty-one million people, nearly two-thirds of the disabled population, have an employment disability. When a physical injury causes permanent disability, it can cost the state, insurance companies, or family members at least $750,000 to support a disabled person for life from the time of the injury. Government programs such as Social Security, Medicaid, and food stamps pay out more than $20 billion per year to unemployed people with disabilities. When a person with a disability wants to work but cannot get a job, all of society loses.

In 2004 only 35 percent of the disabled population was employed full or part time, compared to 78 percent of people without disabilities, according to the National Organization on Disability/Harris Survey of Americans with Disabilities. Three times as many Americans with disabilities were living in poverty, with annual household incomes below $15,000, the survey found. Such polls also indicate that most disabled individuals want to work. However, incorrect perceptions, unfair employment practices, accessibility barriers, and technology deficits still stand in the way.

In 1990 one of the most far-reaching and beneficial pieces of legislation to help the physically challenged become self-supportive became law. It was the Americans with Disabilities Act (ADA). The ADA was designed to make jobs and public facilities more accessible to people with disabilities. It is illegal for a company to fire or refuse to hire someone because that person has a disability unless the disability would prevent the individual from performing the basic function of the job. Employers must improve access at the worksite and provide accommodations for people with disabilities. A company is not required to make changes that would place an "undue burden" on the business, however.

The law applies to people with physical disabilities as well as those with mental illness, AIDS, and obesity. Originally, the law's ban on employment discrimination against people with disabilities pertained only to companies with twenty-five or more workers. The threshold is now fifteen or more employees. The change has caused a 150 percent increase in the number of companies affected by the law. According to the EEOC, 666,000 businesses now come under the ADA.

Following the ADA came the Developmental Disabilities Assistance and Bill of Rights Act, which establishes Protection and Advocacy (P&A) Systems to empower, protect the safety of, and advocate on behalf of persons with developmental disabilities. P&As act as independent agencies within each state to protect the legal and human rights of the physically challenged. In 2004 P&As and Client Assistant Programs provided advocacy services to more than 7,500 people, training to over 65,000 people, and information and referrals to almost 50,000 people. P&As helped adults with developmental disabilities secure jobs, encouraged businesses to employ this population, intervened on behalf of the disabled in cases of ADA employer discrimination, assisted persons with developmental disabilities to have homes of their own, and favorably resolved abuse complaints. In March 1998 the Presidential Task Force on Employment of Adults with Disabilities was implemented to create a coordinated and aggressive national policy to increase the employment rate of the physically challenged.

As employers feel the pressure of tight labor markets and repercussions from the ADA, they may find themselves more motivated to hire people who are physically challenged. Many employers may believe, however, that they cannot afford to buy the devices necessary for an individual with a severe disability to get the job done. The reality is that the cost of technology that enables such a person to work is falling. More than ten years ago, voice recognition technology cost about $10,000. Today the application and computer for such technology can be purchased for $2,000 or less. For $100, voice recognition software is available, and the top-end program Dragon NaturallySpeaking Professional is about $700.

New technology is continually being developed. Microsoft, Apple, IBM, and other technology companies are focusing on making their mainstream products accessible to people with disabilities. A Department of Labor fact sheet states that more than half of accommodations cost nothing, and of those accommodations that do cost money, the typical expenditure averages $600.

Accommodations for employees who have disabilities can be as simple as hitting a switch to run an electric stapler or copy machine. Raising an ordinary desk or worktable on blocks may allow the user to move his or her wheelchair up to the work area to work comfortably. Specially designed workstations, including those that can be raised and lowered mechanically, are now available. Moving equipment from one side of a workstation to the other may be all that is necessary.

A variety of devices that can be used with telephones to amplify hearing and speech are already on the market. Rubber-tipped pens and pencils bound to the hands of employees with disabilities can give them the ability to use computers. Raised lettering or braille symbols on signs and elevator buttons can assist employees who are visually impaired. Switches that can be operated with one's mouth or a head stick or even by rolling a wheelchair across a strip on the floor can be installed.

Numerous resources are available to employers and to the physically challenged to assist both in dealing with the challenges of the workplace. The Job Accommodation Network (JAN) was established by the President's Committee on Employment of People with Disabilities in 1984. In 1991 the service of JAN was expanded to provide public access information to businesses and services needing to comply with the ADA. JAN is an information and consulting service that provides individualized accommodation solutions to inquiries about enabling people with disabilities to work. In addition to its database of more than twenty thousand specific accommodations, JAN can also provide employers with specific resources to assist in solving difficult or unique accommodation adaptation problems.

The Office of Special Education and Rehabilitation Services of the U.S. Department of Education funds pilot-supported work programs in selected states. These programs can be used as an alternative vocational rehabilitative tool. In supported work programs, job coaches work with several individuals with handicaps who are placed in private sector employment settings with nonhandicapped workers. The job coaches typically provide six to twelve months of extensive training and actually perform the job where necessary.

At the state and local levels, employers and employees can contact their state governor's committee or local mayor's committee on employment of people with disabilities, as well as occupational therapy departments at local hospitals. Colleges and universities are yet another source of information on programs for people with disabilities. For example, the MEED (Microcomputer Education for Employment of the Disabled) program is a comprehensive business computer training program that enables unemployed physically challenged adults to become microcomputer (PC) applications specialists. The program awards up to forty-one college credits toward an associate of science degree in the computer science discipline through Miami-Dade Community College in Miami, Florida. The principal objectives of the program are to train people with severe physical disabilities in a variety of practical microcomputer software skills. MEED has had a strong partnership with local corporations and businesses. It has its own business advisory council, and more than one hundred corporate executives are personally involved with student activities ranging from financial and equipment contributions to field trips, internships, mentor programs, employment opportunities, and classroom instruction. MEED was the first private-public partnership to offer comprehensive personal computer software applications training for adults with disabilities. Since its inception in 1986, MEED has trained more than 150 individuals. Twenty-six adults with disabilities completed the program in 2004. Approximately 80 percent of MEED participants have achieved competitive employment within South Florida businesses.

Local efforts also include the work of organizations such as Calidad Industries, a subsidiary of Goodwill Industries of the Greater East Bay, in Oakland, California, which strives to place disabled individuals in government-agency, skilled-labor, and food-service occupations. Cheryl Sudduth, a special-needs advocate at Calidad and winner of *Working Mother* magazine's Maverick Award in 2005, has put together a network of volunteers so that when a prospective employer voices concerns about needing a sign-language interpreter, for example, she can solve the problem by providing a volunteer to do the job.

Working in Cyberspace

Melissa J. Doak

In the modern workplace, there is no denying the indispensability of the computer. According to a report issued by the U.S. Bureau of Labor Statistics (BLS) in 2005, seventy-seven million workers, or 55.5 percent of the entire American workforce, used a computer on the job in 2003. That is more than double the number of workplace computer users in 1984, and the numbers will almost certainly continue to grow.

In the past decade alone, one major use of computers at work has grown at breakneck speed: accessing the Internet. More than two in five (41.7 percent) of American workers accessed the Internet or used e-mail at work in 2003. The Internet and the World Wide Web have become so pervasive in the workplace that signs of their influence can be seen everywhere. Instead of making a phone call to a colleague or client, workers now send e-mail or an instant message. Rather than mailing a document, employees simply send a file over the Internet. Print and television advertisements for nearly every company—large or small, old or new—contain a Web address. Business is no longer just business, commerce, or retail—now it is also "e-business," "e-commerce," or "e-tail." Thousands of companies conduct business solely on the Web, without any storefront. Although these Internet companies, often called "dot-coms," have had their ups and downs, the strongest have survived and are flourishing.

For many workers in the twenty-first century, the Internet has become an indispensable tool. According to the BLS, workers in managerial and professional specialty occupations, especially finance, management, and business, are the largest users of computers (79.6 percent) and the Internet (67.1 percent). Over two-thirds (67.3 percent) of those in sales and office occupations used a computer at work; almost one-half (47.9 percent) used the Internet. On the other hand, only 27.5 percent of service workers, 26.4 percent of those in natural resources, construction, and maintenance occupations, and 26 percent of those in production, transportation, and material moving occupations used a computer at work, and even lower percentages of those workers used the Internet.

Some jobs involve working directly in cyberspace, either creating or maintaining the Internet. These workers still make up a fairly small percentage of the overall workforce, however. For other workers, even though they are not involved directly in the development or maintenance of cyberspace features and components, the Internet is a tool that makes their job easier and their time more productive. Many have decided to use the capabilities of the Internet to telecommute or begin a home-based business. However, with the explosion of Internet and e-mail use, also come problems that should be addressed.

Melissa J. Doak is a freelance writer of reference books and educational materials.

WORKING IN CYBERSPACE

In the early 1990s it was the exception rather than the rule for even a large corporation to have its own Web site. Today, it is practically unheard of for any company, even a tiny mom-and-pop operation, to not have a professionally designed site. In fact, for many smaller companies, a Web site is the only way to reach a large market for their products and services. This proliferation of Web sites has led to a significant increase in the number of jobs in cyberspace.

Network, Database, and Computer Systems Administrators

The rapid spread of computers and Internet use has resulted in a great demand for trained professionals to develop and maintain these systems. Storing, managing, and extracting data quickly and efficiently has become ever more complex as the Internet and electronic business generate huge and growing volumes of data. Database administrators work with database software, determining how to organize and store this large volume of data. These workers must set up computer databases to meet user requirements, as well as test and maintain the databases. Database administrators often are responsible for planning and implementing security measures. The Bureau of Labor Statistics predicts that the number of positions for database administrators will increase by 38.2 percent between 2004 and 2014, from approximately 104,000 to 144,000 jobs.

Because networks are configured in many ways, network systems and data communications analysts and administrators are needed to design, test, evaluate, and oversee systems that range from local connections between two offices in the same building to vast global networks. Voice mail and e-mail systems, local and wide area networks, the Internet and intranets (self-contained internal networks within an organization that use wireless technology) are among the data communications systems these professionals work with. The Bureau of Labor Statistics predicts that network systems and data communications analysts will be the second-fastest-growing occupation between 2004 and 2014, with the number of positions increasing by 54.6 percent during that time. Network and computer systems administrators will also be a fast-growing occupation; the number of positions for this group is projected to increase by 38.4 percent over the decade.

Design, Development, and Maintenance

The growth of the Web has generated a variety of other occupations related to the design, development, and maintenance of Web sites and their servers. The Internet, accessed with a few clicks of a mouse, seems deceptively simple. But a great deal of work goes on behind the scenes to keep the Web running smoothly. The people who develop and maintain the internal workings of the Internet, as well as private networks called intranets that operate through Internet technology, are some of the most highly skilled professionals in cyberspace. Examples of jobs in Web design and maintenance include computer programmers, Web site developers and designers, information security specialists, and information architects. As the number of job openings in this area is greater than the number of qualified people, workers in Web design and maintenance are in great demand.

Electronic business (e-business), any process that a business organization conducts over a computer network, is a rapidly growing sector of the Internet. One part of e-business, electronic commerce (e-commerce), is the buying and selling of goods and services online. As e-commerce expands, there is a corresponding growth of firms that specialize in developing and maintaining sites on the World Wide Web for business clients, as well as firms that develop and maintain intranets. These firms recruit computer specialists, including programmers, software engineers, systems analysts, Web designers, and content developers. Teams of these computer professionals design computer networks, implement upgrades or conversions, custom design software programs, develop and maintain Web sites, and maintain networks on a day-to-day basis.

With the growth of e-commerce has also come an increased focus on security. Threats include computer viruses that can disable entire business systems and credit card fraud, which threatens the consumers e-businesses are trying to attract. Security consulting firms employ specialists who analyze vulnerability and specialize in providing protection, including virus protection and firewalls, to make computer networks safe. Cyberspace security professionals will be in increasing demand as e-commerce continues to grow.

CYBERSPACE ON THE JOB

The Internet has become indispensable in many jobs. The Bureau of Labor Statistics found that more than two of every five employed persons used e-mail or connected to the Internet while working. Workers use the Internet to communicate with others, to conduct research, to transfer information, and to solve problems.

Communication Revolutionized

The single most common use of the Internet at work is for communication with others. E-mail has revolutionized the way that workers communicate with supervisors, coworkers, clients, and customers. E-mail and the Web have allowed many small businesses to expand their customer base from their local area to a national or even international arena. Customers can use e-mail to place orders, check their order status, and ask questions. Some companies can streamline their business by using e-mail instead of expensive toll-free phone numbers staffed by order takers and customer service representatives.

E-mail is extremely useful in communicating within businesses and organizations as well. Gone are the days when paper memos littered inboxes. In the modern office, memos regarding everything from the latest sales figures to the company picnic are circulated via e-mail. An interoffice e-mail can be sent to one recipient or hundreds of recipients with the click of a button. (The downside of this capability, of course, is that it is equally easy for confidential information to be inadvertently disseminated to hundreds of recipients.) With interoffice e-mail, photocopying time and expense are reduced, and crucial or confidential memos are less likely to get lost on workers' desks. In the global marketplace, e-mail also allows colleagues on opposite sides of the world to communicate without the expense of long-distance telephone calls. In addition, time zones are of little consequence because e-mail can be answered at the convenience of the recipient.

For colleagues who are working online at the same time, instant messaging is becoming a useful tool. Instant messaging (IM) is a quick and easy way to communicate with one or more people online in real time—sort of a cross between e-mail and a telephone call. With instant messaging software and a list of contact names (often called screen names) to communicate with, users can send and receive on-screen messages with any of their contacts that are online at the same time. Some corporations are deploying enterprise-wide instant messaging systems to increase productivity and interoffice communication. About eleven million people already use instant messaging at work, according to a report issued in 2004 by the Pew Internet & American Life Project.

Videoconferencing is another form of office communication that takes place over the Internet, revolutionizing the way meetings are conducted. Rather than having to meet physically in one conference room at a given location, workers can meet in cyberspace, "face-to-face," in real time, from multiple locations. With a high-speed Internet connection, a small video camera, and a headset, people can meet in cyberspace using the video functions of free instant messaging programs or other Web collaboration tools like Macromedia Breeze, Wired-Red, or GroupSystems. Because people can actually see and hear one another, videoconferencing is often more useful than e-mail or phone calls for meetings that involve several people. It allows for collaboration and teamwork, as if all workers were in the same room instead of hundreds or thousands of miles away from one another. An executive on a business trip to Europe can continue to get a daily update from her assistants in New York City. A designer in Los Angeles can meet face-to-face with a prospective client in Chicago, without leaving his office. Useful applications for this technology are endless.

Research

With the proliferation of information available in cyberspace, the Internet has become a useful research tool. Investigating the pros and cons of starting a home-based business? The mega-search engine Google can help. Putting together a presentation for the company board meeting? Find needed facts and figures on the Internet. Need some historical or biographical information for a report? Access the database resources of the local library with a few clicks of the computer mouse. The Internet is an incredible resource for finding information.

The Internet is particularly useful in locating the most up-to-date information about a subject. Not only are this week's currency exchange rates available, but so are this afternoon's closing stock quotes and next week's weather forecast. Unlike printed research materials, such as books and magazines, Internet "pages" can be quickly and continually updated, which can make the most current news available almost as soon as it happens.

Information found on the Internet, however, is not infallible. Not only is there an overwhelming amount of information available to sort through, there is the reliability factor to consider. When books, journal articles, and newspaper and magazine articles are published in paper form, they generally go through a rigorous fact-checking process to make sure the information contained in them is accurate. No such process exists for much of the information published on the Internet. Anyone with basic Web authoring tools and a Web hosting service can publish whatever they want— fact or fiction—in cyberspace. Trying to filter out the accurate from the dubious or downright wrong information can be an arduous and time-consuming task. Although it is important to know how to search the Internet, it is equally, if not more, important to know which sources to trust.

Fortunately, there are some guidelines to follow when evaluating information on the Internet. A good place to start is with the letters following the "dot" at the end of the Web address. These letters indicate the Web site type or purpose. A Web address that ends in ".com," for example, is usually a commercial site. If the Web site is for a company that is in business to sell products or services, the information provided—much like any other form of advertising—may be biased. On the other hand, the online editions of major newspapers, magazines, and other traditional media sources are usually found at Web sites that use the ".com" extension. Information retrieved from these sites can generally be considered as reliable as whatever is published in their print editions.

A Web site address ending in ".gov" denotes an official site of the U.S. government. Statistical information obtained from a government site, for example, is almost always factually accurate, although researchers should keep in mind that some government resources are partisan in content or funding support, and thus may also be biased. Information found at (or linked to) college or other educational Web sites (those ending in ".edu") and at sites for nonprofit organizations (".org") are generally thought to be trustworthy.

Regardless of where data or information is posted, asking several questions can help a user determine its trustworthiness. Who is the author, and what are her qualifications (education, experience) that relate to the information she is presenting? Is the piece you have found peer reviewed? Are there sources or a bibliography included? Are there obvious errors (in grammar or spelling, for example) that offer the clue that this is not a reliable source? Is the page biased, or does it use inflammatory language? What is the purpose of the page? Was it published recently, or is the information outdated? Taking the time to evaluate the information found in cyberspace is well worth the effort.

Information Transfer

Years ago, information transfer involved typing a document on a typewriter, photocopying it, and sending it by mail to its destination. If the document needed to travel a great distance, it could take days or even weeks to arrive. In more recent years, overnight courier services and fax machines greatly improved the speed at which information could be transferred. But the Internet has made even these improvements seem outmoded. With the Internet, files can be transferred from one computer to another in a matter of seconds, and the information to be sent is not limited to just a few pages of text. Today, complex documents, photographs, and even entire software programs can be quickly and easily transferred across cyberspace.

The business world has greatly benefited from this ability to quickly transfer information over great distances. Administrators can work on annual reports while on business trips and send huge documents, charts and graphs, or Power-Point presentations back to their home offices. Independent contractors can work on assignments that can be sent to companies around the world. Educators on sabbatical in other countries can respond to the work of their at-home peers and students almost as easily as if they were down the hall. And all of this information transfer can be done instantaneously, literally with the click of a button.

Help and Problem Solving

The Internet is also a valuable resource for finding solutions to problems in a wide variety of areas, especially technical ones. To solve a problem with a computer printer, for example, a user might first consult the printer manufacturer's Web site. If the problem affects the way the computer interacts with the printer, and if many users have encountered the same problem, there might be a "patch," or a software file, available for immediate download that can correct the problem. If not, there is usually a list of frequently asked questions (FAQs) posted by the manufacturer that might provide a solution. Another option might be to send an e-mail to the company's tech support team or begin an online instant message conversation with a customer service representative. Perhaps the manufacturer maintains a message board for discussions about its products. A message board is a Web feature that allows a group "conversation" to take place over a period of time. One participant posts a question on the message board, and others can post answers and other comments. Newsgroup postings and message boards from outside the company's Web site can also be searched for someone describing the same printer problem. Of the millions of people in the cyber community, chances are someone else has experienced the same problem and has posted a helpful suggestion for solving it.

In addition, print manuals for software programs are now a thing of the past. Until recent years, software programs came packaged with large printed manuals. Software programs now generally come only with a small printed "getting started" manual. For more extensive help, users access the software's help function, which includes a table of contents and an index of help topics. These topics are linked to the manufacturer's online manual. These manuals are interactive and quite user friendly.

WORKPLACE ISSUES

Productivity and Privacy

Although increased productivity is an important reason for using the Internet, this same tool can also cause decreased productivity. The problem stems from workers enjoying cyberspace diversions—such as "surfing" the Web, trading stocks online, hanging out in online chat rooms, sending and receiving personal e-mails, and playing Web-based games—during work hours. A Bureau of Labor Statistics survey found that 87.5 percent of employees thought it was appropriate for them to visit non-work-related Web sites during work hours and that 83.7 percent believed it was appropriate to send personal e-mail during the workday.

Surprisingly, in the same survey, about the same percentage of employers believed it was appropriate for their employees to surf non-work-related Web sites (82.2 percent) and send personal e-mail during the work day (83.7 percent). Still, productivity concerns have led many employers to crack down on employees who spend too much unnecessary time in cyberspace. Although employees often believe that their use of Internet and e-mail at work is and should be private, courts have consistently permitted employers to monitor that use, and even keep that monitoring secret. In *Smyth v. The Pillsbury Company*, for example, the Federal District Court for the Eastern District of Pennsylvania found that there should be no reasonable expectation of privacy in e-mails sent at work, despite the company's statements that e-mail correspondence would be confidential. According to an American Management Association survey, more than 75 percent of U.S. businesses monitor their employees' Internet usage, e-mail, phone calls, and correspondence.

While some companies have removed Internet access or even fired employees because of personal Internet use, one problem is how to best go about monitoring Internet use without spending an inordinate amount of time and money doing so. Charles J. Muhl, in an article published in the *Monthly Labor Review* (February 2003), suggests that all employers should clearly detail to employees what are and what are not permissible uses of the Internet and e-mail at work, as well as which personal uses are allowed, if any. Employers should alert employees that e-mail and Internet use is not private, confidential, or privileged, and will be monitored. *Infoworld*, an online resource for the infrastructure technology (IT) industry, suggests that many companies find that establishing alerts based on keywords or particular behavior patterns is the most cost-effective method for monitoring Internet use. When a keyword is typed, the IT staff is alerted and full-scale monitoring can occur. A small New England insurance company posts a list in the office of Web sites recently frequented by employees. According to the insurance company, this technique has been an effective deterrent against employees wasting too much time on the Web.

Telecommuting

Telecommuting is any method a worker uses to work productively while away from the traditional office, and it is a fast-growing trend in American society in the twenty-first century. This form of work is advantageous for everyone. From a business standpoint, allowing employees to telecommute reduces high overhead costs. From an employee's view, telecommuting reduces commuting costs, an important consideration as gas prices increase and more employees live at greater distances from their workplaces than ever before. A study conducted in 2005 by the technology research firm Gartner, Inc., states that 82.5 million Americans currently work from home at least once a week. The study predicts that that number will increase to 100 million by 2008. Although home-based workers currently represent a minority of the nation's workforce, their numbers have been rising dramatically in recent years. In large part, this is due to a drastic shift away from agriculture and manufacturing toward a service-based economy. A majority of Americans today are involved in work that creates and processes information.

The work of processing information has traditionally been done in corporate offices; however, the modern office is in transition. Companies are emphasizing efficiency over bureaucracy. With computers, fax machines, high-speed Internet connections, videoconferencing, email, and other technological tools, companies are able to save time and money while achieving their goals. This technology has also meant that for many workers, working together inside office buildings is no longer necessary. Home-based workers can communicate quickly and easily with coworkers and clients using accessible and affordable technological tools.

Of course not all employees are able to work from home. Workers employed, for example, in transportation, storefront retail sales, production and material distribution, or public school education must be in their respective workplaces in order to perform their jobs.

There are downsides to the accessibility of technological tools that make working from home so easy. An estimated seventeen million Americans work from their homes at least once a month but do not get paid for their work. These workers bring work home with them after putting in regular office hours because their employer expects them to get it done. According to the Bureau of Labor Statistics, 75 percent of employees who continue to work once they get home do not get paid for their extra time. These workers, on average, spend seven hours at home on unpaid work each week.

Self-Employment

The availability of low-cost computer equipment and high-speed Internet access has also made it easier for many people to work for themselves. Each year, computers, Internet connections, and Internet service providers become more powerful and less expensive. For many self-employed people, such as desktop publishers and Web site designers, a computer and Internet access is necessary for producing and delivering their goods or services. But even if a home business produces merchandise for sale, the Internet has become an indispensable marketing tool.

Home-based businesses made up more than half (53 percent) of small businesses in fiscal year 2003. Home-based business owners may get all of their income from their business, or they may work at their home business on nights and weekends. Most of these businesses (91 percent) reported no paid employees. These businesses ran the gamut of industrial sectors: 60 percent were in service industries, 16 percent in construction, 14 percent in retail trade, and the rest were scattered across manufacturing, finance, transportation, communications, and wholesale trade. Writers, Web designers, bookkeepers, financial planners, customer support personnel, computer programmers, graphic designers, day care providers, and craftspeople have all begun successful home businesses. Almost any service can become the basis for a home-based business. For example, some people seek work preparing resumes, creating Web sites, or writing advertising copy. Cyberspace makes marketing and providing goods and services much easier than it once was.

Some people who begin home businesses choose to manufacture products such as gourmet, ready-made meals, educational toys, or custom-made jewelry. These production-oriented business people may rely on the Internet to research marketing techniques or potential new products, to advertise, to purchase supplies, and to sell their wares. Some small business owners work from home on a computer while their employees do much of the labor associated with their product in a factory setting elsewhere.

Other people specialize in buying and selling products online. For example, people may scour online sites, yard sales, or even the attics and basements of their families and friends, and then sell these objects through online auction sites such as eBay, Amazon.com, and Yahoo! Auctions. People sell a wide range of products online, from antiques and vintage clothing to used computers and nostalgic childhood toys. In 2003 online retailing grew 51 percent to a $114 billion industry, with a significant portion of this coming from online auction sites.

Independent contractors, also called freelancers, also rely on the Internet to procure and deliver work. These individuals work for companies on a project, or contract, basis, rather than as salaried employees. Some independent contractors work in the arts and include writers, photographers, and artists. Others provide consulting or clerical services, or perform work for hire such as construction and landscape design or maintenance. Most freelancers today are dependent on the Internet, as high-speed Internet connections provide the ability to instantly send files to clients located thousands of miles away. For example, an independent contractor who specializes in creating educational content for Web sites might work for publishers in Los Angeles, Cleveland, and Miami, while living and working in rural North Dakota. The Internet has greatly improved the potential client base of independent contractors.

THE FUTURE OF WORKING IN CYBERSPACE

Job Growth

According to the Bureau of Labor Statistics, five of the fifteen fastest-growing jobs between 2004 and 2014 will be in the computer field; these occupations will add nearly 650,000 new jobs to the economy over the ten-year period. The top five computer-related occupations will be network systems and data communications analysts, software application engineers, systems software engineers, network and database administrators, and database administrators. Some of these jobs will come from Internet companies, Web site designers, Internet service providers, search engines, software consulting firms, and telecommunications companies.

Clearly, jobs working in cyberspace are growing exponentially. Meanwhile the use of the Internet as an integral part of many jobs in the Information Age is here to stay. Regardless of whether one works directly in cyberspace or simply uses the Internet as a tool, the Internet has transformed both the workplace and the way people do their jobs. Cyberspace allows companies to expand geographically in terms of both employees and customers. In addition, workers benefit from Internet access by being able to do their jobs more quickly and efficiently.

The Demise of "The Job"?

As the twenty-first century progresses, the boundaries between the workplace and the home most likely will continue to blur. The number of home-based workers has increased steadily in recent years and will continue to do so. Some theorists have argued that cyberspace has not just transformed the way workers do their jobs, but in fact, is contributing to the disappearance of the very job itself. While people continue to work, that work won't be contained within what we now call "jobs." Note the amount of unpaid work, at home, that many workers today must do. Instead of a set number of hours each day that one must work in a job, work will become task- or project-oriented. Independent contractors exemplify this trend. They contract their services by the project; whether they work a typical nine-to-five day, fifteen hours a day, or a few hours at a time on evenings and weekends until the work is done is immaterial.

In 1995 Peter Leyden, in the *Minneapolis-St. Paul Star Tribune*, argued that our economy is losing "the job" as the concept behind how we organize work. "Our economy," he writes, "driven by the proliferation of digital technologies, is hurtling toward a time when working in jobs as we know them will not be the predominant way we get things done. In the Digital Age, we will still work. We will still earn livings. We will still produce things and provide services. But the majority of us likely won't go off to 'jobs' each day."

Contemplate that as you imagine *your* future working in cyberspace.

Career Information for Canada

The following pages provide some basic information about the Canadian job market. Included are background information on the Canada Employment and Immigration Commission, a list of Canadian departments of education, and selected listings of Canadian trade and professional associations. To find out more about any of the jobs included in a specific volume of the Career Information Center, contact the trade and professional associations listed for that volume.

THE CANADA EMPLOYMENT AND IMMIGRATION COMMISSION

The Canada Employment and Immigration Commission provides, through a national network of more than 450 Canada Employment Centres, employment services to both clients and employers. These centers offer programs and services related to counseling, registration, placement, and employer-market development.

The Canadian Jobs Strategy programs, available through Canada Employment Centres, provide employment training and development opportunities to those Canadians most in need.

The Skill Investment program brings help to workers whose jobs are threatened by changing technology and economic conditions. Participants have the chance to learn new skills before they are laid off or their existing skills are no longer needed.

The Job Entry program helps young people and women who face difficulties entering the labor market through a combination of training and work experience.

The Job Development program offers assistance for the long-term unemployed, with individualized skill development and practical employment opportunities.

The Skill Shortages program deals with the problem of critical skill shortages, filling employers' needs for workers with specialized training.

The Community Futures program offers help for workers in communities facing chronic high unemployment, plant closures, and mass layoffs.

The Innovations program provides funds for pilot and demonstration projects that test new solutions to labor market problems.

The Job Accommodation Network (JAN) is a telephone consulting service with a data bank containing thousands of examples of how employers have accommodated their workers who have disabilities. By calling the service, employers can get information from the data bank, advice from a trained consultant, and the name of an employer who has successfully accommodated similar limitations.

Information about these and other programs and services offered by the Canada Employment and Immigration Commission can be obtained at any Canada Employment Centre.

Canadian Departments of Education

ALBERTA

Alberta Advanced Education and Career Development
City Centre
10155 One Hundred Second Street, Seventh Floor
Edmonton T5J 4L5
http://www.aecd.gov.ab.ca

Alberta Education
Communications Branch
Devonian Building
11160 Jasper Avenue, Second Floor
Edmonton T5K 0L2
http://www.learning.gov.ab.ca

MANITOBA

Manitoba Education and Training
Planning and Policy Coordination Branch No. 409
1181 Portage Avenue
Winnipeg R3G 0T3
http://www.gov.mb.ca/educate/

NEW BRUNSWICK

Department of Education
P.O. Box 6000
Fredericton E3B 5H1
http://www.gov.nb.ca/education/

NORTHWEST TERRITORIES

Department of Education, Culture, and Employment
Government of the Northwest Territories
Department of the Executive
P.O. Box 1320
Yellowknife, NT X1A 2L9
http://siksik.learnnet.nt.ca

NOVA SCOTIA

Department of Education and Culture
P.O. Box 578
2021 Brunswick Street, Suite 402
Halifax B3J 2S9
http://www.ednet.ns.ca

ONTARIO

Ministry of Education and Training
Public Inquiries and Correspondence Unit
14th Floor, Mowat Block
900 Bay Street
Toronto M7A 1L2
http://www.edu.gov.on.ca

PRINCE EDWARD ISLAND

Department of Education
Information Centre
Second Floor, Sullivan Building
P.O. Box 2000
16 Fitzroy Street
Charlottetown C1A 7N8
http://www.gov.pe.ca/educ/

QUEBEC

Ministère de l'Éducation
Direction des communications
Edifice Marie-Guyart, 28e Étage
1035 rue De La Chevrotière
Quebec G1R 5A5
http://www.meq.gouv.qc.ca

SASKATCHEWAN

Saskatchewan Education Resource Centre
2220 College Avenue
Regina S4P 3V7

www.sasked.gov.sk.ca

YUKON

Yukon Education
P.O. Box 2703
Whitehorse Y1A 2C6
http://www.gov.yk.ca/depts/education/

Canadian Trade and Professional Associations

Agribusiness, Environment, and Natural Resources

VOLUME 1

ALBERTA

Canadian Association of Oilwell Drilling Contractors
540 Fifth Avenue SW, Suite 800
Calgary T2P 0M2

Canadian Association of Petroleum Landmen
500 4th Avenue SW, Suite 2800
Calgary T2P 2V6

Canadian Association of Petroleum Producers
350 7th Avenue SW, Suite 2100
Calgary T2P 3N9

Canadian Gas Processors Association
900 6th Avenue SW, Suite 500
Calgary T2P 3K2

Canadian Ground Water Association
P.O. Box 60
Lousana T0M 1K0

Canadian Society of Petroleum Geologists
160540 5th Avenue SW
Calgary T2P 0M2

Coal Association of Canada
205 Ninth Avenue SE, Suite 502
Calgary T2G 0R3

Petroleum Services Association of Canada
1150, 800-6th Avenue SW
Calgary T2P 3G3

Recycling Council of Alberta
Box 40552, Highfield Post Office
Calgary T2G 5G8

BRITISH COLUMBIA

Canadian Farmworkers Union
12414 82nd Avenue, Suite 109
Surrey V3W 3E9

Forest Action Network
Box 625
Bella Coola V0T 1C0

MANITOBA

Canada Grains Council
360 Main Street, Suite 330
Winnipeg R3C 3Z3

Canadian International Grains Institute
303 Main Street, Suite 1000
Winnipeg R3C 3G7

NEWFOUNDLAND

Geologic Society of Canada
Alexander Murray Building, Room ER4063
Memorial University of Newfoundland
St. John's A1B 3X5

NOVA SCOTIA

Ecology Action Centre
1568 Argyle Street, Suite 31
Halifax B3J 2B3

Friends of Nature Conservation Society
P.O. Box 281
Chester B0J 1J0

Northwest Altantic Fisheries Organization
P.O. Box 638
Dartmouth B2Y 3Y9

ONTARIO

Agricultural Institute of Canada
141 Laurier Avenue W, Suite 1112
Ottawa K1P 5J3

Agricultural Groups Concerned About Resources and the Environment
40 Eglinton Avenue E, 5th Floor
Toronto M4P 3B1

Animal Defense League of Canada
P.O. Box 3880, Station C
Ottawa K1Y 4M5

Aquatic Conservation Network
P.O. Box 67011
Westboro RPO
Ottawa K2A 4E4

Canadian Agri-Food Research Council
Central Experimental Farm
Heritage House, Building 60
Ottawa K1A 0C6

Canadian Animal Health Institute
160 Research Lane, Suite 102
Guelph N1G 5B2

Canadian Association of Mining Equipment and Services for Export
345 Renfrew Drive, Suite 101
Markham L3R 9S9

Canadian Association of Recycling Industries
682 Monarch Avenue, Unit 11
Ajax L1S 4S2

Canadian Association on Water Quality
Environmental Technology Center
Environment Canada
3439 River Road S
Gloucester K1A 0H3

Canadian Council on Animal Care
350 Albert Street, Suite 315
Ottawa K1P 5J3

Canadian Dairy Commission
1525 Carling Avenue
Ottawa K1A 0Z2

Canadian Drilling Association
222 McIntyre Street W, Suite 206
North Bay P1B 2Y8

Canadian Environmental Network
300-945 Wellington Street
Ottawa K1Y 2X5

Canadian Federation of Agriculture
75 Albert Street, Suite 1101
Ottawa K1P 5E7

Canadian Feed Industry Association
325 Dalhousie Street, Suite 625
Ottawa K1N 7G2

Canadian Forestry Association
185 Somerset Street W, Suite 203
Ottawa K2P 0J2

Canadian Gas Association
20 Eglinton Avenue W, Suite 1305
Toronto M4R 1K8

Canadian Horticultural Council
1101 Prince of Wales Drive, Suite 310
Ottawa K2C 3W7

Canadian Institute of Food Science and Technology
P.O. Box 152
Apple Hill K0C 1B0

Canadian Institute of Forestry
151 Slater Street, Suite 606
Ottawa K1P 5H3

Canadian Lumbermen's Association
27 Goulburn Avenue
Ottawa K1N 8C7

Canadian Meteorological and Oceanographic Society
McDonald Building, Suite 112
150 Louis Pasteur Avenue
Ottawa K1N 6N5

Canadian Nature Federation
1 Nicholas Street, Suite 606
Ottawa K1N 7B7

Canadian Organic Growers
P.O. Box 6408, Station J
Ottawa K2A 3Y6

Canadian Petroleum Products Institute
275 Slater Street, Suite 1000
Ottawa K1P 5H9

Canadian Seed Growers Association
P.O. Box 8455
Ottawa K1G 3T1

Canadian Seed Trade Association
39 Robertson Road, Suite 302
Nepean K2H 8R2

Canadian Society of Agronomy
141 Laurier Avenue W, Suite 1112
Ottawa K1P 5J3

Canadian Society of Animal Sciences
141 Lauier Avenue West, Suite 1112
Ottawa K1P 5J3

Canadian Society of Environmental Biologists
PO Box 962, Station F
Toronto M4Y 2N9

Canadian Veterinary Medical Association
339 Booth Street
Ottawa K1R 7K1

Canadian Water and Wastewater Association
45 Rideau Street, Suite 402
Ottawa K1N 5W8

Canadian Water Quality Association
151 Frobisher Drive, Suite A 201
Waterloo N2V 2C9

Canadian Water Resources Association
P.O. Box 1329
Cambridge N1R 7G6

Canadian Wildlife Foundation
350 Michael Copeland Drive
Kanata K2M 2W1

Canadian Wood Council
1400 Blair Place, Suite 210
Ottawa K1J 9B8

Federation of Ontario Naturalists
335 Lesmill Road
Don Mills M3B 2W8

Independent Order of Foresters
789 Don Mills Road
Toronto M3C 1T9

International Council of Metals and the Environment
506-294 Albert Street
Ottawa K1P 6E6

National Dairy Council of Canada
221 Laurier Avenue East
Ottawa K1N 6P1

Planetary Association for Clean Energy
100 Bronson, No. 1001
Ottawa K1R 6G8

Women's Association of the Mining Industry of Canada Foundation
P.O. Box 207, Station A
Toronto M5W 1B2

QUEBEC

Agricultural Producers Union
555 Roland-Therrien
Longueuil J4H 3Y9

Canadianne Cattle Breeders Association
468 rue Dolbeau
Sherbrooke J1G 2Z7

Canadian Institute of Mining,
Metallurgy, and Petroleum
Xerox Tower, Suite 1210
3400 de Maisonneuve Boulevard West
Montréal H3Z 3B8

SASKATCHEWAN

Back to the Farm Research Foundation
P.O. Box 69
Davidson S0G 1A0

Canadian Consulting Agrologists
Association
502-45th Street West, 2nd Floor
Saskatoon S7L 6H2

Canadian Society of Agricultural
Engineering
RPO University
P.O. Box 381
Saskatoon S7N 4J8

National Farmers Union, Canada
2717 Wentz Avenue
Saskatoon S7K 4B6

COMMUNICATIONS AND THE ARTS

VOLUME 2

ALBERTA

Canadian Popular Theatre Alliance
11039 Saskatchewan Drive
Edmonton T6G 2B4

Canadian Society for Traditional Music
P.O. Box 4232, Station C
Calgary T2T 5N1

Caviar Players Drama Society
P.O. Box 733
Bon Accord T0A 0K0

BRITISH COLUMBIA

Canadian Dance Teachers Association
8160 Lucas Road
Richmond V6Y 1G3

NOVA SCOTIA

Atlantic Film Festival
P.O. Boc 36139
Halifax B3J 3S9

ONTARIO

Algonquin Arts Council
Heritage Way, Unit 2, 8 Hastings
P.O. Box 1360
Bancroft K0L 1C0

Alliance of Canadian Cinema,
Television, and Radio Artists
2239 Yonge Street, 3rd Floor
Toronto M4S 2B5

Association of Canadian Publishers
110 Eglinton Avenue West, Suite 401
Toronto M4R 1A3

Black Music Association of Canada
59 Chester Hill Road
Toronto M4K 1X4

Canadian Academy of Recording Arts
and Sciences
124 Merton Street, Suite 305
Toronto M4S 2Z2

Canadian Actors Equity Association
44 Victoria Street, 12th Floor
Toronto M5C 3C4

Canadian Artists Network-Black Artists
in Action
54 Wolseley Street, 2nd Floor
Toronto M5T 1A5

Canadian Arts Presenting Association
17 New York Street, Suite 200
Ottawa K1N 9J6

Canadian Association for Photographic
Art
31858 Hopedale Avenue
Clearbrook V2T 2G7

Canadian Association of Broadcast
Employees
250 Main Street, Suite 1
Hamilton L8P 1J8

Canadian Association of Broadcasters
P.O. Box 627, Station B
Ottawa K1P 5S2

Canadian Association of Ethnic Radio
Broadcasters
622 College Street
Toronto M6G 1B6

Canadian Association of Journalists
St. Patrick's Building
Carleton University
1125 Colonel By Drive
Ottawa K1S 5B6

Canadian Association of Photographers
and Illustrators in Communications
100 Broadview Avenue, Suite 322
Toronto M4M 3H3

Canadian Association of Professional
Dance Organizations
99 Fourth Avenue, Suite E
P.O. Box 4130
Ottawa K1S 2L0

Canadian Authors Association
P.O. Box 419
Campbellford K0L 1L0

Canadian Cable Television Association
360 Albert Street, Suite 1010
Ottawa K1R 7X7

Canadian Community Newspapers
Association
90 Eglinton Avenue E, Suite 206
Toronto M4P 2Y3

Canadian Conference of the Arts
804-130 Albert Street
Ottawa K1P 5G4

Canadian Council for the Arts
P.O. Box 1047
350 Albert Street
Ottawa K1P 5V8

Canadian Film Centre
2489 Bayview Avenue
Toronto M2L 1A8

Canadian Film Institute
2 Daly Street, First Floor
Ottawa K1N 6E2

Canadian Independent Telephone
Association
2442 St. Joseph Boulevard, Suite 107
Orleans K1C 1G1

Canadian League of Composers
20 St. Joseph Street
Toronto M4Y 1J9

Canadian Magazine Publishers
Association
Suite 202, 130 Spadina Avenue
Toronto M5V 2L4

Canadian Media Guild
144 Front Street W, Suite 300
Toronto M5J 2L7

Canadian Native Arts Foundation
77 Mowat Avenue, Suite 508
Toronto M6K 3E3

Canadian Newspaper Association
890 Yonge Street, Suite 200
Toronto M4W 3P4

Canadian Society for Education
Through Art
University of Western Ontario
Faculty of Education
1137 Western Road
London N6G 1G7

Canadian Society of Cinematographers
571 Jarvis Street
Toronto M4Y 2J1

Canadian Wireless
Telecommunications Association
275 Slater Street, Suite 509
Ottawa K1P 5H9

Canadian Women in Communications
67 Younge Street, Suite 804
Toronto M5E 1J8

Centre for Indigenous Theatre
401 Richmond Street W, Suite 260
Toronto M5V 1X3

Commonwealth Association for
Education in Journalism and
Communication
Faculty of Law
University of Western Ontario
London N6A 3K7

Editors Association of Canada
35 Spadina Road
Toronto M5R 2S9

Film Studies Association of Canada
Department of Film Studies
Queen's University
Kingston K7L 3N6

Inuit Art Foundation
2081 Merivale Road
Nepean K2G 1G9

Motion Picture Theatre Associations of
Canada
146 Bloor Street W, 4th Floor
Toronto M5S 1P3

Music Industries Association of Canada
1210 Sheppard Avenue E, Suite 109
Toronto M2K 1E3

Orchestras Canada
56 The Esplanade, Suite 311
Toronto M5E 1A7

Society of Graphic Designers of Canada
P.O. Box 2728, Station D
Ottawa K1P 5W7

Visual Arts Ontario
1153A Queen Street West
Toronto M6J 1J4

Writers Union of Canada
24 Ryerson Avenue
Toronto M5T 2P3

QUEBEC

Association for the Study of Canadian
Radio and Television
Center for Broadcasting Studies
Concordia University, CJC-1590
1455 Boulevard de Maisonneuve
Montréal H3G 1M8

Canadian Amateur Musicians
1751 Richardson, No. 2509
Montréal H3K 1G6

Canadian Literary and Artistic
Association
1981 McGill College, Suite 1100
Montréal H3A 3C1

Canadian Overseas
Telecommunications Union
440 Boulevard Rene Levesque W, Bureau
801
Montréal H2Z 1V7

Dramatists Centre
3450 rue St. Urbain
Montréal H2X 2N5

Freelance Professionals Network
933, Station H
Montréal H3G 2M9

General Cinema and Television Union,
National Office of Film Section
2360 Lucerne, bureau 5/6A
Montréal H3R 2J8

Independent Film and Video Alliance
4550 Garnier
Montréal H2J 3S5

International Federation of Translators
2021, Avenue Union
Bureau 1108
Montréal H3A 2S9

National Film Board of Canada
P.O. Box 6100, Station Centre-ville
Montréal H3C 3H5

Union des Artistes
3433 rue Stanley
Montréal H3A 1S2

World Association of Community Radio
Broadcasters
3575, Boulevard St.-Laurent, Suite 611
Montréal H2X 2T7

World Association of Women
Journalists and Writers, Canada
3945 St. Martin Boulevard West
Laval H7T 1B7

SASKATCHEWAN

Photographers Gallery Association
12-23rd Street SE, 2nd Floor
Saskatoon S7K 0H5

COMPUTERS, BUSINESS, AND OFFICE

VOLUME 3

ONTARIO

Alliance of Independent Businesses
P.O. Box 280, Station R
Toronto M4G 3Z9

Association of Administrative
Assistants
P.O. Box 5107, Station A
Toronto M5W 1N4

Association of Collegiate Entrepreneurs
and Young Business Owners
180 Renfrew Drive, Suite 200
Markham L3R 8B7

Association of Professional Computer
Consultants
P.O. Box 24261, Hazeldean RPO
Kanata K2M 2C3

Canadian Association for Business
Economics
P.O. Box 828, Station B
Ottawa K1P 5P9

Canadian Association of Certified
Executive Accountants
2380 Holly Lane, Suite 201
Ottawa K1V 7P2

Canadian Bankers Association
Commerce Court W, Suite 3000
P.O. Box 348
Toronto M5L 1G2

Canadian Centre for Business in the
Community
255 Smyth Road
Ottawa K1H 8M7

Canadian Computer Dealer Association
2 Philosopher Trail, Unit 1A
Brampton L6S 4C9

Canadian Information Processing
Society
One Yonge Street, Suite 2401
Toronto M5E 1E5

Canadian Institute of Actuaries
Constitution Square
360 Albert Street, Suite 820
Ottawa K1R 7X7

Canadian Institute of Certified
Administrative Managers
2 Saint Clair Avenue, Suite 800
Toronto M4W 3R1

Canadian Institute of Chartered
Accountants
277 Wellington Street W
Toronto M5V 3H2

Canadian Institute of Management
2175 Sheppard Avenue E, Suite 310
North York M2J 1W8

Credit Institute of Canada
5090 Explorer Drive, Suite 501
Mississauga L4W 3T9

Electronic Commerce Council of
Canada
885 Don Mills Road, Suite 301
Don Mills M3C 1V9

International Facility Management
Association, Toronto Chapter
Gordon Baker Road, Suite 900
Toronto M2H 3R1

International Personnel Management
Association
329 March Road, Suite 232, Box 11
Kanata K2K 2E1

Society of Professional Accountants of
Canada
37 Cosentino Drive
Scarborough M1P 3A3

QUEBEC

Canadian Economics Association
855 Sherbrooke Street W
McGill University
Montréal H3A 2T7

CONSTRUCTION

VOLUME 4

ONTARIO

Bricklayers and Masons Independent
Union of Canada
1263 Wilson Avenue, Suite 105
Toronto M3M 3G3

Building and Construction Trades
Department-Canadian Office
350 Sparks Street, Suite 910
Ottawa K1R 7S8

Canadian Concrete Masonry Producers
Association
1013 Wilson Avenue, Suite 101
Downsview M3K 1G1

Canadian Home Builders Association
150 Laurier Avenue West, Suite 500
Ottawa K1P 5J4

Canadian Institute of Plumbing and
Heating
295 West Mall, Suite 330
Toronto M9C 4Z4

Canadian Institute of Steel
Construction
201 Consumers Road, Suite 300
Willowdale M2J 4G8

Canadian Refrigeration and Air
Conditioning Contractors
Association
5045 Orbitor Drive, Building 11, Suite
300
Mississsauga L4W 4Y4

Centra-Cam Vocational Training
Association
P.O. Box 1443
Camrose T4V 1X4

Heating, Refrigeration, and Air
Conditioning Institute of Canada
Building 11, Suite 300
5045 Orbitor Drive
Mississauga L4W 4Y4

Royal Architectural Institute of Canada
55 Murray Street, Suite 330
Ottawa K1N 5M3

QUEBEC

Canadian Centre for Architecture
1920 rue Baile Street
Montréal H3H 2S6

HOMEMAKING AND PERSONAL SERVICES

VOLUME 5

BRITISH COLUMBIA

Canadian Administrative Housekeepers
Association
4570 Canada Way, Suite 201
Burnaby V7E 1J7

MANITOBA

Canadian Home Economics
Association Foundation
303 Ashland Avenue
Winnipeg R3L 1L6

NEW BRUNSWICK

International Institute of Public
Appraisers
P.O. Box 3132, Station B
Fredericton E3A 5G9

ONTARIO

Aquatic Gardeners Association
83 Cathcart Street
London N6C 3L9

Canadian Association for Research in
Home Economics
Nutrition, Consumer and Family
Studies Department
Ryerson Polytechnic University
350 Victoria Street
Toronto M5B 2K3

Canadian Cosmetic, Toiletry, and
Fragrance Association
420 Britannia E, Suite 102
Mississauga L4Z 3L5

Canadian Nursery Landscape
Association
7856 Fifth Line S
RR 4
Milton L9T 2X8

National Association of Security
Personnel
P.O. Box 160
Mississauga L4T 3B6

Organization for Nutritional Education
Woodlawn Postal Outlet
P.O. Box 20025
Guelph N1H 8H6

QUEBEC

International Association of Personal
Protection Agents
414 Lafleur, Suite 4C
LaSalle H8R 3H6

SCIENCE AND TECHNOLOGY

VOLUME 6

ALBERTA

Canadian Congress of Neurological
Sciences
P.O. Box 5456, Station A
Calgary T2H 1X8

Canadian Neurological Society
906 12th Avenue, Suite 810
Calgary T2R 1K7

Canadian Society for Plant Molecular
Biology
Department of Biological Science
University of Calgary
Calgary T2N 1N4

Canadian Society for Professional
Engineers
203 College Street, Suite 303
Toronto M5T 1P9

Canadian Society of Exploration
Geophysicists
510 5th Street SW, Room 905
Calgary T2P 3S2

International Association of Science
and Technology for Development
4500 16th Avenue NW, Suite 80
Calgary T3B 0M6

BRITISH COLUMBIA

Society for Canadian Women in Science
and Technology
417-535 Hornby Street
Vancouver V6C 2E8

MANITOBA

Biophysical Society of Canada
435 Ellice Avenue
Winnipeg R3B 1Y6

ONTARIO

Association of Canadian Map Libraries
and Archives
National Archives of Canada
Ottawa K1A 0N3

Association of Consulting Engineers of
Canada
130 Albert Street, Suite 616
Ottawa K1P 5G4

Canadian Academy of Engineering
130 Alberta Street, Suite 1414
Ottawa K1P 5G4

Canadian Association of Medical
Microbiologists
711 Concession Street
Hamilton L8V 1C3

Canadian Association of Physicists
McDonald Building, Suite 112
150 Louis Pasteur Drive
Ottawa K1N 9N5

Canadian Astronomical Society
Department of Physics
Queen's University
Kingston K7L 3N6

Canadian Botanical Association
University of Guelph
Guelph N1G 2W1

Canadian Council of Professional
Engineers
116 Albert Street, No. 401
Ottawa K1P 5G3

Canadian Council of Technicians and
Technologists
285 McLeod Street
Ottawa K2P 1A1

Canadian Historical Association
395 Wellington Street
Ottawa K1A 0N3

Canadian Hospital Engineering Society
4 Cataraqui, Suite 310
Kingston K7K 1Z7

Canadian Medical and Biological
Engineering Society
Building M19, Room 220
Ottawa K1A 0R8

Canadian Nuclear Society
144 Front Street West, Suite 475
Toronto M5J 2L7

Canadian Society for Chemical
Engineering and Technology
130 Slater Street, Suite 550
Ottawa K1P 6E2

Canadian Society for Chemistry
130 Slater Street, Suite 550
Ottawa K1P 6E2

Canadian Society for Mechanical
Engineering
P.O. Box 23027
Westgate Postal Outlet
Cambridge N1S 4Z6

Canadian Society for Medical
Laboratory Science
P.O. Box 2830 LCD 1
Hamilton L8N 3N8

Canadian Society of Clinical Chemists
4 Cataraqui Street, Suite 310
P.O. Box 1570
Kingston K7L 5C8

Canadian Society of Microbiologists
1200 Prince of Wales Drive, Suite E
Ottawa K2C 1M9

Canadian Society of Safety Engineering
10435 Islington Avenue
P.O. Box 294
Kleinburg L0J 1C0

Canadian Union of Operating
Engineers
2077 Dundas E, Unit 202
Mississauga L4X 1M2

Engineering Institute of Canada
Building M-19, Room 220
Montréal Road
Ottawa K1A 0R6

Information Technology Association of
Canada
28000 Skymark Avenue, Suite 402
Mississauga L4W 5A6

QUEBEC

Association of Canadian
Pharmaceutical Physicians
2150 Boulevard Saint-Elzear W
Laval H7L 4A8

Canadian Association for Clinical
Microbiologists and Infectious
Diseases
20045 Montee Sainte-Marie
Montréal H9X 3R5

Canadian Association of Medical
Biochemists
Hotel-Dieu de Quebec, 11
Cote du Palais G1R 2S6

Canadian Economics Association
McGill University
855 Sherbrooke Street West
Montréal H3A 2T7

Canadian Orthopaedic Association
1440 St. Catherine Street W, Suite 320
Montréal H3G 1R8

Canadian Society for Civil Engineering
2155 Guy Street, Suite 840
Montréal H3H 2R9

Canadian Society for Industrial
Engineering
92016 P.O. Box Portobello
Brossard J4W 3K8

Canadian Society for Nutritional
Sciences
MacDonald Campus
McGill University
21111 Lakeshore
Ste.-Anne-de-Bellevue H9X 3V9

Canadian Sociology and Anthropology
Association
c/o Concordia University
1455 boulevard de Maisonneuve West
Bureau LB-615
Montréal H3G 1M8

Engineers and Scientists Association
600 Frederick Phillips Drive
St. Laurent H4M 2S9

French Canadian Association for the
Advancement of the Sciences
425 rue de la Gauchetiere E
Montréal H2L 2M7

SASKATCHEWAN

Canadian Archaeological Association
Department of Anthropology and
Archaeology
University of Saskatchewan
Saskatoon S7N 5B1

HEALTH

VOLUME 7

ALBERTA

Canada's Health Informatics
Association
5782 172nd Street
Edmonton T6M 1B4

Canadian Association of Public Health
Dentisry
8230 105th Street
Edmonton T6E 5H9

Canadian Federation of Mental Health
Nurses
Faculty of Nursing
Clinical Sciences Building, 3rd Floor
University of Alberta
Edmonton T6G 2G3

Canadian Neurosurgery Society
906 12th Avenue, Suite 810
Calgary T2E 1K7

Canadian Orthoptic Council
506 71st Avenue SW, Suite 5
Calgary T2V 4V4

BRITISH COLUMBIA

Canadian Academy of Child Psychology
C1012638 Coventry Hills Way NE
Calgary T3K 4Z7

Canadian Association of Nuclear
Medicine
Nuclear Medicine Department
Foothills Hospital
1403 29th Street SW
Calgary T2N 2T9

Canadian College of Physicists in
Medicine
399 Royal Avenue
Kelowna V1Y 5L3

Canadian Occupational Health Nurses
Association
3777 Kingsway, Suite 5
Burnaby V5H 3Z7

MANITOBA

Denturist Association of Canada
PO Box 46114, RPO Westdale
Winnipeg R3R 3S3

Opticians Association of Canada
214-160 Hargrave Street
Winnipeg R3C 3H3

NEWFOUNDLAND

Canadian Association of General
Surgeons
Health Sciences Center
300 Prince Phillip Drive
St. John's A1B 3V6

NOVA SCOTIA

Community Health Nurses Association
of Canada
106 Bellevista Drive
Dartmouth B2W 2X7

ONTARIO

Association of Canadian Medical
Colleges
774 Echo Drive
Ottawa K1S 5P2

Canadian Academy of Facial Plastic and
Reconstructive Surgery
3206 Barwell Road
Mississauga L5L 4L6

Canadian Academy of Sport Medicine
1010 Poytek Street, Unit 14, Suite 100
Gloucester K1J 9H9

Canadian Anaesthetists Society
1 Eglinton Avenue East, Suite 208
Toronto M4P 3A1

Canadian Association for Health,
Physical Recreation, and Dance
1600 James Naismith Drive
Gloucester K1B 5N4

Canadian Association of Critical Care
Nurses
P.O. Box 25322
London N6C 6B1

Canadian Association of Emergency
Physicians
1785 Alta Vista Drive, Suite 104
Ottawa K1G 3Y6

Canadian Association of Optometrists
234 Argyle Avenue
Ottawa K2P 1B9

Canadian Association of Physical
Medicine and Rehabilitation
774 Echo Drive
Ottawa K1S 5N8

Canadian Association of Speech-
Language Pathologists and
Audiologists
130 Albert Street, Suite 2006
Ottawa K1P 5G4

Canadian Centre for Occupational
Health and Safety
250 Main Street E
Hamilton L8N 1H6

Canadian Chiropractic Association
1396 Eglinton Avenue W
Toronto M6C 2E4

Canadian Council on Multicultural
Health
1017 Wilson Avenue, Suite 400
Downsview M3K 1Z1

Canadian Dental Association
1815 Alta Vista Drive
Ottawa K1G 3Y6

Canadian Dental Hygienists
Association
96 Centerpointe Drive
Nepean K2G 6B1

Canadian Gerontological Nursing
Association
911 Maitland Street
London N5Y 2X2

Canadian Health Economics Research
Association
Abramsky Hall, 3rd Floor
Queen's University
Kingston K7L 3N6

Canadian Health Record Association
1090 Don Mills Road, Suite 501
Don Mills M3C 3R6

Canadian Healthcare Association
17 York Street, Suite 100
Ottawa K1N 9J6

Canadian Medical Association
1867 Alta Vista Drive
Ottawa K1G 3Y6

Canadian Mental Health Association
2160 Yonge Street
Toronto M4S 2Z3

Canadian Nurses Association
50 Driveway
Ottawa K2P 1E2

Canadian Occupational Therapy
Foundation
55 Eglinton Avenue, Suite 602
Toronto M4P 1G8

Canadian Osteopathic Association
575 Waterloo Street
London N6B 2R2

Canadian Pharmacists Association
1785 Alta Vista Drive
Ottawa K1G 3Y6

Canadian Psychiatric Association
260-441 McLaren Street
Ottawa K2P 2H3

Canadian Public Health Association
400-1565 Carling Avenue
Ottawa K1Z 8R1

Canadian Red Cross Society
1430 Blair Place, 3rd Floor
Gloucester K1J 9N2

Canadian Society for International
Health
1 Nicholas Street, Suite 1105
Ottawa K1N 7B7

Canadian Society for Medical
Laboratory Science
PO Box 2830 LCD 1
Hamilton L8N 3N8

Canadian Society of Geriatric Medicine
1053 Carling Avenue
Ottawa K1Y 4E9

Canadian Society of Respiratory
Therapists
1785 Alta Vista Drive, Suite 102
Ottawa K1G 3Y6

International Society of Radiographers
and Radiological Technologists
170 West Donway, Suite 404
Don Mills M3C 2G3

QUEBEC

Canadian Association of Pediatric
Nurses
2300 rue Tupper
Montréal H3H 1P3

Canadian Association of Pediatric
Surgeons
3175 Catherine Road
Montréal H3T 1C5

Canadian Association of Radiologists
5101 rue Buchan, Bureau 510
Montréal H4P 2R9

HOSPITALITY AND
RECREATION

VOLUME 8

ALBERTA

Associated Canadian Travellers
116 16th Avenue NE
Calgary T2E 1J5

Canadian Association of Fairs and
Exhibitions
P.O. Box 1172, Station Main
Edmonton T5J 2M4

Canadian Camping Association
P.O. Box 74030 Peppertree Post
Edmonton T5K 2S7

Commonwealth Association of
Museums
P.O. Box 30192
Chinook Postal Outlet
Calgary T2H 2V9

BRITISH COLUMBIA

Association of Tourism Professionals
1185 W Georgia, Suite 800
Vancouver V6E 4E6

Canadian Art Museum Directors
Organization
101-465 Victoria Street
Kamloops V2C 2A9

World Leisure and Recreation
Association
WLRA Secretariat
Site 81 C, Compo
Okanagan Falls V0H 1R0

MANITOBA

Backpackers International
168 Maryland Street
Winnipeg R3G 1L3

NORTHWEST TERRITORIES

Nunavut Tourism
P.O. Box 1450
Iqaluit X0A 0H0

ONTARIO

Alliance of Canadian Travel
Associations
1729 Bank Street, Suite 201
Ottawa K1V 7Z5

Athletics Canada
606-1185 Eglinton Avenue E
Toronto M3C 3C6

Banking Association of Canada
7895 Tranmere Drive, Suite 202
Mississauga L5S 1V9

Canadian Association of Retail Travel
Agents
765 Barton Street E
Hamilton L8L 3A9

Canadian Association of Tour Operators
200 N Service Road W, Unit 1, Suite 416
Oakville L6M 2V1

Canadian Association of Zoos and
Aquariums
361A Finch Avenue
Scarborough M1B 5K7

Canadian Colleges Athletic Association
Windmill Point
Cornwall K6H 4Z1

Canadian Federation of Chefs and
Cooks
325 Dalhousie, Suite 904
Ottawa K1N 7G2

Canadian Football Hall of Fame and
Museum
58 Jackson Street W
Hamilton L8P 1L4

Canadian Institutes of Travel
Counsellors
41 Richwood Drive
Markham L3P 3Y7

Canadian Inter-University Athletic
Union
1600 James Naismith Drive
Gloucester K1B 5N4

Canadian Intramural Recreation
Association
1600 James Naismith Drive
Gloucester K1B 5N4

Canadian Museums Association
280 Metcalfe Street, Suite 400
Ottawa K2P 1R7

Canadian Parks and Recreation
Association
1600 James Naismith Drive, Suite 306
Gloucester K1B 5N4

Canadian Parks and Wilderness Society
880 Wellington Street, Suite 506
Ottawa K1R 6K7

Canadian Recreational Canoeing
Association
P.O. Box 398
446 Main Street W
Merrickville K0G 1N0

Canadian Restaurant and Foodservices
Association
316 Bloor Street West
Toronto M5S 1W5

Canadian Sports Council
1600 James Naismith Drive, Suite 406
Gloucester K1B 5N4

Canadian Tourism Research Institute
255 Smyth Road
Ottawa K1H 8M7

Canadian Union of Restaurant and
Related Employees
94 Kenhar Drive
Weston M9L 1N2

Hotel Association of Canada
130 Albert Street, Suite 1206
Ottawa K1P 5G4

Tourism Industry Association of
Canada
130 Albert Street, Suite 1016
Ottawa K1P 5G4

QUEBEC

Canadian Sporting Goods Association
455 St. Antoine Street West, Suite 510
Montréal H2Z 1J1

YUKON

Klondike Visitors Association
P.O. Box 389 W
Dawson City Y0B 1G0

MANUFACTURING

VOLUME 9

ALBERTA

Architectural Woodwork Manufacturers
Association of Canada
516 4th Street
High River T1V 1B6

ONTARIO

Aerospace Industries Association of
Canada
60 Queen Street, Suite 1200
Ottawa K1P 5Y7

Alliance of Manufacturers and
Exporters of Canada
5995 Azebury Road, Suite 900
Mississauga L5R 3P9

Amalgamated Clothing and Textile
Workers Union
15 Gervais Drive, Suite 700
Don Mills M3C 1Y8

Association of International
Automobile Manufacturers of
Canada
438 University Avenue, Suite 1618
P.O. Box 60
Toronto M5G 2K8

Automotive Industries Association of
Canada
1272 Wellington Street
Ottawa K1Y 3A7

Automotive Parts Manufacturers
Association
195 The West Mall, Suite 516
Toronto M9C 5K1

Canadian Aeronautics and Space
Institute
130 Slater Street, Suite 818
Ottawa K1P 6E2

Canadian Apparel Federation
130 Slater Street, Suite 1050
Ottawa K1P 6E2

Canadian Appliance Manufacturers
Association
5800 Explorer Drive, Suite 200
Mississauga L4W 5K9

Canadian Association of Footwear
Importers
210 Dundas Street W, Suite 700
Toronto M5G 2E8

Canadian Association of Moldmakers,
Inc.
424 Tecumseh Road East
Windsor N8X 2R6

Canadian Association of Wholesale
Sales Representatives
1771 Avenue Road
Box 54546
Toronto M5M 4N5

Canadian Auto Workers
205 Placer Court
North York M2H 3H9

Canadian Boiler Society
3256 Cindy Crescent
Mississauga L4Y 3J6

Canadian Book Manufacturers
Association
75 Albert Street, Suite 906
Ottawa K1P 5E7

Canadian Ceramic Society
2175 Sheppard Avenue East, Suite 110
Willowdale M2J 1W8

Canadian Chemical Producers
Association
350 Sparks Street, Suite 805
Ottawa K1R 7S8

Canadian Drug Manufacturers
Association
4120 Yonge Street, Suite 409
Toronto M2P 2B8

Canadian Glass Manufacturers
Association of Canada
27 Goulburn Avenue
Ottawa K1N 8C7

Canadian Hardware and Housewares
Manufacturers Association
1335 Morningside Avenue, Suite 101
Scarborough M1B 5M4

Canadian Manufactured Housing
Institute
150 Laurier Avenue West, Suite 500
Ottawa K1P 5J4

Canadian Manufacturers of Chemical
Specialties Association
56 Sparks Street, Suite 500
Ottawa K1P 5A9

Canadian Mining Equipment
Manufacturers Association
116 Albert Street, Suite 4000
Ottawa K1P 5G3

Canadian Paper Box Manufacturers
Association
701 Evans Avenue, Suite 400
Etobicoke M9C 1A3

Canadian Pharmacists Association
1785 Alta Vista Drive
Ottawa K1G 3Y6

Canadian Plastics Industry Association
5925 Airport Road, Suite 500
Misssissauga L4W 1W1

Canadian Shirt Manufacturers
Association
36 Homer Avenue
Toronto M8Z 5Y1

Canadian Steel Producers Association
50 O'Connor Street, Suite 1425
Ottawa K1P 6L2

Canadian Textiles Institute
66 Slater Street, Suite 1720
Ottawa K1P 5H1

Canadian Toy Manufacturers
Association
PO Box 294
Kleinberg L0J 1C0

Canadian Vehicle Manufacturers
Association
25 Adelaide Street E, Suite 1602
Toronto M5C 3A1

Confectionery Manufacturers
Association of Canada
885 Don Mills Road, Suite 301
Don Mills M3C 1V9

Machinery and Equipment
Manufacturers Association of
Canada
116 Albert Street, Suite 701
Ottawa K1P 5G3

Pharmaceutical Manufacturers
Association of Canada
302-1111 Prince of Wales Drive
Ottawa K2C 3T2

Shipbuilding Association of Canada
222 Queen Street, Suite 1502
Ottawa K1P 5V9

United Steelworkers of America,
Canadian Branch
234 Eglinton Avenue East, Suite 700
Toronto M4P 1K7

QUEBEC

Canadian Association for Composite
Structures and Materials
75 de Mortagne Blvd.
Boucherville J4B 6Y4

Canadian Pulp and Paper Association
1155 Metcalfe Street, Suite 1900
Montréal H3B 4T6

Men's Clothing Manufacturers
Association
555 rue Chabanel , Bureau 801
Montréal H2N 2H8

Sectoral Association of Transportation
Equipment and Machines
Manufacturing
3565 rue Jarry E, Bureau 202
Montréal H1Z 4K6

Shoe Manufacturers Association of
Canada
P.O. Box 223
Beaconsfield H9W 5T7

MARKETING AND DISTRIBUTION

VOLUME 10

ALBERTA

Canadian Organization of Small
Business
P.O. Box 11246
Edmonton T5K 3J5

NEWFOUNDLAND

Agricultural Products Marketing Board
Provincial Agriculture Building
Brookfield Road
P.O. Box 8700
St. John's A1B 4J6

NOVA SCOTIA

Natural Products Marketing Council
P.O. Box 550
Truro B2N 5E3

ONTARIO

Association of Canadian Insurers
151 Yonge Street, Suite 1800
Toronto M5C 2W7

Canadian Advertising Research
Foundation
175 Bloor Street East, South Tower, Suite
307
Toronto M4W 3R8

Canadian Association of Equipment
Distributors
1272 Wellington Street, Suite 300
Ottawa K1Y 3A7

Canadian Association of Marketing
Research Organizations
2121 Argenpia Road, Suite 404
Mississauga L5N 2X4

Canadian Association of Mutual
Insurance Companies
325 Dalhousie Street, Suite 907
P.O. Box 117, Station B
Ottawa K1P 6C3

Canadian Booksellers Association
789 Don Mills Road, Suite 700
Toronto M3C 1T5

Canadian Exporters Association
1 Nicholas Street, Suite 1500
Ottawa K1N 7B7

Canadian Food Brokers Association
100-58 Meadowbrook Lane
Unionville L3R 2N9

Canadian Importers Association
438 University Avenue, Suite 1618,
Box 60
Toronto M5G 2K8

Canadian Marketing Association
1 Concorde Gate, Suite 607
Don Mills M3C 3N6

Canadian Produce Marketing
Association
1101 Prince of Wales Drive, Suite 310
Ottawa K2C 3W7

Canadian Professional Sales
Association
145 Wellington W, Suite 610
Toronto M5J 1H8

Canadian Real Estate Association
344 Slater Street, Suite 1600
Ottawa K1R 7Y3

Canadian Retail Hardware Association
2121 Argentia Road, Suite 102
Mississauga L5N 2X4

Independent Life Insurance Brokers of
Canada
2175 Sheppard Avenue E, Suite 310
North York M2J 1W8

Insurance Brokers Association of
Canada
181 University Avenue, Suite 1902
Toronto M5H 3M7

Insurance Bureau of Canada
151 Younge Street, 18th Floor
Toronto M5C 2W7

QUEBEC

Association of Footwear Industry
7910 Pelletier
Brossard J4X 1J7

Canadian Council of Grocery
Distributors
P.O. Box 1082, Place du Parc
Montréal H2W 2P4

PUBLIC AND COMMUNITY SERVICES

VOLUME 11

ALBERTA

Canadian Association of Firefighters
11 J Rayburn Crescent
St. Albert T8N 5C3

Canadian College of Teachers
P.O. Box 57157, Eastgate Post Office
2010A Sherwood Drive
Sherwood Park T8A 5L7

BRITISH COLUMBIA

Canadian Association of School
  Administrators
2835 Country Woods Drive
Surrey V4A 9P9

ONTARIO

Alliance of Canadian Travel
  Associations
1729 Bank Street, Suite 201
Ottawa K1V 7Z5

Ambedkar Center for Justice and Peace
P.O. Box 846, Station P
Toronto M5S 2Z2

Association of Universities and Colleges
  of Canada
350 Albert Street, Suite 600
Ottawa K1R 1B1

Bereavement Services and Community
  Education
1403 Bayview Avenue
Toronto M4G 3A8

Canadian Association for Adult
  Education
29 Prince Arthur Avenue
Toronto M5R 1B2

Canadian Association of Chiefs of
  Police
130 Albert Street, Suite 1710
Ottawa K1P 5G4

Canadian Association of Children's
  Librarians
200 Elgin Street, Suite 602
Ottawa K2P 1L5

Canadian Association of College and
  University Libraries
200 Elgin Street, Suite 602
Ottawa K2P 1L5

Canadian Association of Fire Chiefs
1066 Somerset Street W, Suite 301
Ottawa K1Y 4T3

Canadian Association of Law Libraries
4 Cataraqui Street, Suite 310
P.O. Box 1570
Kingston K7L 5C8

Canadian Association of Public
  Libraries
200 Elgin Street, Suite 602
Ottawa K2P 1L5

Canadian Association of Social Workers
383 Parkdale Avenue, Suite 402
Ottawa K1Y 4R4

Canadian Bar Association
50 O'Connor Street, Suite 902
Ottawa K1P 6L2

Canadian Career Information
  Association
720 Spadina Avenue, Suite 300
Toronto M5S 2T9

Canadian Criminal Justice Association
383 Parkdale Avenue, Suite 304
Ottawa K1Y 4R4

Canadian Library Association
200 Elgin Street, Suite 602
Ottawa K2P 1L5

Canadian Police Association
141 Catherine Street, Suite 100
Ottawa K2P 1C3

Canadian Society for the Study of
  Education
260 Dalhousie Street, Suite 204
Ottawa K1N 7E4

Canadian Society for the Study of
  Religion
Religious Studies
Queen's University
Kingston K7L 3N6

Canadian Teachers Federation
110 Argyle Avenue
Ottawa K2P 1B4

Canadian Union of Postal Workers
377 Bank Street
Ottawa K2P 1Y3

QUEBEC

Canadian Association of Legal
  Assistants
P.O. Box 967, Station B
Montréal H3B 3K5

Canadian Institute for the
  Administration of Justice
University of Montréal
Faculty of Law, Room 3430
CP 6128 Succursal Centre-ville
Montréal H3C 3J7

Canadian Maritime Law Association
240 St. Jacques W, Suite 300
Montréal H2X 1L9

International Center for Comparative
  Criminology
Universite of Montréal
Case Postale 6128, Succursale Centre-
  ville
Montréal H3C 3J7

TRANSPORTATION

VOLUME 12

BRITISH COLUMBIA

Association of Tourism Professionals
1185 West Georgia, Suite 800
Vancouver V6E 4E6

British Columbia Maritime Employers
  Association
500-349 Railway Street
Vancouver V6A 1A4

Canadian Union of Transportation
  Employees
625 Vancouver Street
Prince George V2L 5R6

NEW BRUNSWICK

Aircraft Maintenance Engineers
  Association
837 Charlotte Street
Fredericton E3B 1M7

ONTARIO

Air Transport Association of Canada
255 Albert Street, Suite 1100
Ottawa K1P 6A4

Air Transportation Association of
  Canada
255 Albert Street, Suite 1100
Ottawa K1P 6A9

Canadian Automotive Repair and
  Service Council
1272 Wellington Street, 3rd Floor
Ottawa K1Y 3A7

Canadian Bus Association
610 Alden Road, Suite 201
Markham L3R 9Z1

Canadian Council of Motor Transport
  Administrators
2323 St. Laurent Boulevard
Ottawa K1G 4J8

Canadian Institute of Traffic and
  Transportation
10 King Street East, Fourth Floor
Toronto M5C 1C3

Canadian Trucking Alliance
130 Slater Street, Suite 1025
Ottawa K1P 6E2

Canadian Urban Transit Association
55 York Street, Suite 901
Toronto M5J 1R7

Freight Carriers Association of Canada
427 Garrison Road
Ft. Erie L2E 6E6

Transportation Association of Canada
2323 St. Laurent Boulevard
Ottawa K1G 4J8

QUEBEC

Canadian Marine Officers Union
9670 rue Notre Dame East
Montréal H1L 3P8

International Air Transport
  Association-Canada
800 Place Victoria
P.O. Box 113
Montréal H42 1M1

International Federation of Air Traffic
  Controllers Associations
1255 University Street, Suite 408
Montréal H3B 3B6

Publications

The Career and Vocational Education Concept

"Apprenticeships: Career Training, Credentials—and a Paycheck in Your Pocket," Olivia Crosby. *Occupational Outlook Quarterly*, vol. 46, no. 2, Summer 2002.

The Community College Role in Welfare to Work, C. David Lisman, ed. San Francisco: Jossey-Bass, 2001.

Do School-to-Work Programs Help the "Forgotten Half"? David Neumark and Donna Rothstein. Cambridge, MA: National Bureau of Economic Research, 2005.

Educating At-Risk Students, Sam Stringfield and Deborah Land, eds. Chicago: University of Chicago Press, 2002.

School-to-Career Programs and Transitions to Employment and Higher Education, David Neumark and Donna Rothstein. Cambridge, MA: National Bureau of Economic Research, 2003.

"School to Career: Reworking the Model," Barry Burke. *Technology & Learning*, vol. 24, no. 6, p. 26, January 2004.

Skill Specific Rather Than General Education: A Reason for U.S.-Europe Growth Differences? Dirk Krueger and Krishna B. Kumar. Cambridge, MA: National Bureau of Economic Research, 2002.

"Transition from School to Work," Alan C. Kerckhoff. *The Changing Adolescent Experience: Societal Trends and the Transition to Adulthood*, Jeylan T. Mortimer and Reed Larson, eds. New York: Cambridge University Press, 2002.

Vocational Education: Current Issues and Prospects, R. Nata. New York: Nova Science, 2003.

Vocational Education, Peter Jarvis and Colin Griffin. London: Routledge, 2003.

Career Development and Career Counseling

Applying Career Development Theory to Counseling, 4th ed., Richard S. Sharf. Belmont, CA: Brooks/Cole Publishing, 2006.

"Basic Confidence Predictors of Career Decision-Making Self-Efficacy," Alisa M. Paulsen and Nancy E. Betz. *Career Development Quarterly*, vol. 53, no. 4, p. 354, June 2004.

"Career Centers for the Future," Allyson D. Brathwaite. *Journal of Career Development*, vol. 29, no. 3, p. 147, Spring 2003.

"Career Centers for the Millennium," Lynn C. McKinnon. *Journal of Career Development*, vol. 28, no. 3, p. 155, Spring 2002.

Career Choice and Development, 4th ed., Duane Brown. San Francisco: Jossey-Bass, 2002.

"Career Coaching: Practice, Training, Professional, and Ethical Issues," Y. Barry Chung and M. Coleman Allen Gfroerer. *Career Development Quarterly*, vol. 52, no. 2, p. 141, December 2003.

Career Counseling: A Holistic Approach, Vernon G. Zunker. Belmont, CA: Thomson/Brooks-Cole, 2006.

"Career Counseling and the Information Highway: Heeding the Road Signs," Theresa M. O'Halloran, Alicia V. Fahr, and Jenny R. Keller. *Career Development Quarterly*, vol. 50, no. 4, p. 371, June 2002.

Career Counseling: Applied Concepts of Life Planning, 6th ed., Vernon G. Zunker. Pacific Grove, CA: Brooks/Cole Publishing, 2001.

Career Counseling: Foundations, Perspectives, and Applications, Dave Capuzzi and Mark D. Stauffer. Boston: Pearson/Allyn and Bacon, 2006.

"Career Counseling in the Future: Constructing, Collaborating, Advocating," Mei Tang. *Career Development Quarterly*, vol. 52, no. 1, p. 61, September 2003.

"Career Counseling in the Twenty-First Century: Beyond Cultural Encapsulation," Mark Pope. *Career Development Quarterly*, vol. 52, no. 1, p. 54, September 2003.

Career Counseling: Process, Issues, and Techniques, Norman C. Gysbers, Mary J. Heppner, and Joseph A. Johnston. Boston: Allyn and Bacon, 2003.

Career Development and Counseling: Putting Theory and Research to Work, Steven D. Brown and Robert W. Lent, eds. Hoboken, NJ: Wiley, 2005.

"Career Myths and How to Debunk Them," Olivia Crosby. *Occupational Outlook Quarterly*, vol. 49, no. 3, Fall 2005.

"Continuity in Life-Span Career Development: Career Exploration as a Precursor to Career Establishment," David A. Jepsen and Ginger L. Dickson. *Career Development Quarterly*, vol. 51, no. 3, p. 217, March 2003.

"Contributions of Self-Efficacy Theory to Career Counseling: A Personal Perspective," Nancy E. Betz. *Career Development Quarterly*, vol. 53, no. 4, p. 340, June 2004.

"Cultural Context of Career Choice: Meta-Analysis of Race/Ethnicity Differences," Nadya A. Fouad and Angela M. Byars-Winston. *Career Development Quarterly*, vol. 53, no. 3, p. 223, March 2005.

Essential Elements of Career Counseling: Processes and Techniques, Norman E. Amundson, JoAnn Harris-Bowlsbey, and Spencer G. Niles. Upper Saddle River, NJ: Pearson, 2005.

"The Legacy of Parsons: Career Counselors and Vocational Psychologists as Agents of Social Change," Karen M. O'Brien. *Career Development Quarterly*, vol. 50, no. 1, p. 66, September 2001.

"Matching Yourself with the World of Work," Henry T. Kasper. *Occupational Outlook Quarterly*, vol. 48, no. 3, Fall 2004.

"Multicultural Career Counseling: Ten Essential for Training," Lisa Y. Flores and Mary J. Heppner. *Journal of Career Development*, vol. 28, no. 3, p. 181, Spring 2002.

"Testing a Model of Men's Nontraditional Occupational Choices," Zuzanne H. Lease. *Career Development Quarterly*, vol. 51, no. 3, p. 244, March 2003.

Overviews of Career and Vocational Education Programs

"Academic Readiness and Career/Life Planning: A Collaborative Partnership Focused on Student Learning," Susan J. Lindahl, Patricia N. Long, and Renee Arnett. *Journal of Career Development*, vol. 28, no. 4, p. 247, Summer 2002.

But What If I Don't Want to Go to College? A Guide to Success through Alternative Education, 3rd ed., Harlow G. Unger. New York: Ferguson, 2006.

High School to Career. Video Series, 5 vols. Indianapolis: JIST Publishing.

Other Ways to Win: Creating Alternatives for High School Graduates, 3rd ed., Kenneth C. Gray and Edwin L. Herr. Thousand Oaks, Calif.: Corwin Press, 2006.

"The Power of Partnerships," Antone Gonsalves. *Technology & Learning*, vol. 23, no. 7, p. 16, February 2003.

School-to-Work: Basic Steps to Employment for the Learning Disabled Student, Kelli M. Gienger. Salem, OR: Western Baptist College, 2001.

School-to-Work: Making a Difference in Education, Katherine L. Hughes, Thomas R. Bailey, and Melinda J. Mechur. New York: Institute on Education and the Economy, Columbia University, 2001.

Career and Vocational Education in the Elementary and Middle School

"Career Development in Middle Childhood: A Qualitative Inquiry," Donna E. Palladino Schultheiss, Thomas V. Palma, and Alberta J. Manzi. *Career Development Quarterly*, vol. 53, no. 3, p. 246, March 2005.

"Children's Career Development: A Research Review from a Learning Perspective," Mark Watson and Mary McMahon. *Journal of Vocational Behavior*, vol. 67, no. 2, p. 119, October 2005.

"Child Vocational Development: A Review and Reconsideration," Paul J. Hartung, Erik J. Porfeli, and Fred W. Vondracek. *Journal of Vocational Behavior*, vol. 66, no. 3, p. 385, June 2005.

"Evaluation of an Intervention to Increase Non-Traditional Career Interests and Career-Related Self-Efficacy among Middle-School Adolescents," Sherri L. Turner and Richard T. Lapan. *Journal of Vocational Behavior*, vol. 66, no. 3, p. 516, June 2005.

"It Takes a Team to Run a Restaurant: Introducing Elementary Students to the Interrelatedness of Occupations," Andrew V. Beale. *Journal of Career Development*, vol. 29, no. 3, p. 211, Spring 2003.

"Occupational Information: What Children Want to Know," Mary McMahon and Mark Watson. *Journal of Career Development*, vol. 31, no. 4, p. 239, Summer 2005.

"Parent/Guardian Visualization of Career and Academic Future of Seventh Graders Enrolled in Low-Achieving Schools," Janet Usinger. *Career Development Quarterly*, vol. 53, no. 3, p. 234, March 2005.

"The Use of Genograms in Career Counseling with Elementary, Middle, and High School Students," Donna M. Gibson. *Career Development Quarterly*, vol. 53, no. 4, p. 353, June 2005.

"Using the Self-Directed Search: Career Explorer with High-Risk Middle School Students," Debra S. Osborn and Robert C. Reardon. *Career Development Quarterly*, vol. 54, no. 3, p. 269, March 2006.

"Vocational Interests and Career Efficacy Expectations in Relation to Occupational Sex-Typing Beliefs for Eighth Grade Students," Peter Y. Ji, Richard T. Lapan, and Kevin Tate. *Journal of Career Development*, vol. 31, no. 2, p. 143, Winter 2004.

Career and Vocational Education in the Secondary School

"Career Choice Patterns and Behavior of Work-Bound Youth during Early Adolescence," Jay W. Rojewski and Heeja Kim. *Journal of Career Development*, vol. 30, no. 2, p. 89, Winter 2003.

"Career Self-Efficacy and Perceptions of Parent Support in Adolescent Career Development," Sherri Turner and Richard T. Lapan. *Career Development Quarterly*, vol. 51, no. 1, p. 44, September 2002.

"The Effect of Career Interventions Designed to Increase Self-Knowledge on the Self-Concepts of Adolescents," Lisette Portnoi, Jean Guichard, and Noelle Lallemand. *Journal of Vocational Behavior*, vol. 65, no. 3, p. 484, December 2004.

"Family Interaction Patterns, Career Planning Attitudes, and Vocational Identity of High School Adolescents," Byron K. Hargrove, Arpana G. Inman, and Randy L. Crane. *Journal of Career Development*, vol. 31, no. 4, p. 263, Summer 2005.

"Hidden Resources and Barriers in Career Learning Assessment with Adolescents Vulnerable to Discrimination," Margo A. Jackson and Christian D. Nutini. *Career Development Quarterly*, vol. 51, no. 1, p. 56, September 2002.

"Reducing Adolescent Career Indecision: The ASVAB Career Exploration Program," Harley E. Baker. *Career Development Quarterly*, vol. 50, no. 4, p. 359, June 2002.

"The Relationship of Ethnic Identity, Career Decision-Making Self-Efficacy and Outcome Expectations among Latino/a High School Students," George V. Gushue. *Journal of Vocational Behavior*, vol. 68, no. 1, p. 85, February 2006.

"The Role of Work-Related Skills and Career Role Models in Adolescent Career Maturity," Eirini Flouri and Ann Buchanan. *Career Development Quarterly*, vol. 51, no. 1, p. 36, September 2002.

Adult and Postsecondary Career Programs

Adult and Continuing Education: Major Themes in Education, Peter Jarvis. London: Routledge, 2003.

"Associate Degree: Two Years to a Career or a Jump Start to a Bachelor's Degree," Olivia Crosby. *Occupational Outlook Quarterly*, vol. 46, no. 4, Winter 2002–2003.

"Career Counseling Strategies to Facilitate a Welfare-to-Work Transition: The Case of Jeanetta," Donna L. McDonald. *Career Development Quarterly*, vol. 50, no 4., p. 326, June 2002.

"Career Development among Ethnic and Age Groups of Community College Students," Loretta Y. Teng, George A. Morgan, and Sharon K. Anderson. *Journal of Career Development*, vol. 28, no. 2, p. 115, Winter 2001.

"The Changing Role of Community College," Henry T. Kasper. *Occupational Outlook Quarterly*, vol. 46, no. 4, Winter 2002–2003.

Chronicle Vocational School Manual: A Directory of Accredited, Approved, Certified, Licensed or Registered Vocational and Technical Schools, 2003–2004. Moravia, NY: Chronicle Guidance Publications, 2003.

"Considering Community College?" Mark Rowh. *Career World*, vol. 34, no. 5, p. 14, February/March 2006.

"Counseling Adults in Career Transition: Reflections of a Counselor-in-Training," Christopher M. Scott. *Journal of Career Development*, vol. 28, no. 3, p. 215, Spring 2002.

"Distance Learning in Postsecondary Education: Learning Whenever, Wherever," Matthew Mariani. *Occupational Outlook Quarterly*, vol. 45, no. 2, Summer 2001.

"A Person-Centered Perspective to Welfare-to-Work Services: In Pursuit of the Elusive and the Unattainable," Stephen G. Weinrach. *Career Development Quarterly*, vol. 52, no. 2, p. 153, December 2003.

"Tech Jobs of Tomorrow," Monika G. Vaccaro. *Career World*, vol. 32, no. 6, p. 24, April/May 2004.

Career and Vocational Education to Meet Special Needs

"Career Counseling with Clients Who Have a Severe Mental Illiness," Robyn A. Caporoso and Mark S. Kiselica. *Career Development Quarterly*, vol. 52, no. 3, p. 235, March 2004.

"Career Counseling with Lesbian, Gay, Bisexual, and Transgendered Persons: The Next Decade," Y. Barry Chung. *Career Development Quarterly*, vol. 52, no. 1, p. 78, September 2003.

"Career Counseling with Persons Living with HIV: An Ecological Approach," Casey A. Barrio and Marie F. Shoffner. *Career Development Quarterly*, vol. 53, no. 4, p. 325, June 2005.

"Career Development and Guidance Programs Across Cultures: The Gap between Policies and Practices," Jane Goodman and Sunny Hansen. *Career Development Quarterly*, vol. 54, no. 1, p. 57, September 2005.

"Career Rehabilitation: Integration of Vocational Rehabilitation and Career Development in the Twenty-First Century," Michael Shahnasarian. *Career Development Quarterly*, vol. 49, no. 3, p. 275, March 2001.

"Conceptions of Work among Adolescents and Young Adults with Mental Retardation," Rachel Gali Cinamon and Limor Gifsh. *Career Development Quarterly*, vol. 52, no. 3, p. 212, March 2004.

"Culturally Appropriate Career Counseling with Gay and Lesbian Clients," Mark Pope, Bob Barret, Dawn M. Szymanski, Y. Barry Chung, et al. *Career Development Quarterly*, vol. 53, no. 2, p. 158, December 2004.

"INCOME: A Culturally Inclusive and Disability-Sensitive Framework for Organizing Career Development Concepts and Interventions," David B. Hersenson. *Career Development Quarterly*, vol. 54, no. 2, p. 150, December 2005.

Life Centered Career Education: A Competency-Based Approach, Donn E. Brolin. Reston, VA: Council for Exceptional Children, 2004.

Program Manual for the High School/High Tech Program: Providing Careers in Technology for Youth with Disabilities. Washington, DC: Office of Disability Employment Policy, 2003.

"A Qualitative Study of Latino Lesbian and Gay Youths' Experiences with Discrimination and the Career Development Process," Eve M. Adams, Betsy J. Cahill, and Stacy J. Ackerlind. *Journal of Vocational Behavior*, vol. 66, no. 2, p. 199, April 2005.

Vocational Rehabilitation: Better Measures and Monitoring Could Improve the Performance of the VR Program. Washington, DC: U.S. Government Accounting Office, 2005.

Planning, Implementing, Evaluating, and Improving Career and Vocational Education

"21st Century Accountability: Perkins III and WIA," David W. Stevens. University of Minnesota, St. Paul, National Research Center for Career and Technical Education, 2001, http://www.nccte.org/publications/infosynthesis/infopaper/infopaper02/infopaper02.html

"Major Needs of Career and Technical Education in the Year 2000: Views from the Field," Morgan V. Lewis. Columbus: National Dissemination Center for Career and Technical Education, The Ohio State University, 2001 (National Dissemination Center for Career and Technical Education Research Report No.RR1003).

Next Steps for the Community College, Trudy H. Bers and Harriott D. Calhoun, eds. San Francisco: Jossey-Bass, 2002.

"The Predictive Validity of a Computer-Assisted Career Decision-Making System: A Six-Year Follow-Up," Itamar Gati, Reuma Gadassi, and Naama Shemesh. *Journal of Vocational Behavior*, vol. 68, no. 2, p. 205, April 2006.

"Reforming Career and Technical Education Teacher Preparation and Licensure: A Public Policy Synthesis," Kenneth C. Gray and Richard A. Walter. University of Minnesota, St. Paul, National Research Center for Career and Technical Education, 2001, http://www.nccte.org/publications/infosynthesis/infopaper/infopaper01/infopaper01.html

"School-to-Career: Reworking the Model," Barry Burke. *Technology & Learning*, vol. 24, no. 6, p. 26, January 2004.

Lists and Indexes

Career and Vocational Information

250 Best Jobs through Apprenticeships, Michael Farr and Laurence Shatkin. Indianapolis: JIST Publishing, 2005.

300 Best Jobs without a Four-Year Degree, Michael Farr. Indianapolis: JIST Publishing, 2006.

Best Jobs for the 21st Century, 4th ed, Michael Farr. Indianapolis: JIST Publishing, 2006.

The Career Guide: Dun's Employment Opportunities Directory. Parsippany, NJ: Dun and Bradstreet Information Services, annual.

*Dictionary of Occupational Titles, with O*NET Definitions*, 5th ed. Baton Rouge: Claitor's, 2003.

Occupational Outlook Handbook, 2006–2007. Indianapolis: JIST Publishing, 2006.

Occupational Outlook Handbook, 2006–2007, U.S. Department of Labor, Bureau of Labor Statistics. Washington, DC: U.S. Government Printing Office, 2005.

"O*NET Update," Matthew Mariani. *Occupational Outlook Quarterly*, vol. 45, no. 3, Fall 2001.

Professional Careers Sourcebook: Where to Find Help Planning Careers that Require College or Technical Degrees, 7th ed, Amy Darga. Detroit: Gale Group, 2002.

Vertical File Index. New York: H. W. Wilson, monthly.

Internet Sites

Clearinghouses for Vocational Information

Career and Education Resource Center
http://www.careers.org

Find Trade Schools
http://www.trade-school.org/

JIST Publishing
http://www.jist.com

Jobweb
http://www.jobweb.org/

National Centers for Career and Technical Education
http://www.nccte.org

Office of Vocational and Adult Education
http://www.ed.gov/about/offices/list/ovae/index.html?src=mr

Online Career Center
http://www.monster.com

Online Job Search Guide and Research Directory
http://www.job-hunt.org

Trade Schools, Colleges & Universities
http://www.trade-schools.net/

Professional Resources

American Counseling Association
http://www.counseling.org

American School Counselor Association
http://www.schoolcounselor.org

Association for Career and Technical Education
http://www.acteonline.org

National Board for Certified Counselors
http://www.nbcc.org

National Centers for Career and Technical Education
http://www.nccte.org/

Online Information and References

Federal Jobs Digest
http://www.jobsfed.com

GaleNet
http://galenet.gale.com

Job Finders Online
http://www.jobfindersonline.com

Occupational Outlook Handbook
http://www.bls.gov/oco/

Occupational Outlook Quarterly Online
http://www.bls.gov/opub/ooq/ooqhome.htm

U.S. Bureau of Labor Statistics Home Page
http://www.bls.gov/

U.S. Department of Labor
http://www.dol.gov

Yahoo! Business and Economy
http://www.yahoo.com/Business

Dictionary of Occupational Titles/Occupational Information Network/Group Numbers

The following list contains the three-digit occupational group numbers from the United States Department of Labor's *Dictionary of Occupational Titles* (DOT). The DOT, for many years the most important publication for occupational information, has been replaced by O*NET, which is based on the Standard Occupational Classification (SOC) system that has been adopted by the U.S. government. DOT numbers have been included here because some libraries and career guidance centers may still file career information according to the DOT numbers. O*NET occupational profiles can be found on the Web at http://online.onetcenter.org/.

Accountants, 160
Actors, 150
Actuaries, 020
Acupuncturists, 079
Administrative assistants, 169
Admitting clerks, 205
Adult education workers, 099
Advertising account executives, 141, 164
Advertising copywriters, 131
Advertising managers, 164
Aerospace engineers, 002
Agricultural engineers, 013
Agricultural supply sales workers, 272
Agricultural technicians, 013, 162, 272, 523
Agronomists, 040
AIDS counselors, 195
Air conditioning and heating technicians, 007
Air conditioning engineers, 007
Air conditioning, heating, and refrigeration mechanics, 637, 827, 862
Air pollution control technicians, 029
Air traffic controllers, 193
Aircraft mechanics, 621, 806
Airline baggage and freight handlers, 357, 912, 919
Airline dispatchers, 912
Airline flight attendants, 352

Airline reservations agents, 238
Airline ticket agents, 238
Airplane pilots, 196
Airport managers, 184
Airport utility workers, 912
All-round machinists, 600
Ambulance drivers, 375, 913
Amusement and recreation attendants, 342, 349
Anatomists, 041
Anesthesiologists, 070
Announcers, 159
Anthropologists, 055
Appliance service workers, 637, 723, 827
Appraisers, 191
Archaeologists, 055
Architects, 001
Architectural drafters, 001
Architectural model makers, 777
Armed services careers, 101, 166, 235, 378, 620, 623, 639, 829, 911–912
Art and music therapists, 195
Art directors, 141
Artificial intelligence specialists, 003
Artists, 141, 144
Assemblers, 700–703, 706, 720–729, 806, 820–82893197C
Astronomers, 021
Athletic coaches, 153

Athletic trainers, 153
Auctioneers, 294
Auditors, 160
Auto body repairers, 807, 845
Auto parts counter workers, 279, 620
Auto sales workers, 273
Automated manufacturing managers, 638
Automobile driving instructors, 099
Automotive exhaust emissions technicians, 010, 620
Automotive mechanics, 620
Avionics technicians, 823

Bank clerks, 203, 209–210, 214–217, 219, 249
Bank officers, 186
Bank tellers, 211
Barbers and hairstylists, 330, 332
Bartenders, 312
Bicycle repairers, 639
Biochemists, 041
Biological technicians, 049, 078, 199
Biologists, 041
Biomedical engineers, 019
Biomedical equipment technicians, 019, 719
Blacksmiths and forge shop workers, 610–612
Blood bank technologists, 078

Master Index

The master index is a comprehensive index of all thirteen volumes of *Career Information Center*. It includes subject terms from Volumes 1 through 13 and lists all the jobs that are mentioned in the twelve volumes of job profiles. Entries that appear in all capital letters have separate occupational profiles in one of the twelve volumes. Entries that are not capitalized refer to jobs that do not have a separate profile but for which information is given

Under some capitalized entries there is a section titled "Profile includes." This lists jobs that are mentioned in the profile.

Some entries are followed by a job title in parentheses after the page number on which it can be found. This job title is the occupational profile in which the entry is discussed.

Some index entries include the line *See Getting Into section of individual volumes*. The Getting Into section is identical in volumes 1 through 12 with the exception of the Trade and Professional Journals list at the end of each volume.

Mathematician, Mechanical engineer, Metallurgist, Office worker, Painter, Physicist, Plater, Power hammer operator, Power shear operator, Production worker, Punch press operator, Riveter, Scientist, Sheet metal worker, Technician, Tool/die maker, Tube bender, Welder)

Affirmative action: employment trends, 13:88–89; overview of, 13:16–17. *See also Getting Into section of individual volumes*

Age: labor force changes, 13:1–2; older employees, 13:90–92

Age Discrimination in Employment Act (ADEA), 13:18, 92

"Age of Industry," 3:1

Agile production, 9:7–8

Agribusiness: farming in U.S. today, 1:1–4; food processing, 1:4–5; jobs in, 1:6, 12; summer jobs, 1:10; trade/professional journals, 1:28–29

AGRICULTURAL ENGINEER, 1:103–104 (Profile)

AGRICULTURAL INSPECTOR, 1:104–105 (Profile)

Agricultural microbiologist, 6:146 (Microbiologist)

Agricultural pilot, 12:116 (Airline pilot)

AGRICULTURAL TECHNICIAN, 1:65–67 (Profile includes: Farm sales representative, Field representative, Food processing field agent, Grain dryer, Technical farm worker)

Agriculture, 9:3–4

Agriculture quarantine inspector, 11:95 (Government inspector/examiner)

AGRONOMIST, 1:106–107 (Profile)

Agronomist, 6:101 (Botanist)

AI (artificial intelligence), 6:9

AIDS, 13:17–18, 37–38

AIDS COUNSELOR, 7:49–51 (Profile)

Air pollution control engineer, 6:139 (Mechanical engineer)

AIR POLLUTION CONTROL TECHNICIAN, 1:67–69 (Profile includes: Field technician, Inspector, Laboratory technician)

AIR TRAFFIC CONTROLLER, 12:113–115 (Profile)

Air transport industry: snapshot, 12:4; summer jobs in, 12:6; trade/professional journals, 12:26

AIR-CONDITIONING ENGINEER, 6:82–84 (Profile)

Air-conditioning/heating/refrigeration mechanic, 9:60 (Stationary engineer/boiler operator)

AIR-CONDITIONING/HEATING/REFRIGERATION MECHANIC/

INSTALLER, 4:27–29 (Profile includes: Air-conditioning/refrigeration mechanic, Furnace installer, Gas burner mechanic, Oil burner mechanic)

Air-conditioning/refrigeration mechanic, 4:27 (Air-conditioning/heating/refrigeration mechanic/installer), 9:94 (Electronics industry), 110 (Office machine/computer industry)

AIRCRAFT DISPATCHER, 12:84–85 (Profile)

AIRCRAFT MECHANIC, 12:86–87 (Profile includes: Line maintenance crew)

Airframe mechanic. *See* AIRCRAFT MECHANIC

Air-gun operator, 4:49 (Demolition worker)

AIRLINE BAGGAGE/FREIGHT HANDLER, 12:27–28 (Profile)

AIRLINE FLIGHT ATTENDANT, 12:88–89 (Profile)

Airline industry: economy and, 8:1; hotel industry and, 8:2; overview of, 12:7

AIRLINE PILOT, 12:115–118 (Profile includes: Agricultural pilot, Business pilot, Captain, Check pilot, Copilot, Helicopter pilot, Test pilot)

AIRLINE RESERVATIONS AGENT, 12:28–29 (Profile)

AIRLINE TICKET AGENT, 12:30–31 (Profile)

AIRPORT MANAGER, 12:118–120 (Profile)

AIRPORT UTILITY WORKER, 12:31–32 (Profile)

Alaskan Arctic National Wildlife Refuge, 1:9

"All-girl-getaway," 8:11

Allied health professionals, 7:7, 9

All-suite hotels, 8:3

Alternate work schedules, 13:66

ALTERNATIVE FUELS VEHICLE TECHNICIAN, 6:33–34 (Profile)

Alternative medicine professionals, 7:7

ALUMINUM INDUSTRY, 9:81–83 (Profile includes: Annealer, Casting operator, Charge gang weigher, Coiler operator, Hot metal crane operator, Overhead crane operator, Pot tender, Remelt operator, Rolling mill operator, Scalper operator, Soaking pit operator, Stretcher level operator, Stretcher level operator helper, Tapper, Tapper helper, Wire draw operator). *See also* COPPER INDUSTRY

AMBULANCE DRIVER, 7:51–52 (Profile includes: Emergency medical technician, Paramedic)

Ambulatory surgical centers, 7:7, 11–12

American Counseling Association. *See Getting Into section of individual volumes*

American Society of Anesthesiologists, 7:11–12

Americans with Disabilities Act (ADA): overview of, 13:17–18; workplace trends, 13:93

Ampoule examiner, 9:120 (Pharmaceutical industry)

Ampoule filler, 9:120 (Pharmaceutical industry)

Amtrak, 12:9

AMUSEMENT/RECREATION ATTENDANT, 8:29–31 (Profile)

Analyst, 10:91 (Marketing research worker)

Analytical chemist, 6:111 (Chemist)

ANATOMIST, 6:84–86 (Profile)

Anatomist, 6:96 (Biologist)

ANESTHESIOLOGIST, 7:95–98 (Profile)

Anesthesiologist, 7:136 (Physician)

Animal biologist. *See* ZOOLOGIST

Animal breeder, 5:49 (Pet care worker)

ANIMAL CARETAKER, 8:31–32 (Profile)

Animal curator, 8:118 (Zookeeper)

Animal groomer, 5:49 (Pet care worker)

Animal pathologist, 6:153 (Pathologist)

Animal physiologist, 6:176 (Zoologist)

ANIMAL SCIENTIST, 1:107–108 (Profile)

Animal scientist, 8:118 (Zookeeper)

Animal sticker, 1:50 (Meat packing worker)

Animal taxonomist, 6:176 (Zoologist)

ANIMAL TRAINER, 1:69–71 (Profile)

Animator. *See* CARTOONIST/ANIMATOR

Annealer, 9:82 (Aluminum industry), 97 (Foundry industry)

ANNOUNCER, 2:55–57 (Profile includes: Disc jockey, Radio announcer, Television announcer)

Anodizer, 9:94 (Electronics industry)

ANTHROPOLOGIST, 6:87–89 (Profile includes: Archaeologist, Cultural anthropologist, Linguistic anthropologist, Physical anthropologist)

Anti-affirmative action. *See* Affirmative action

Antiques appraiser, 5:93 (Appraiser)

Anti-Spam Act, 2:5

APPAREL INDUSTRY, 9:84–87 (Profile includes: Assembler, Bundler, Busheler, Cutter, Dressmaker, Fashion designer, Finish presser, Fitter, Fur cutter, Fur finisher, Fur machine operator, Fur nailer, Fusing machine operator, Hand sewer, Hand spreader, Hat maker, Industrial engineer, Knitting mill operator, Machine spreader, Marker, Milliner, Pattern grader, Patternmaker, Presser, Production manager, Quality control technician, Sewing machine operator, Tailor)

Appellate court judge, 11:98 (Judge)

Appliance repair, 5:3

APPLIANCE SERVICE WORKER, 5:59–60 (Profile includes: Bench worker, Field worker)

Appliances, communications, 2:1

Application form, job. *See Getting Into section of individual volumes*

Applications programmer, 3:121 (Computer programmer)

Applications software engineer, 3:127 (Computer software engineer)

Applied artist, 2:57 (Artist)

Applied arts trade/professional journals, 2:30

APPRAISER, 5:93–95 (Profile includes: Antiques, Estate, Fine art, Jewelry)

Apprenticeships: job finding and, 13:42–43; retraining via, 13:56–57

Aquaculture, 1:11–12

Arbitrator, 9:74 (Labor relations specialist)

Archaeological tourism, 8:2

Archaeologist, 6:6, 87 (Anthropologist)

ARCHITECT, 4:126–128 (Profile). *See also* LANDSCAPE ARCHITECT

ARCHITECTURAL DRAFTER, 4:98–100 (Profile includes: Checker, Junior drafter, Senior drafter, Tracer)

Architectural drafter, 9:48 (Drafter)

ARCHITECTURAL MODEL MAKER, 4:100–101 (Profile)

Architecture: industry overview, 4:3; summer jobs in, 4:6; trade/professional journals, 4:26

Archivist, 6:130 (Historian)

Area specialist, 1:133 (Geographer)

Arkadelphia, Arkansas, 9:9

Armed services: careers in, 11:5; industry snapshot, 11:7; retraining opportunities in, 13:57; trade/professional journals, 11:28

ARMED SERVICES CAREER, 11:31–33 (Profile)

ART DIRECTOR, 2:94–96 (Profile includes: Advertising art director)

Artificial intelligence (AI), 6:9

ARTIFICIAL INTELLIGENCE SPECIALIST, 6:89–90 (Profile)

Artist, 2:35 (Lithographic worker)

ARTIST, 2:57–60 (Profile includes: Applied artist, Fine artist, Painter, Printmaker, Sculptor)

Artist's model, 2:40 (Model)

Arts: communications *vs.*, 2:1–2; newspaper editor, 2:109 (Editor, newspaper); overview of, 2:4, 14; summer jobs in, 2:7

Ash, Mary Kay, 13:30

Assembler, 5:42 (Laundry worker), 9:79 (Aerospace industry), 85 (Apparel industry), 94 (Electron-

ics industry), 100 (Furniture industry), 109 (Office machine/computer industry)

ASSEMBLER/FABRICATOR, 9:31–33 (Profile includes: Assembly line worker, Bench assembler, Floor assembler, Precision assembler)

Assembly inspector, 9:79 (Aerospace industry)

Assembly line, 3:1

Assembly line worker, 9:31 (Assembler/fabricator)

Assistant camera operator, 2:65 (Camera operator)

Assistant laboratory animal technician, 7:39 (Laboratory animal care worker)

Assistant professor, 11:130 (Teacher, college)

Associate editor, 2:109 (Editor, newspaper)

Associate professor, 11:130 (Teacher, college)

Association executive. *See* MEETING PLANNER

ASTRONOMER, 6:91–93 (Profile)

Astronomer, 9:78 (Aerospace industry)

Astronomy: in natural sciences, 6:2; trade/professional journals, 6:28

Astrophysicist, 6:158 (Physicist). *See also* ASTRONOMER

Athlete. *See* PROFESSIONAL ATHLETE

ATHLETIC COACH, 8:95–97 (Profile)

Athletic director, 10:107 (Sports management professional)

ATHLETIC TRAINER, 8:97–99 (Profile)

Athletics trade/professional journals, 8:28

Atmospheric scientist. *See* METEOROLOGIST

Attorney. *See* Estate tax attorney; LAWYER; LAWYER, CORPORATE; LAWYER, PUBLIC SERVICE

AUCTIONEER, 10:60–62 (Profile)

Audio control technician, 2:63 (Broadcast technician)

Audio recording technician, 2:63 (Broadcast technician)

AUDIOLOGIST, 7:98–99 (Profile)

Auditing clerk, 3:39 (Bookkeeper)

AUDITOR, 3:105–106 (Profile includes: External auditor, Internal auditor)

Auto body painter, 12:33 (Auto body repairer)

AUTO BODY REPAIRER, 12:32–34 (Profile includes: Auto body painter)

AUTO PARTS COUNTER WORKER, 10:29–31 (Profile includes: Service writer)

AUTO SALES WORKER, 10:31–33 (Profile)

Automation: in agile manufacturing, 9:8; flexible, 9:6–7; in manufacturing, 9:5–6

Automation system engineer, 6:162 (Robotics engineer)

Automobile assembler, 9:88 (Automotive industry)

AUTOMOBILE DRIVING INSTRUCTOR, 12:90–91 (Profile)

Automobile industry: history of in U.S., 12:2–3; overview of, 12:3–5; parts/dealerships, 12:5. *See also* Motor vehicle industry

Automobiles, 3:1, 8:2

Automotive designer, 9:87 (Automotive industry)

Automotive engineer, 6:139 (Mechanical engineer), 9:88 (Automotive industry)

AUTOMOTIVE EXHAUST EMISSIONS TECHNICIAN, 12:92–93 (Profile)

AUTOMOTIVE INDUSTRY, 9:87–90 (Profile includes: Automobile assembler, Automotive designer, Automotive engineer, Automotive technician, Chemist, Drafter, Electrician, Electroplater, Industrial engineer, Industrial machinery repairer, Industrial upholsterer, Inspector, Machine operator, Machine tool operator, Machinist, Metal finisher, Metal polisher, Millwright, Mock-up builder, Model maker, Patternmaker, Physicist, Plant engineer, Production manager, Production painter, Production planner, Shop supervisor, Stylist, Test driver, Tool/die maker)

AUTOMOTIVE MECHANIC, 12:93–95 (Profile)

Automotive technician, 6:50 (Mechanical engineering technician), 9:88 (Automotive industry)

Automotive trade/professional journals, 12:26

Aviation inspector, 12:109 (Transportation inspector)

Aviation safety officer, 11:95 (Government inspector/examiner)

Aviation/air transport trade/professional journals, 12:26

AVIONICS TECHNICIAN, 12:95–96 (Profile)

Baby boomers, 8:7

Back tender, 9:115 (Paper industry)

Backcountry ranger, 8:107 (Park ranger)

Backer, 2:32 (Bookbinder)

Backhoe operator, 4:85 (Septic tank installer/servicer)

Back-of-the-house employees, 8:4

Bacteria, 7:2–3

Bacteriologist, 6:145 (Microbiologist)

Baggage porter, 8:50 (Hotel bellhop/porter)

Bagger, **5:**32 (Dry cleaning worker), **5:**43 (Laundry worker)

BAKER, **1:**31–32 (Profile)

Baker, **12:**101 (Merchant marine steward/cook). *See also* PASTRY CHEF/BAKER

Bakery clerk, **10:**52 (Supermarket worker)

Ball-and-chain operator, **4:**49 (Demolition worker)

Ballet dancer, **2:**74 (Dancer)

Ballistic technician, **11:**61 (Crime laboratory technician)

Band saw operator, **1:**51 (Meat packing worker)

BANK CLERK, **3:**33–34 (Profile includes: Bookkeeping clerk, Business machine operator, Data entry keyer, Exchange clerk, File clerk, Interest clerk, Loan clerk, Mail handler, Messenger, New account clerk, Proof operator, Securities clerk)

Bank investment manager, **3:**107 (Bank officer/manager)

BANK OFFICER/MANAGER, **3:**107–109 (Profile includes: Bank investment manager, Branch manager, Credit department manager, Financial manager, Loan officer, Operations manager, Real estate loan officer, Trust officer)

BANK TELLER, **3:**34–36 (Profile includes: Vault teller)

BANKER, INVESTMENT, **3:**155–156 (Profile)

Banking industry, **3:**7–8, 10–11

BARBER/HAIRSTYLIST, **5:**60–62 (Profile)

Barker operator, **1:**48 (Lumber mill worker)

BARTENDER, **8:**33–34 (Profile)

Batch loader, **9:**112 (Paint/varnish/lacquer industry)

BBC News, **1:**9

Beamster, **9:**107 (Leather/shoe industry)

Beater engineer, **9:**114 (Paper industry)

Bell captain, **8:**50 (Hotel bellhop/porter)

Bench assembler, **9:**32 (Assembler/fabricator)

Bench hand, **8:**85 (Pastry chef/baker)

Bench molder, **9:**97 (Foundry industry)

Bench technician, **6:**35 (Cable television/telecommunications technician), 72 (Wireless communications technician)

Bench worker, **5:**59 (Appliance service worker)

Benefits, employee: additional financial, **13:**64–65; alternate work schedules, **13:**66; cafeteria plans, **13:**66; child care, **13:**65; disability/life insurance, **13:**63; eco-nomic change and, **13:**66–67; employee counseling/professional services, **13:**65; employee/employer advantages, **13:**59–60; federal law, **13:**20; mandatory, **13:**60–61; medical/health, **13:**61–63; overview of, **13:**60; pension plans, **13:**63–64; time off, **13:**65–66. *See also specific job profiles*

BENEFITS/COMPENSATION ANALYST, **3:**111–112 (Profile)

BENU, **7:**12

BICYCLE MECHANIC, **12:**34–35 (Profile)

Big Three, **12:**3–4

Bilingual secretary, **3:**91 (Secretary), **10:**88 (Import/export worker)

Bilingual teacher, **11:**132 (Teacher, preschool/kindergarten/elementary)

BILLING CLERK, **3:**37–38 (Profile)

Binder layer, **1:**62 (Tobacco industry worker)

Bindery worker, **2:**31 (Bookbinder)

Binding/cellophaning machine operator, **1:**62 (Tobacco industry worker)

Bingham Canyon (UT) copper mine, **1:**11

BIOCHEMIST, **6:**93–96 (Profile)

Biochemist, **6:**96 (Biologist)

Biochemistry, **6:**3

Biological scientist. *See* ANATOMIST

BIOLOGICAL TECHNICIAN, **6:**75–77 (Profile)

Biological technician, **9:**119 (Pharmaceutical industry)

BIOLOGIST, **6:**96–98 (Profile includes: Anatomist, Biochemist, Biophysicist, Botanist, Geneticist, Marine biologist, Microbiologist, Nutritionist, Pathologist, Pharmacologist, Physiologist, Zoologist)

Biologist, **9:**119 (Pharmaceutical industry)

Biology: in natural sciences, **6:**2; overview of, **6:**3

BIOMEDICAL ENGINEER, **6:**99–100 (Profile)

BIOMEDICAL EQUIPMENT TECHNICIAN, **7:**53–54 (Profile)

Biophysicist, **6:**96 (Biologist)

Biostatistician, **3:**179 (Statistician)

Biotechnologist. *See* GENETIC ENGINEERING RESEARCH SCIENTIST

Biotechnology, **6:**7, 11, **7:**9

Bird flu, **7:**4

Blacksmith, **12:**62 (Railroad maintenance worker)

Blaster, **1:**55 (Miner, metal), **4:**48–49 (Demolition worker)

Blender, **1:**34 (Cheese industry worker), **9:**112 (Paint/varnish/lac-quer industry), 122 (Plastics industry)

Blind ad. *See Getting Into section of individual volumes*

Block setter, **1:**48 (Lumber mill worker)

Blower, **9:**130 (Steel industry)

BLS (Bureau of Labor Statistics). *See* Labor force

Bodyguard, **11:**65 (Detective)

Boiler operator, **11:**48 (Power plant worker). *See also* STATIONARY ENGINEER/BOILER OPERATOR

Boiler tender, **9:**60 (Stationary engineer/boiler operator)

BOILERMAKER, **9:**43–45 (Profile)

Boilermaker, **9:**104 (Industrial chemical industry), 127 (Shipbuilding industry), **12:**62 (Railroad maintenance worker)

Bonus clerk, **3:**64–65 (Payroll clerk)

BOOKBINDER, **2:**31–32 (Profile includes: Backer, Bindery worker, Folding machine operator, Gatherer, Stitcher)

BOOKKEEPER, **3:**38–40 (Profile includes: Accounts payable clerk, Accounts receivable clerk, Auditing clerk)

Bookkeeper, **10:**51 (Supermarket worker)

Bookkeeping clerk, **3:**33 (Bank clerk)

Bookmobile librarian, **11:**107 (Librarian, public)

Boom operator, **2:**63 (Broadcast technician), 89 (Sound engineering technician)

BORDER PATROL AGENT, **11:**54–55 (Profile)

Botanist, **6:**96 (Biologist)

BOTANIST, **6:**101–103 (Profile includes: Agronomist, Economic botanist, Marine botanist, Plant physiologist)

Bouncer, **11:**65 (Detective)

Boyle, Brian, **1:**8

Branch manager, **3:**107 (Bank officer/manager)

Brick-cutting machine operator, **9:**133 (Structural clay products industry)

BRICKLAYER, **4:**30–31 (Profile includes: Hod carrier)

Bridge jobs, **13:**91

BRIDGE/LOCK TENDER, **12:**35–36 (Profile)

Broadcast media: CDs, recording industry, **2:**11; film, **2:**12–13; overview of, **2:**10–11; radio, **2:**11–12; television, **2:**12

BROADCAST NEWS ANALYST, **2:**60–62 (Profile includes: Meteorologist, Newscaster, Sportscaster, Weathercaster)

Broadcast scriptwriter, **2:**137–138 (Scriptwriter)

BROADCAST TECHNICIAN, 2:62–65 (Profile includes: Audio control technician, Audio recording technician, Boom operator, Camera operator, Chief technician, Color control technician, Control technician, Director, Engineer, Field technician, Lighting technician, Maintenance technician, Master control engineer, Radio broadcast technician, Technical director, Transmitter technician, Video control technician, Video recording technician)

Broadcasting industry: overview of, 2:4; summer jobs in, 2:6; trade/professional journals, 2:30

BROKERAGE CLERK, 3:40–42 (Profile includes: Dividend clerk, Margin clerk, Purchase-and-sale clerk, Receive-and-deliver clerk, Transfer clerk)

Bronx Zoo, 8:9

Brusher, 9:91 (Ceramics industry)

Bucker, 1:46 (Logger)

Budget accountant, 3:99 (Accountant, management)

Budget examiner, 11:95 (Government inspector/examiner)

BUILDING CUSTODIAN, 11:33–34 (Profile)

BUILDING INSPECTOR, 4:102–104 (Profile includes: Electrical inspector, Elevator inspector, Plumbing inspector, Public works inspector)

Bull chain operator, 1:48 (Lumber mill worker)

Bulldozer operator, 1:55 (Miner, metal)

BULLDOZER/GRADER/PAVING MACHINE OPERATOR, 4:32–33 (Profile)

Bundle wrapper, 5:43 (Laundry worker)

Bundler, 9:85 (Apparel industry)

Bureau of Labor Statistics (BLS). See Labor force

Burnisher, 9:108 (Leather/shoe industry)

Bus driver, 12:45 (Local transit operator). See also INTERCITY BUS DRIVER; SCHOOL BUS DRIVER; SPECIAL SERVICE BUS DRIVER

Bus transport trade/professional journals, 12:26

Busboy. See DINING ROOM ATTENDANT

Bush, George W.: defense budget, 6:12; national parks, 8:10; worker training, 13:50

Busheler, 9:85 (Apparel industry)

Business: alternative work styles in, 3:11; description of, 3:1–2; future of, 3:13–14; occupations, 13:9; services, 13:4; top-paying jobs in, 3:9;

training in small/mid-sized, 13:72; travelers, 8:3–4; trends, 3:6–7; workforce, 3:5–6

Business editor, 2:109 (Editor, newspaper)

BUSINESS FAMILY/CONSUMER SCIENTIST, 5:95–97 (Profile)

Business machine operator, 3:33 (Bank clerk)

BUSINESS MACHINE OPERATOR, 3:42–44 (Profile)

Business pilot, 12:116 (Airline pilot)

Business-to-business marketing, 10:11–12

Butcher, 1:50 (Meat packing worker), 10:52 (Supermarket worker). See also RETAIL BUTCHER

Buyer. See PURCHASING AGENT

Cabinetmaker, 4:34 (Carpenter), 9:100 (Furniture industry)

Cable splicer, 11:38 (Electric power transmission/distribution worker)

Cable system installer, 6:35 (Cable television/telecommunications technician)

Cable television, 2:12

CABLE TELEVISION ENGINEER, 6:103–105 (Profile)

CABLE TELEVISION/TELECOMMUNICATIONS TECHNICIAN, 6:35–37 (Profile includes: Bench technician, Cable system installer, Chief cable technician, Service technician, Trunk technician)

CAD (Computer-assisted design), 4:8

CAFETERIA ATTENDANT, 8:35–36 (Profile includes: Dining room attendant, Food runner)

Cafeteria plans, 13:66

Cage cashier. See GAMING CAGE WORKER

Calender operator, 9:122 (Plastics industry), 124–125 (Rubber industry)

CaliforniaChoice, 7:12

Camera operator, 2:63 (Broadcast technician)

CAMERA OPERATOR, 2:65–67 (Profile includes: Assistant camera operator, Grip, Still photographer)

Camera operator, color separation, 2:35 (Lithographic worker)

Camera operator, halftone, 2:34 (Lithographic worker)

Camera operator, line, 2:34 (Lithographic worker)

Camp counselor, 8:87 (Recreation worker)

Camps, 8:11

Can inspector, 1:45 (Food canning/freezing worker)

Candy feeder, 1:33 (Candy manufacturing worker)

Candy maker, 1:32 (Candy manufacturing worker)

Candy maker helper, 1:32 (Candy manufacturing worker)

CANDY MANUFACTURING WORKER, 1:32–34 (Profile includes: Candy feeder, Candy maker, Candy maker helper, Candy packer, Enrober machine operator, Hand dipper, Weigher)

Candy packer, 1:33 (Candy manufacturing worker)

CAN-Spam Act, 10:12

Capper operator, 9:112 (Paint/varnish/lacquer industry)

Captain, 12:115 (Airline pilot), 127 (Merchant marine captain)

CAR RENTAL/LEASING AGENT, 12:96–98 (Profile includes: Customer service representative, Station manager)

Car repairer, 12:62 (Railroad maintenance worker)

CAR WASH WORKER, 12:37–38 (Profile includes: Cashier, Manager)

Carcass splitter, 1:50 (Meat packing worker)

Card tender, 9:136 (Textile industry)

Cardiac emergency nurse, 7:147 (Registered nurse)

CARDIAC MONITOR TECHNICIAN, 7:55–56 (Profile)

CARDIAC PERFUSIONIST, 7:100–101 (Profile)

CARDIOLOGY TECHNOLOGIST, 7:56–58 (Profile)

Career counseling. See Getting Into section of individual volumes

Career planning. See Getting Into section of individual volumes

CareerBuilder. See Getting Into section of individual volumes

Careers, public sector: armed services, 11:5; education, 11:5–6; federal government, 11:4–5; law, 11:6; overview of, 11:3–4; protective services, 11:7; social work, 11:6; state/local government, 11:5

CARPENTER, 4:34–36 (Profile includes: Cabinetmaker, Finish carpenter, Millworker, Rough carpenter)

Carpenter, 9:127 (Shipbuilding industry)

Carpet cleaner. See RUG/CARPET CLEANER

Carrier Corporation, 9:9–10

CARTOGRAPHER, 1:108–110 (Profile includes: Cartographic drafter, Cartographic supervisor, Geographic information specialist, Mosaicist, Photogrammetrist, Project cartographer)

Cartographer, 1:133 (Geographer)

Flight superintendent. *See* AIRCRAFT DISPATCHER

Floor assembler, **9:**31 (Assembler/fabricator)

FLOOR COVERING INSTALLER, **4:**54–57 (Profile)

FLOOR SANDER/FINISHER, **4:**57–59 (Profile)

Floor secretary. *See* WARD CLERK

FLORAL DESIGNER, **5:**74–76 (Profile)

Fluid physicist, **6:**158 (Physicist)

Fluid power technician. *See* HYDRAULIC/PNEUMATIC TECHNICIAN

Flyer, **2:**49 (Stagehand)

Folding machine operator, **2:**31 (Bookbinder)

Food, **1:**3–4. *See also* Agribusiness

Food and Drug Administration, **1:**5

FOOD BROKER, **10:**62–63 (Profile)

FOOD CANNING/FREEZING WORKER, **1:**45–46 (Profile includes: Can inspector, Cooker, Double-seamer operator, Filling machine operator, Freezer tunnel operator, Freezing room worker, Hand packer, Hand peeler, Hand sorter, Hand trimmer, Processor, Quantity fill inspector, Temperature checker, Washer operator)

Food processing, **1:**4–5, 10

Food processing field agent, **1:**65–66 (Agricultural technician)

FOOD PROCESSING TECHNICIAN, **1:**81–83 (Profile includes: Inspector, Laboratory technician, Production supervisor)

Food runner, **8:**35 (Cafeteria attendant)

FOOD SCIENCE TECHNICIAN, **1:**83–84 (Profile)

FOOD SCIENTIST, **1:**129–130 (Profile includes: Dairy technologist)

Food service industry: overview of, **8:**4; snapshot, **8:**10; summer jobs in, **8:**6; trends in, **8:**4–5; workers, **8:**5

Food service manager, **8:**101 (Lodging manager)

Food services trade/professional journals, **8:**28

Food technologist. *See* FOOD SCIENTIST

Food/drug inspector, **11:**95 (Government inspector/examiner)

Ford, Henry, **3:**1, **9:**4, 6, **12:**2

Foreign representative, **10:**87 (Import/export worker)

Foreign service officer, **11:**91 (Foreign service worker)

Foreign service reserve officer, **11:**92 (Foreign service worker)

Foreign service staff, **11:**92 (Foreign service worker)

FOREIGN SERVICE WORKER, **11:**91–93 (Profile includes: Commercial-economic officer, Consular officer,

Foreign service officer, Foreign service reserve officer, Foreign service staff, Political officer)

Foreign student adviser, **11:**86 (College student personnel worker)

Foreign tourism, **8:**3

Foreman/forewoman. *See* CONSTRUCTION SUPERVISOR

Forensic pathologist, **6:**153 (Pathologist)

Forensic science technician. *See* CRIME LABORATORY TECHNICIAN

FORENSIC SCIENTIST, **6:**126–127 (Profile)

Forensics nurse, **7:**148–149 (Registered nurse)

Forest ranger, **1:**131 (Forester)

FORESTER, **1:**131–132 (Profile includes: Forest ranger, Service forester)

Forester, **9:**115 (Paper industry)

Forestry, **1:**8, 10

Forestry industry, **13:**10

FORESTRY TECHNICIAN, **1:**85–86 (Profile)

Forklift operator. *See* INDUSTRIAL TRUCK OPERATOR

Forming machine operator, **9:**101 (Glass industry)

Fossil fuels, **1:**8–11

FOUNDRY INDUSTRY, **9:**96–98 (Profile includes: Annealer, Bench molder, Casting inspector, Chipper, Coremaker, Crane operator, Grinder, Hand molder, Machine coremaker, Machine molder, Machinist, Maintenance mechanic, Millwright, Patternmaker, Sand mixer, Shakeout worker, Shot blaster, Tumbler operator)

Frame spinner, **9:**136 (Textile industry)

Frame wirer, **6:**68 (Telecommunications central office technician)

Free trade agreements, **1:**2, 3

Freelancer. *See* Contractors, independent

Freelancing, **3:**11

Freezer tunnel operator, **1:**45 (Food canning/freezing worker)

Freezing room worker, **1:**45 (Food canning/freezing worker)

Freight handler. *See* AIRLINE BAGGAGE/FREIGHT HANDLER

Fringe benefits, **13:**59

Front office clerk. *See* HOTEL/MOTEL/RESORT DESK CLERK

Front-end machine operator, **4:**49 (Demolition worker)

Front-of-the-house employees, **8:**4

Fry cook, **8:**72 (Cook/chef)

Full professor, **11:**130 (Teacher, college)

Functional resume. *See Getting Into* section of individual volumes

FUND-RAISER, **11:**93–95 (Profile)

FUNERAL DIRECTOR, **5:**109–111 (Profile)

Funeral services, **5:**3, 9

Fur cutter, **9:**85 (Apparel industry)

Fur farmer, **1:**97 (Small animal breeder)

Fur finisher, **9:**85 (Apparel industry)

Fur machine operator, **9:**85 (Apparel industry)

Fur nailer, **9:**85 (Apparel industry)

Furnace installer, **4:**27 (Air-conditioning/heating/refrigeration mechanic/installer)

Furnace operator, **9:**130 (Steel industry)

Furniture designer, **9:**99 (Furniture industry)

FURNITURE INDUSTRY, **9:**99–101 (Profile includes: Assembler, Cabinetmaker, Drafter, Finisher, Furniture designer, Lumber handler, Machine operator, Model maker, Stock handler)

Fusing machine operator, **9:**85 (Apparel industry)

Gaffer, **2:**78 (Lighting technician), **9:**102 (Glass industry)

Galilei, Galileo, **6:**1

GAMING CAGE WORKER, **8:**44–45 (Profile)

GAMING DEALER, **8:**46–47 (Profile)

GAMING SURVEILLANCE OFFICER, **8:**76–77 (Profile)

Gang leader, **10:**58 (Warehouse worker)

GARAGE DOOR MECHANIC, **4:**59–61 (Profile)

GARDENER/GROUNDSKEEPER, **5:**34–36 (Profile includes: Greenskeeper)

Gas burner mechanic, **4:**27 (Air-conditioning/heating/refrigeration mechanic/installer)

Gas compressor operator, **1:**59 (Petroleum/natural gas exploration/production worker)

GAS STATION CASHIER, **12:**40–41 (Profile)

Gasoline plant operator, **1:**59 (Petroleum/natural gas exploration/production worker)

Gatherer, **2:**31–32 (Bookbinder), **9:**102 (Glass industry)

GATT (General Agreement on Tariffs and Trade), **3:**1

Gauger, **1:**59 (Petroleum/natural gas exploration/production worker)

Gear repairer, **12:**39 (Dockworker)

Gem cutter, **5:**79 (Jeweler)

Gemologist, **5:**79 (Jeweler)

Gender, **13:**1

General Agreement on Tariffs and Trade (GATT), **1:**2, 3, **3:**1

Health exams, **13:**33

Health information technician. *See* MEDICAL RECORDS/HEALTH INFORMATION TECHNICIAN

Health information Web sites, **7:**3

Health maintenance organizations (HMOs), **7:**9, 12

Health management programs, **13:**34

Health physicist, **1:**150 (Occupational health/safety specialist), **6:**158 (Physicist)

Health physics technician, **6:**55 (Nuclear technician)

Health screening, **13:**34–35

Health services, employee. *See* Employee health services

Health services manager. *See* MEDICAL/HEALTH SERVICES MANAGER

HEALTH/SAFETY ENGINEER, **1:**138–140 (Profile)

Heat treater, **9:**78 (Aerospace industry)

Heater, **9:**130 (Steel industry)

Heavy equipment diesel mechanic, **12:**99 (Diesel mechanic)

Heeler, **9:**108 (Leather/shoe industry)

Helicopter pilot, **12:**116 (Airline pilot)

Help-desk technician, **3:**129 (Computer support specialist)

Help-wanted ads. *See Getting Into section of individual volumes*

Herbologists, **7:**7

Heritage travel, **8:**2

Herpetologist, **6:**176 (Zoologist)

Hershey, Milton, **10:**3

Hidden job market, **13:**45–46

High-definition television (HDTV), **2:**12

High-pressure hydraulic press operator, **9:**133 (Structural clay products industry)

HIGHWAY ENGINEER, **4:**137–139 (Profile includes: Construction specialist, Planning engineer, Research specialist)

HIGHWAY INSPECTOR, **4:**113–115 (Profile)

HIGHWAY MAINTENANCE WORKER, **11:**43–44 (Profile)

Hippocrates, **7:**2, 3

Hippocratic Oath, **7:**2

Hispanic origin employees, **13:**2–3

HISTORIAN, **6:**130–132 (Profile includes: Archivist)

Historians, **6:**6

History, transportation industry, **12:**1–3

Histotechnician, **7:**58 (Clinical laboratory technician)

HIV/AIDS nurse, **7:**147 (Registered nurse)

HMOs (Health maintenance organizations), **7:**9, 12

Hod carrier, **4:**30 (Bricklayer), 45 (Construction laborer)

Hoist and winch operator, **4:**108 (Crane operator)

Hollywood, **2:**13

HOME CATERER, **5:**36–38 (Profile)

HOME HEALTH AIDE, **7:**37–39 (Profile)

HOME SECURITY CONSULTANT, **5:**76–78 (Profile)

Home shopping television networks, **10:**11

Home study, **13:**57

Home-based employment. *See* Employment, home-based

Home-based health care, **7:**8

HOMEMAKER, **5:**38–40 (Profile)

Homemaking services: global view, **5:**5; industry snapshot, **5:**3; overview of, **5:**1–2, 7; summer jobs in, **5:**2; top-paying jobs in, **5:**6; trade/professional journals, **5:**26

Homeopaths, **7:**7

Horticulture, **1:**8, 10

Hose operator, **11:**39 (Firefighter)

Hospices, **7:**8

HOSPITALITY CASHIER, **8:**48–49 (Profile)

Hospitality/recreation industry: employment outlook for, **8:**11; overview of, **8:**1–2

Hospitals: cost of health care, **7:**11, 12; industry snapshot, **7:**9; services of, **7:**1–2

Host/hostess. *See* RESTAURANT HOST/HOSTESS

Hot metal crane operator, **9:**82 (Aluminum industry), 130 (Steel industry)

Hot-cell technician, **6:**55 (Nuclear technician)

HOTEL BELLHOP/PORTER, **8:**50–51 (Profile includes: Baggage porter, Bell captain, Head porter, Housekeeping porter)

HOTEL HOUSEKEEPER, **8:**52–53 (Profile)

Hotel industry, **8:**28; business travelers, **8:**3–4; conventions, **8:**4; overview of, **8:**2–3; snapshot, **8:**10; summer jobs in, **8:**6; trends in, **8:**3; worker teams, **8:**4

HOTEL/CASINO/RESORT CONCIERGE, **8:**77–78 (Profile)

HOTEL/MOTEL/RESORT DESK CLERK, **8:**54–55 (Profile includes: Information clerk, Key clerk, Mail clerk, Rack clerk, Reservation clerk)

House detective, **11:**65 (Detective)

HOUSEKEEPER, DOMESTIC, **5:**40–42 (Profile includes: Day worker)

Housekeeping porter, **8:**50 (Hotel bellhop/porter)

Human factors engineer. *See* ERGONOMIST

Human Genome Project, **6:**11, **7:**9

Human resource development specialist. *See* TRAINING/DEVELOPMENT SPECIALIST

HUMAN RESOURCES ASSISTANT, **3:**55–56 (Profile)

HUMAN RESOURCES MANAGER, **3:**148–150 (Profile)

Hydraulic engineer, **4:**129 (Civil engineer)

HYDRAULIC/PNEUMATIC TECHNICIAN, **6:**48–50 (Profile)

Hydrogen, **1:**9–10

Hydrogen furnace operator, **9:**94 (Electronics industry)

HYDROLOGIST, **1:**140–142 (Profile)

Hypotheses, **6:**1

Icer, **8:**85 (Pastry chef/baker)

Ichthyologist, **6:**176 (Zoologist)

Icing mixer, **8:**85 (Pastry chef/baker)

ILLUSTRATOR/GRAPHIC DESIGNER, **2:**114–117 (Profile includes: Medical illustrator, Technical illustrator)

Image consultant, **5:**5

Immigrants, **13:**87–90

Immunizations, **13:**36

Immunologist, **6:**145 (Microbiologist)

Import specialist, **11:**63 (Customs worker)

IMPORT/EXPORT WORKER, **10:**87–89 (Profile includes: Bilingual secretary, Correspondent, Export broker, Export credit manager, Foreign representative, Translator)

Incentive programs, **13:**64–65

Incinerator operator, **11:**50 (Refuse worker)

Independent contractors. *See* Contractors, independent

INDUSTRIAL CHEMICAL INDUSTRY, **9:**104–106 (Profile includes: Accountant, Boilermaker, Chemical engineer, Chemical operator, Chemical operator helper, Chemical sales representative, Chemical technician, Chemist, Drier operator, Electrical engineer, Filterer, Grinder, Lead burner, Machinist, Mechanical engineer, Mixer, Pipe fitter, Technical writer)

Industrial construction, **4:**6

INDUSTRIAL DESIGNER, **9:**66–68 (Profile)

Industrial designer, **9:**93 (Electronics industry)

INDUSTRIAL ENGINEER, **9:**68–70 (Profile)

Industrial engineer, **9:**78 (Aerospace industry), 86 (Apparel industry), 88 (Automotive industry), 109 (Office machine/computer industry)

Industrial explosion, **9:**3–5

LIBRARIAN, SPECIAL, **11**:110–112 (Profile includes: Head librarian)

Library administrator, **11**:107 (Librarian, public)

LICENSED PRACTICAL NURSE, **7**:74–75 (Profile)

Lid stamper, **9**:112 (Paint/varnish/lacquer industry)

Life insurance, **13**:63

Life sciences, **6**:28–29

Life scientist. *See* BIOLOGIST

LIFEGUARD, **8**:79–80 (Profile)

Lifetime contracts, **13**:50

Lighting designer, **2**:79 (Lighting technician)

LIGHTING TECHNICIAN, **2**:78–80 (Profile includes: Gaffer, Lighting designer, Television lighting technician, Theatrical lighting technician)

Lighting technician, theatrical, **2**:79 (Lighting technician)

Line camera operator, **2**:34 (Lithographic worker)

Line installer/repairer, **11**:38 (Electric power transmission/distribution worker)

Line maintenance crew, **12**:86 (Aircraft mechanic)

Liner, **9**:91 (Ceramics industry)

LINGUIST, **6**:135–136 (Profile)

Linguistic anthropologist, **6**:87 (Anthropologist)

Linotype operator, **2**:45 (Prepress worker)

Literary translator, **2**:148 (Translator/interpreter)

LITERARY/THEATRICAL AGENT, **2**:119–120 (Profile)

LITHOGRAPHIC WORKER, **2**:34–36 (Profile includes: Color separation camera operator, Dot-etcher, Finisher, Halftone camera operator, Letterer, Line camera operator, Lithographic artist, Photoengraver, Platemaker, Retoucher, Router, Scanner operator, Stripper)

Load dispatcher, **11**:37 (Electric power transmission/distribution worker)

Loader engineer, **1**:47 (Logger)

Loading machine operator, **1**:52 (Miner, coal)

Loan clerk, **3**:33 (Bank clerk)

Loan officer, **3**:107 (Bank officer/manager)

Local government, **11**:5

LOCAL TRANSIT OPERATOR, **12**:45–46 (Profile includes: Bus driver, Subway conductor, Subway driver, Trolley driver)

LOCAL TRUCK DRIVER, **12**:47–48 (Profile)

LOCKSMITH, **5**:81–82 (Profile)

Locomotive engineer. *See* RAILROAD ENGINEER

Locomotive operator, **1**:55 (Miner, metal)

LODGING MANAGER, **8**:101–102 (Profile includes: Executive housekeeper, Food service manager, General manager, Personnel manager, Sales manager)

Loft worker, **9**:126 (Shipbuilding industry)

LOGGER, **1**:46–48 (Profile includes: Bucker, Choker, Faller, Loader engineer, Rigging slinger, Scaler, Yarder)

LONG-HAUL TRUCK DRIVER, **12**:48–50 (Profile includes: Moving van driver)

Longshoreman. *See* DOCKWORKER

Longwall machine operator, **1**:53 (Miner, coal)

Loom fixer, **9**:136 (Textile industry)

Loom winder tender, **9**:136 (Textile industry)

Los Angeles County Coroner's Office, **11**:10

Lumber companies, **1**:8

Lumber handler, **9**:99–100 (Furniture industry)

LUMBER MILL WORKER, **1**:48–50 (Profile includes: Barker operator, Block setter, Bull chain operator, Deck worker, Dry kiln operator, Grader, Headsaw crew, Planer mill grader, Planer operator, Pond worker, Pony edger, Scaler, Sorter, Trimmer saw operator)

Machine coremaker, **9**:97 (Foundry industry)

Machine molder, **9**:97 (Foundry industry)

Machine mover/installer, **4**:47 (Construction millwright)

Machine operator, **9**:88 (Automotive industry), 100 (Furniture industry), 107 (Leather/shoe industry)

MACHINE OPERATOR/TENDER, **9**:38–40 (Profile includes: Drill press operator, Turret lathe operator)

MACHINE SETTER, **9**:54–56 (Profile)

Machine setter, **9**:57 (Machinist)

Machine spreader, **9**:85 (Apparel industry)

Machine tender. *See* MACHINE OPERATOR/TENDER

Machine tool operator, **9**:88 (Automotive industry), 110 (Office machine/computer industry)

Machine washer, **5**:42 (Laundry worker)

Machined parts inspector, **9**:79 (Aerospace industry), 110 (Office machine/computer industry)

Machinery manufacturing industry, **9**:3

MACHINIST, **9**:56–58 (Profile includes: Machine setter, Maintenance machinist)

Machinist, **9**:88 (Automotive industry), 97 (Foundry industry), 104 (Industrial chemical industry), 127 (Shipbuilding industry), **12**:62 (Railroad maintenance worker)

Mad Cow Disease, **1**:5

Magazine photographer, **2**:85 (Photographer)

Magazines, **2**:8. *See also* Print media advertising; Trade/professional journals

Magistrate, **11**:98 (Judge)

Magnetic resonance imaging (MRI) scanner, **7**:5

Magnetoencephalography (MEG), **7**:5

Magnuson Fisheries Conservation and Management Act, **1**:11

MAIL CLERK, **3**:58–59 (Profile)

Mail clerk, **8**:54 (Hotel/motel/resort desk clerk)

Mail handler, **3**:33 (Bank clerk)

MAIL SERVICE WORKER, **3**:59–61 (Profile includes: Courier, Customer service agent, Driver, Handler)

Mailman. *See* POSTAL SERVICE WORKER

MAINTENANCE ELECTRICIAN, **4**:115–117 (Profile)

Maintenance industry, **13**:9

Maintenance machinist, **9**:57 (Machinist)

Maintenance mechanic, **9**:97 (Foundry industry)

Maintenance services, **5**:6–7

Maintenance specialist, **4**:47 (Construction millwright)

Maintenance technician, **2**:62 (Broadcast technician)

Maintenance worker, **1**:38 (Diver)

MAKEUP ARTIST, **2**:37–38 (Profile)

Makeup editor, **2**:109 (Editor, newspaper)

Malpractice suits, **7**:11

Managed competition, **7**:12

Management: construction, **4**:7–8, 9; consulting, **3**:7, 10; layers, **13**:50; occupations, **13**:9; positions, **3**:5; trade/professional journals, **3**:30, **4**:26

MANAGEMENT ANALYST/CONSULTANT, **3**:156–158 (Profile)

Manager, **8**:42 (Fast food franchise worker), **12**:37 (Car wash worker)

Managing editor, **2**:103 (Editor, book), 107 (Editor, magazine), 109 (Editor, newspaper)

Mandatory employee benefits, **13**:60–61

Manipulator operator, **9**:130 (Steel industry)

MANUFACTURED HOME ASSEMBLER, **4**:67–68 (Profile)

Manufactured housing, **4**:5

MANUFACTURERS' SALES WORKER, **10**:66–68 (Profile)

Manufacturing engineer, **6**:139 (Mechanical engineer)

Manufacturing industry: contemporary manufacturing, **9**:9–10; employment in, **9**:10–11; factory system, evolution of, **9**:6–9; labor force, projected changes in, **13**:6–7; overview of, **9**:1–6; small manufacturers, **9**:10; trade/professional journals, **9**:28

Manufacturing optician. *See* OPHTHALMIC LABORATORY TECHNICIAN

Mapping scientist. *See* CARTOGRAPHER

MARBLE/TILE/TERRAZZO WORKER, **4**:69–70 (Profile)

Margin clerk, **3**:40 (Brokerage clerk)

Marijuana, medical use of, **7**:7

Marine biologist, **1**:152 (Oceanographer), **6**:96 (Biologist)

Marine botanist, **6**:101 (Botanist)

Marine drafter, **9**:48 (Drafter)

MARINE ENGINEER, **1**:142–143 (Profile)

Marine engineer, **9**:126 (Shipbuilding industry)

Marine geophysicist, **1**:152 (Oceanographer)

Marine microbiologist, **6**:146 (Microbiologist)

Marine operator, **3**:70 (Telephone operator)

Marine squad, **11**:40 (Firefighter)

MARINE TECHNICIAN, **12**:51–52 (Profile)

Marine transportation trade/professional journals, **12**:26

Marker, **5**:32 (Dry cleaning worker), 42 (Laundry worker), **9**:85 (Apparel industry), **10**:50 (Stock clerk)

Market research interviewer, **3**:56 (Interviewer)

Marketing: business-to-business, **10**:11–12; contemporary, **10**:3–5; demographic trends, **10**:5; future of, **10**:12; government, **11**:10; history of, **10**:2–3; interactive, **10**:1–2; product, overview of, **10**:1; services, **10**:12; trade/professional journals, **10**:28

Marketing, self. *See Getting Into* section *of individual volumes*

MARKETING DIRECTOR, **10**:89–91 (Profile)

Marketing research director, **10**:91 (Marketing research worker)

MARKETING RESEARCH WORKER, **10**:91–93 (Profile includes: Advertising researcher, Analyst, Coder, Field worker, Marketing research

director, Statistician, Survey researcher, Tabulator)

MARRIAGE/FAMILY COUNSELOR, **11**:112–113 (Profile)

Mary Kay Cosmetics, **13**:30

Mason. *See* BRICKLAYER; CEMENT MASON; PLASTERER/STUCCO MASON; STONEMASON

Mass production, **9**:4, 6

Mass transit industry, **12**:4, 9

MASSAGE THERAPIST, **5**:82–84 (Profile)

Master control engineer, **2**:63 (Broadcast technician)

Material moving industry, **13**:10

Materials, **4**:8–9

Materials science technician. *See* METALLURGICAL TECHNICIAN

Materials scientists, **6**:3

Mathematical statistician, **3**:180 (Statistician)

MATHEMATICIAN, **6**:137–139 (Profile)

Mathematician, **9**:78 (Aerospace industry), 93 (Electronics industry), 109 (Office machine/computer industry)

Mathematics, **6**:28

Matloff, Norman, **13**:87

McDonald's, **13**:72, 92

Meat cutter, **1**:50 (Meat packing worker). *See also* RETAIL BUTCHER

Meat grader, **11**:95 (Government inspector/examiner)

MEAT PACKING WORKER, **1**:50–52 (Profile includes: Animal sticker, Band saw operator, Butcher, Carcass splitter, Casing-running-machine tender, De-hairing machine tender, Dry curer, Eviscerator, Meat cutter, Offal separator, Shackler, Shaver, Singer, Steamer, Stunner, Trimmer)

Meat wrapper, **10**:52 (Supermarket worker)

Mechanic. *See* AIRCRAFT MECHANIC; AUTOMOTIVE MECHANIC; DIESEL MECHANIC; MOTORBOAT MECHANIC; MOTORCYCLE MECHANIC

Mechanical drafter, **6**:50 (Mechanical engineering technician), **9**:48 (Drafter)

Mechanical engineer, **6**:4, 10; **9**:78 (Aerospace industry), 93 (Electronics industry), 104 (Industrial chemical industry), 109 (Office machine/computer industry), 115 (Paper industry), 125 (Rubber industry)

MECHANICAL ENGINEER, **6**:139–141 (Profile includes: Air pollution control engineer, Automotive engineer, Environmental systems

engineer, Manufacturing engineer)

MECHANICAL ENGINEERING TECHNICIAN, **6**:50–52 (Profile includes: Automotive technician, Diesel technician, Mechanical drafter, Production technician, Tool designer)

Mechanical trade/professional journals, **4**:26

MEDIA BUYER, **10**:94–95 (Profile)

Mediator, **9**:74 (Labor relations specialist)

Medicaid, **7**:11

Medical: insurance, **3**:13; research, **7**:10; schools, **7**:3, 5; science, **7**:3–4; surveillance examinations, **13**:33; technicians, **7**:7

MEDICAL ASSISTANT, **7**:76–77 (Profile)

Medical benefits: flexible spending accounts, **13**:62; health care costs, adjusting to higher, **13**:62; overview of, **13**:61; types of coverage, **13**:61–62

Medical doctor. *See* PHYSICIAN; Physicians

Medical illustrator, **2**:115 (Illustrator/graphic designer)

MEDICAL ILLUSTRATOR, **7**:117–119 (Profile)

Medical microbiologist, **6**:145 (Microbiologist)

Medical pathologist, **6**:152 (Pathologist)

Medical photographer, **2**:85 (Photographer)

MEDICAL PHYSICIST, **7**:119–120 (Profile)

MEDICAL RECORDS/HEALTH INFORMATION TECHNICIAN, **7**:78–79 (Profile)

Medical secretary, **3**:91 (Secretary)

MEDICAL/HEALTH SERVICES MANAGER, **7**:114–117 (Profile includes: Clinical, Generalist, Nonclinical, Specialist)

Medicare, **7**:11, 12

Medicine, **6**:6–7, **7**:2–4. *See also* Health care

MEETING PLANNER, **3**:89–90 (Profile)

MEETING/CONVENTION PLANNER, **8**:103–104 (Profile)

MEG (magnetoencephalography), **7**:5

Melter, **9**:81 (Copper industry), 130 (Steel industry)

Mental health, **7**:30–31

MERCHANDISE DISPLAYER/WINDOW TRIMMER, **2**:38–40 (Profile)

MERCHANT MARINE CAPTAIN, **12**:127–128 (Profile includes: Captain, First mate, Second mate, Third mate)

MERCHANT MARINE ENGINEER, **12**:129–130 (Profile includes:

Chief engineer, Firer, First assistant engineer, Oiler, Second assistant engineer, Third assistant engineer, Water tender, Wiper)

MERCHANT MARINE PURSER, **12:**130–131 (Profile)

MERCHANT MARINE RADIO OFFICER, **12:**132–133 (Profile)

MERCHANT MARINE STEWARD/COOK, **12:**101–102 (Profile includes: Baker, Chief cook, Chief steward, Mess attendant, Second cook, Third cook, Utility hand)

Mergers, bank, **3:**8

Meritor Savings Bank, **13:**19

Mess attendant, **12:**101 (Merchant marine steward/cook)

Messenger, **3:**33 (Bank clerk), **10:**50 (Stock clerk)

MESSENGER SERVICE WORKER, **3:**61–62 (Profile)

Metal finisher, **9:**88 (Automotive industry)

Metal mining, **1:**11

Metal polisher, **9:**88 (Automotive industry)

Metal worker, **2:**72 (Craftsperson)

METALLURGICAL ENGINEER, **6:**142–144 (Profile)

Metallurgical engineer, **9:**81 (Copper industry), 93 (Electronics industry), 130 (Steel industry)

METALLURGICAL TECHNICIAN, **6:**53–54 (Profile)

Metallurgist, **9:**78 (Aerospace industry)

METEOROLOGIST, **1:**144–145 (Profile includes: Climatologist, Physical meteorologist, Synoptic meteorologist)

Meteorologist, **2:**60 (Broadcast news analyst)

Meter installer/repairer, **11:**36 (Electric power service worker)

Microbiologist, **6:**96 (Biologist). *See also* GENETIC ENGINEERING RESEARCH SCIENTIST

MICROBIOLOGIST, **6:**145–147 (Profile includes: Agricultural microbiologist, Bacteriologist, Immunologist, Marine microbiologist, Medical microbiologist, Public health microbiologist, Virologist)

MICROWAVE ENGINEER, **6:**148–149 (Profile)

Middle East oil, **1:**9

Migrant worker, **1:**40 (Farm laborer)

Military. *See* Armed services

Military training: Community College of the Air Force, **13:**81; Credentialing Opportunities On-Line program, **13:**80–81; overview of, **13:**80; United Services Military Apprenticeship Program, **13:**80

Milliken, Roger, **10:**10

Milliner, **9:**85 (Apparel industry)

Millworker, **4:**34 (Carpenter)

Millwright, **9:**89 (Automotive industry), 97 (Foundry industry)

Milton's, **10:**4

Mine worker, **9:**90 (Ceramics industry), 132 (Structural clay products industry)

MINER, COAL, **1:**52–54 (Profile includes: Coal loading machine operator, Continuous mining machine operator, Cutting machine operator, Dragline operator, Drilling machine operator, Fire boss, Fitter, Loading machine operator, Longwall machine operator, Overburden stripping operator, Preparation plant central control operator, Rock dust machine operator, Rotary auger operator, Separation tender, Shot firer, Shuttle car operator, Stopping builder, Tractor operator, Washbox attendant)

MINER, METAL, **1:**55–56 (Profile includes: Blaster, Bulldozer operator, Compressor crew, Crane operator, Dragline operator, Drill supervisor, Driller, Dynamiting crew, Fan operator, Locomotive operator, Mineral preparation engineer, Mucker, Pit supervisor, Power shovel operator, Scaler, Scraper, Shaft sinker, Timber installer, Track installer)

Mineral preparation engineer, **1:**55 (Miner, metal)

Mineralogist, **1:**135 (Geologist)

Mining, metal, **1:**11

MINING ENGINEER, **1:**145–147 (Profile)

Mining industry, **13:**5–6

MINING TECHNICIAN, **1:**90–91 (Profile)

Minorities, **4:**9–10, **13:**87–90

Mixer, **8:**85 (Pastry chef/baker), **9:**104 (Industrial chemical industry)

Mixer operator, **9:**124 (Rubber industry)

Mobile operator, **3:**70 (Telephone operator)

Mock-up builder, **9:**88 (Automotive industry)

MODEL, **2:**40–43 (Profile includes: Artist's model, Fashion model, Fitting model, Photographic model, Print model, Television commercial model)

Model maker, **9:**87 (Automotive industry), 99 (Furniture industry). *See also* ARCHITECTURAL MODEL MAKER

Modeler, **9:**92 (Ceramics industry)

Modular homes, **4:**5

Mold maker, **9:**92 (Ceramics industry)

Molding machine operator, **9:**122 (Plastics industry)

Molecular biologist. *See* BIOCHEMIST

Monster Board. *See Getting Into section of individual volumes*

Monthly Retail Trade Survey, **10:**2, 10

Moonlighting, **13:**26

Mosaicist, **1:**109 (Cartographer)

Motel desk clerk. *See* HOTEL/MOTEL/RESORT DESK CLERK

Motion picture director, **2:**100 (Director)

Motion picture industry, **2:**4, 12–13

MOTION PICTURE PROJECTIONIST, **8:**56–57 (Profile)

Motion picture scriptwriter, **2:**137–138 (Scriptwriter)

Motor vehicle industry: future of, **12:**4; global economy and, **9:**1, 5, 10; overview of, **9:**2

MOTORBOAT MECHANIC, **12:**52–53 (Profile)

MOTORCYCLE MECHANIC, **12:**54–55 (Profile)

MOVER, **12:**56–57 (Profile)

Movie producer, **2:**130–131 (Producer)

Movie theaters, **8:**7

Moving van driver, **12:**49 (Long-haul truck driver)

MRI (magnetic resonance imaging) scanner, **7:**5

MSNBC.com, **1:**9

Mucker, **1:**55 (Miner, metal)

MULTIMEDIA DEVELOPER, **2:**121–122 (Profile)

Multiplex, **8:**7

Multiskilling, **13:**70–71

Municipal court judge, **11:**98 (Judge)

Museum Attendance Report, **8:**7

MUSEUM CONSERVATOR, **8:**104–105 (Profile)

MUSEUM CURATOR, **8:**105–107 (Profile)

Museums, **8:**7–8

MUSIC TEACHER, **2:**81–82 (Profile)

MUSIC VIDEO PRODUCER, **2:**83–84 (Profile)

MUSICIAN, **2:**123–125 (Profile includes: Classical musician, Club musician, Pianist)

NACME (National Council for Minorities in Engineering), **13:**90

NAFTA (North American Free Trade Agreement), **1:**2, **3:**1, 3, **12:**2

NANNY, **5:**84–86 (Profile)

National Council for Minorities in Engineering (NACME), **13:**90

National Fire Academy, **13:**72

National Information Infrastructure (NII), **2:**4–5

National Institutes of Health, **6:**11, 99, 114, **7:**9

National Park Service, **8:**9, 10

Natural gas, **1:**9–10

Natural resources: conservation of, **1:**5; consumption of, **1:**8–9; industry snapshot, **1:**3; jobs in, **1:**6, 12; summer jobs, **1:**10; trade/professional journals, **1:**28, 29; types of, **1:**9–11; water resources, **1:**11–12

NATURAL SCIENCE MANAGER, **1:**147–149 (Profile)

Natural sciences, **6:**2–4

Nautical architect, **9:**126 (Shipbuilding industry)

NAVAL ARCHITECT, **1:**149–150 (Profile)

Nephrology nurse, **7:**147 (Registered nurse)

NETWORK ADMINISTRATOR, **3:**159–160 (Profile)

Network administrator, **13:**96

NETWORK TECHNICIAN, **3:**118–120 (Profile)

Networking. *See Getting Into section of individual volumes*

Networks, communications, **2:**2

Neuropathologist, **6:**153 (Pathologist)

Neurosurgeon, **7:**152 (Surgeon)

New account clerk, **3:**33 (Bank clerk)

NEWS REPORTER/CORRESPONDENT, **2:**126–128 (Profile includes: Newspaper reporter, Television/radio reporter, Wire service reporter)

Newscaster, **2:**60 (Broadcast news analyst)

Newspaper reporter, **2:**126 (News reporter/correspondent)

Newspapers. *See* Print media advertising

NII (National Information Infrastructure), **2:**4–5

Nonclinical manager, **7:**115 (Medical/health services manager)

Noninstructional assistant, **11:**76 (Teacher assistant)

Nonprofit organizations, **11:**10–11, **13:**87

North American Free Trade Agreement (NAFTA), **1:**2, **3:**1, 3, **12:**2

Nuclear energy, **1:**11

NUCLEAR ENGINEER, **6:**150–152 (Profile)

Nuclear engineers, **6:**5

NUCLEAR MEDICINE TECHNOLOGIST, **7:**80–81 (Profile)

Nuclear physicist, **6:**158 (Physicist)

Nuclear reactor operator, **6:**55 (Nuclear technician), **11:**48 (Power plant worker)

NUCLEAR TECHNICIAN, **6:**55–57 (Profile includes: Accelerator operator, Decontamination worker, Health physics technician, Hot-cell technician, Nuclear reactor operator, Radiation monitor, Radiographer)

Numerical-control machine operator, **9:**110 (Office machine/computer industry)

Nurse. *See* REGISTERED NURSE

Nurse-practitioner, **7:**7, 147–148 (Registered nurse)

NURSERY WORKER, **1:**93–95 (Profiles includes: Sales representative)

NURSERY/GREENHOUSE MANAGER, **1:**92–93 (Profile)

Nurses: industry snapshot, **7:**9; overview of, **7:**6–7; role change of, **7:**13; trade/professional journals, **7:**30

NURSING AIDE/ORDERLY, **7:**40–42 (Profile)

Nutritionist, **6:**96 (Biologist). *See also* DIETITIAN/NUTRITIONIST

Oath, physician, **7:**2

Obesity, **7:**11

Obstetrician/gynecologist, **7:**137 (Physician)

Occupational employment: construction/extraction, **13:**9; farming/forestry/fishing, **13:**10; groups, growth by, **13:**7; installation/maintenance/repairs, **13:**9; management/business/financial, **13:**9; office/administrative support, **13:**9; overview of, **13:**7–8; production, **13:**9; professional, **13:**8; sales, **13:**9; service, **13:**8; transportation/material moving, **13:**10

OCCUPATIONAL HEALTH/SAFETY SPECIALIST, **1:**150–152 (Profile includes: Environmental protection officer, Health physicist, Industrial hygienist)

Occupational Safety and Health Act. *See Getting Into section of individual volumes*

Occupational Safety and Health Administration (OSHA), **13:**36–37. *See also Getting Into section of individual volumes*

OCCUPATIONAL THERAPIST, **7:**121–122 (Profile)

OCCUPATIONAL THERAPIST ASSISTANT, **7:**82–83 (Profile)

Occupations: changes in, **13:**10–13; education/training requirements, **13:**12; fastest-growing, **13:**10–11; with largest job decrease, **13:**12, 13; with largest job increase, **13:**11–12; office, **13:**9. *See also* Jobs

OCEANOGRAPHER, **1:**152–153 (Profile includes: Chemical oceanographer, Marine biologist, Marine geophysicist)

O'Connor, Sandra Day, **13:**88–89

Offal separator, **1:**50 (Meat packing worker)

OFFICE CLERK, **3:**63–64 (Profile)

OFFICE MACHINE REPAIRER/COMPUTER, **3:**82–84 (Profile)

OFFICE MACHINE/COMPUTER INDUSTRY, **9:**109–111 (Profile includes: Air conditioning/refrigeration mechanic, Assembler, Computer programmer, Drafter, Electrical engineer, Electrician, Electronic subassembly inspector, Electronics technician, Industrial engineer, Industrial machinery repairer, Instrument repairer, Machine tool operator, Machined parts inspector, Mathematician, Mechanical engineer, Numerical-control machine operator, Physicist, Sales representative, Systems analyst, Technical worker, Test set operator, Testing machine operator, Tool/die maker, Type inspector)

OFFICE MANAGER, **3:**161–163 (Profile)

Office occupations, **13:**9

Office of Special Education and Rehabilitation Services, **13:**94

OFFICE PLANNER, **3:**163–165 (Profile)

Office worker, **9:**79 (Aerospace industry)

Office work/services: positions, **3:**6; trade/professional journals, **3:**30

Offices: alternative work styles in, **3:**11; computers in, **3:**2; development of, **3:**2; environments, **3:**4; evolving workplace, **3:**14; information processing, **3:**3–4; telecommuting, **3:**5; top-paying jobs in, **3:**9

Off-premises sector, **8:**4

Offset press operator, **2:**47 (Printing machine operator)

Oil, **1:**8–9

Oil burner mechanic, **4:**27 (Air-conditioning/heating/refrigeration mechanic/installer)

Oiler, **12:**129 (Merchant marine engineer)

Older employees, **13:**90–92

Online advertising, **10:**8

Online communications, **2:**10

Online job databases. *See Getting Into section of individual volumes*

Online publishing, **2:**10

On-the-job training, **13:**82. *See also specific job profiles*

OPEC (Organization of Petroleum Exporting Countries), **1:**9

Opener tender, **9:**136 (Textile industry)

Operating engineer, **4:**32 (Bulldozer/grader/paving machine operator), 48–49 (Demolition worker), 108 (Crane operator), 117 (Pile-driver operator)

Operating room technician. *See* SURGICAL TECHNOLOGIST

Operations manager, **3:**107 (Bank officer/manager)

Plumbing inspector, 4:102 (Building inspector)

PODIATRIST, 7:140–141 (Profile)

Point-of-sale data, 9:7

Police detective, 11:65 (Detective)

POLICE OFFICER, 11:72–74 (Profile). *See also* STATE POLICE OFFICER

Police science technician. *See* CRIME LABORATORY TECHNICIAN

Polisher, 9:108 (Leather/shoe industry)

Political cartoonist, 2:68 (Cartoonist/animator)

POLITICAL CONSULTANT, 11:115–116 (Profile includes: Corporate lobbyist)

Political officer, 11:91 (Foreign service worker)

POLITICAL SCIENTIST, 6:160–162 (Profile)

Political scientists, 6:6

Pollution, 1:3, 5, 7–8, 11

Polygraph technician, 11:61 (Crime laboratory technician)

Polymerase chain reaction (PCR), 6:11

Pond worker, 1:48 (Lumber mill worker)

Pony edger, 1:49 (Lumber mill worker)

Popular singer, 2:141 (Singer)

Population diversity, 13:89–90

Population sociologist. *See* DEMOGRAPHER

Porter. *See* HOTEL BELLHOP/PORTER

Portrait photographer, 2:85 (Photographer)

Positron-emission tomography (PET) scanner, 7:5, 9

POSTAL SERVICE WORKER, 11:46–47 (Profile includes: Distribution clerk, Letter carrier, Postmaster, Supervisor, Window clerk)

Postmaster, 11:46 (Postal service worker)

Postsecondary education, 11:5

Postsecondary institutions, 13:73

Postsecondary trade schools, 13:78

Pot tender, 9:81 (Aluminum industry)

Potential Rating Index by Zip Marketing (PRIZM New Evolution), 10:4

Potter, 9:91 (Ceramics industry)

Pourer, 9:81 (Copper industry)

Power hammer operator, 9:78 (Aerospace industry)

Power plant mechanic. *See* AIRCRAFT MECHANIC

POWER PLANT WORKER, 11:48–49 (Profile includes: Boiler operator, Nuclear reactor operator, Superintendent, Switchboard operator, Turbine operator, Watch engineer)

Power shear operator, 9:78 (Aerospace industry)

Power shovel operator, 1:55 (Miner, metal), 9:90 (Ceramics industry), 132 (Structural clay products industry)

POWER TOOL REPAIRER, 4:78–79 (Profile)

PPO (preferred provider organization), 7:12

Precision assembler, 9:32 (Assembler/fabricator)

PRECISION INSTRUMENT/EQUIPMENT REPAIRER, 6:62–63 (Profile)

Preferred provider organization (PPO), 7:12

Prefitter, 9:108 (Leather/shoe industry)

Preparation plant central control operator, 1:53 (Miner, coal)

Pre-placement examinations, 13:33

PREPRESS WORKER, 2:45–46 (Profile includes: Compositor, Linotype operator)

Prescription optician. *See* DISPENSING OPTICIAN

Press operator, 2:47 (Printing machine operator), 9:133 (Structural clay products industry)

Press photographer, 2:85 (Photographer)

Presser, 9:85 (Apparel industry), 91 (Ceramics industry), 101 (Glass industry)

Pricing, 10:8

Principal, 11:122 (School administrator)

Print media advertising, 10:7–8

Print model, 2:41 (Model)

PRINTING MACHINE OPERATOR, 2:47–49 (Profile includes: Offset press operator, Press operator, Relief press operator)

Printing trade/professional journals, 2:30

Printmaker, 2:57 (Artist)

Privacy, Internet, 13:100–101

Private employment agencies. *See Getting Into section of individual volumes*

Private investigator, 11:65 (Detective)

Private medical office, 7:1

Privatization, 11:8

PRIZM (Potential Rating Index by Zip Marketing) New Evolution, 10:4

PROBATION OFFICER, 11:117–118 (Profile)

Process engineer, 9:115 (Paper industry)

Processor, 1:45 (Food canning/freezing worker)

Procter & Gamble, 10:3

Procurement clerk, 10:50 (Stock clerk)

Produce clerk, 10:52 (Supermarket worker)

PRODUCER, 2:130–132 (Profile includes: Movie, Television, Theatrical)

PRODUCT MANAGER, 10:95–97 (Profile)

Product promoter. *See* SALES DEMONSTRATOR/PRODUCT PROMOTER

Product sales: business-to-business marketing, 10:11–12; direct sales, 10:10–11; home-based business, 13:30; retailing, 10:9–10; wholesalers/distributors, 10:8–9

Product sampling, 10:8

Production: agile, 9:7–8; flexible, 9:6–7; mass, 9:4, 6; occupations, 13:9

Production editor, 2:103 (Editor, book), 3:125 (Computer software documentation writer)

Production manager, 9:86 (Apparel industry), 89 (Automotive industry)

Production painter, 9:88 (Automotive industry)

Production planner, 9:88 (Automotive industry)

Production supervisor, 1:81 (Food processing technician)

Production technician, 6:50 (Mechanical engineering technician)

Production worker, 1:36 (Dairy industry worker), 9:78 (Aerospace industry)

Professional associations retraining opportunities, 13:56

PROFESSIONAL ATHLETE, 8:109–111 (Profile)

Professional benefits administrator. *See* EMPLOYEE BENEFITS MANAGER

Professional occupations, 13:8

PROFESSIONAL ORGANIZER, 5:51–52 (Profile)

Professional services: employee benefits, 13:65; job growth in, 13:4

Professional/trade journals. *See specific profession/trade*

Professor. *See* TEACHER, COLLEGE

Programmer. *See* COMPUTER PROGRAMMER

Project cartographer, 1:109 (Cartographer)

Projectionist. *See* MOTION PICTURE PROJECTIONIST

Promotion/development director, 10:107 (Sports management professional)

Promotions, 10:8

Proof operator, 3:33 (Bank clerk)

PROOFREADER, 2:87–89 (Profile)

Proofreader/format designer, 3:74 (Word processor)

Prop stagehand, 2:49 (Stagehand)

PROPERTY/REAL ESTATE/COMMUNITY ASSOCIATION MANAGER, 8:111–113 (Profile)

Prospecting computer, 1:58 (Petroleum/natural gas exploration/production worker)

Prosthesis software, 7:5

Prosthetist. *See* ORTHOTIST/PROSTHETIST

Sales. *See* Product sales; Retailing; Wholesalers

SALES DEMONSTRATOR/PRODUCT PROMOTER, **10**:47–49 (Profile)

SALES ENGINEER, **10**:104–105 (Profile)

Sales manager, **8**:101 (Lodging manager)

SALES MANAGER, **10**:105–106 (Profile)

Sales occupations, **13**:9

Sales representative, **1**:93–94 (Nursery worker), **3**:72 (Telephone service representative), **9**:109 (Office machine/computer industry), 113 (Paint/varnish/lacquer industry). *See also* MANUFACTURERS' SALES WORKER; RETAIL STORE SALES WORKER

Salvage diver, **1**:38 (Diver)

Sample-taker operator, **1**:59 (Petroleum/natural gas exploration/production worker)

San Diego Zoo, **8**:9

Sand mixer, **9**:97 (Foundry industry)

Sanitary engineer, **4**:129 (Civil engineer)

Satellite radio, **2**:12

Satellite TV, **2**:12

Sawmill worker. *See* LUMBER MILL WORKER

Scale car operator, **9**:129 (Steel industry)

Scaler, **1**:46 (Logger), 48 (Lumber mill worker), 55 (Miner, metal)

Scalper operator, **9**:82 (Aluminum industry)

Scanner operator, **2**:35 (Lithographic worker)

Schedules, alternate work, **13**:66

SCHOOL ADMINISTRATOR, **11**:122–124 (Profile includes: Federal administrator, Principal, State administrator, Superintendent)

SCHOOL BUS DRIVER, **12**:70–71 (Profile)

SCHOOL COUNSELOR, **11**:124–126 (Profile)

SCHOOL MEDIA SPECIALIST, **11**:126–127 (Profile)

School nurse, **7**:147 (Registered nurse)

School psychologist, **7**:144 (Psychologist)

Science: definition of, **6**:1; employment opportunities, **6**:3, 11–12; examples of, **6**:1–2; global view, **6**:2; industry snapshot, **6**:7; natural sciences, **6**:2–4; new developments, **6**:9–11; specialized areas, **6**:6–7, 9; top-paying jobs in, **6**:8; trade/professional journals, **6**:28–29

Science photographer, **2**:85 (Photographer)

Scientific method, **7**:2

Scientific theories, **6**:1–2

Scientist, **9**:93 (Electronics industry), **9**:78 (Aerospace industry)

Scout, **1**:87 (Geological/petroleum technician)

Scrap crane operator, **9**:130 (Steel industry)

Scrap metal processing worker, **1**:95 (Recycling/reclamation worker)

Scraper, **1**:55 (Miner, metal)

Screen maker, **9**:136 (Textile industry)

Screen printer, **2**:72 (Craftsperson), **9**:136 (Textile industry)

Screen printing artist, **9**:136 (Textile industry)

SCRIPTWRITER, **2**:137–139 (Profile includes: Broadcast scriptwriter, Continuity writer, Motion picture scriptwriter)

Sculptor, **2**:57 (Artist)

Sea transport summer jobs, **12**:6

Seaman. *See* SAILOR

Second assistant engineer, **12**:129 (Merchant marine engineer)

Second cook, **12**:101 (Merchant marine steward/cook)

Second mate, **12**:127 (Merchant marine captain)

Second officer. *See* FLIGHT ENGINEER

Secondary education, **11**:5

SECRETARY, **3**:90–92 (Profile includes: Bilingual, Legal, Medical)

Secretary, **10**:51 (Supermarket worker). *See also* ADMINISTRATIVE ASSISTANT

Securities analyst. *See* FINANCIAL ANALYST

SECURITIES BROKER, **3**:174–176 (Profile)

Securities clerk, **3**:33 (Bank clerk)

SECURITY GUARD, **11**:52–53 (Profile)

Self-employment, **13**:26, 101–102

Self-evaluation. *See Getting Into section of individual volumes*

Self-inventory chart. *See Getting Into section of individual volumes*

Self-marketing. *See Getting Into section of individual volumes*

SEMICONDUCTOR PROCESSOR, **6**:66–67 (Profile)

Senior drafter, **4**:98 (Architectural drafter), **9**:48 (Drafter)

Senior writer, **3**:125 (Computer software documentation writer)

Separation tender, **1**:53 (Miner, coal)

September 11, 2001, **2**:1, **8**:1

SEPTIC TANK INSTALLER/SERVICER, **4**:85–87 (Profile includes: Backhoe operator, Laborer)

Sequoia National Forest (CA), **1**:8

Service forester, **1**:131 (Forester)

Service industry: educational services, **13**:5; health care/social assistance, **13**:4–5; occupations, **13**:8; overview of, **3**:6, **13**:4; professional/business services, **13**:4

Service representative, **11**:36 (Electric power service worker)

SERVICE STATION ATTENDANT, **12**:71–73 (Profile)

Service technician, **6**:35 (Cable television/telecommunications technician). *See also* FARM EQUIPMENT MECHANIC

Service writer, **10**:30 (Auto parts counter worker)

Services: computer, **3**:7; industry, **5**:9; marketing, **10**:12

SET/EXHIBIT DESIGNER, **2**:139–141 (Profile)

Sewer, **5**:69 (Custom upholsterer), **9**:108 (Leather/shoe industry)

Sewing machine operator, **9**:84 (Apparel industry)

Sexual harassment, **13**:18–19

Shackler, **1**:50 (Meat packing worker)

Shaft sinker, **1**:55 (Miner, metal)

Shakeout worker, **9**:97 (Foundry industry)

Sharecropper, **1**:119 (Farmer, cotton/tobacco/peanut)

Shaver, **1**:50 (Meat packing worker)

Shear operator, **9**:131 (Steel industry)

SHEET METAL WORKER, **4**:87–89 (Profile)

Sheet metal worker, **9**:78 (Aerospace industry), 127 (Shipbuilding industry), **12**:62 (Railroad maintenance worker)

SHIPBUILDING INDUSTRY, **9**:126–128 (Profile includes: Boilermaker, Carpenter, Caulker, Construction supervisor, Coremaker, Crane operator, Drafter, Electrician, Electronics technician, Loft worker, Machinist, Marine engineer, Nautical architect, Painter, Patternmaker, Pipe fitter, Rigger, Sheet metal worker, Shipfitter, Ships' carpenter, Shipwright, Tool/die maker, Welder)

Shipfitter, **9**:127 (Shipbuilding industry)

Shipping clerk, **10**:58 (Warehouse worker). *See also* RECEIVING/SHIPPING/TRAFFIC CLERK

Shipping industry snapshot, **12**:4

Shipping receiver, **10**:58 (Warehouse worker)

Shipping/receiving worker, **10**:50 (Stock clerk)

Ships' carpenter, **9**:126 (Shipbuilding industry)

Shipwright, **9**:126 (Shipbuilding industry)

Shoe industry. *See* LEATHER/SHOE INDUSTRY

SHOE REPAIRER, **5**:54–55 (Profile)

Shop supervisor, **9**:88 (Automotive industry)

Wages, **13:**4, 6. *See also specific job profiles*
WAITER, **8:**67–69 (Profile)
Wall Street Journal, **13:**86
"War on Terror," **6:**12
WARD CLERK, **7:**47–48 (Profile)
WAREHOUSE WORKER, **10:**57–59 (Profile includes: Checker, Gang leader, Handler, Order filler, Records clerk, Shipping clerk, Shipping receiver, Stock clerk)
WARN (Worker Adjustment and Retraining Notification Act), **13:**22
Warp tying machine tender, **9:**136 (Textile industry)
Warper tender, **9:**136 (Textile industry)
Washbox attendant, **1:**53 (Miner, coal)
Washer operator, **1:**45 (Food canning/freezing worker)
Waste management, **1:**7–8
WASTEWATER TREATMENT PLANT OPERATOR, **1:**63–64 (Profile)
Watch engineer, **9:**60 (Stationary engineer/boiler operator), **11:**48 (Power plant worker)
WATCH REPAIRER, **5:**88–90 (Profile)
Water resources, **1:**11–12
Water tender, **12:**129 (Merchant marine engineer)
Water transportation industry, **12:**7–8
WATER TREATMENT PLANT/SYSTEM OPERATOR, **1:**101–102 (Profile)
WATER WELL DRILLER, **4:**123–125 (Profile includes: Pump service rig helper, Pump service rig operator, Well driller helper)
Weathercaster, **2:**60 (Broadcast news analyst)
Weaver, **2:**72 (Craftsperson), **9:**136 (Textile industry)
WEB DESIGNER, **2:**152–154 (Profile)
Web sites. *See* World Wide Web (WWW)
WEBMASTER, **2:**155–157 (Profile)
WebMD, **7:**3
WEDDING CONSULTANT, **5:**90–92 (Profile)
Wedding consulting, **5:**5
Weigher, **1:**32 (Candy manufacturing worker)
WELDER, **4:**95–97 (Profile)
Welder, **9:**78 (Aerospace industry), 126 (Shipbuilding industry)
Well driller helper, **4:**123 (Water well driller)

Well puller, **1:**59 (Petroleum/natural gas exploration/production worker)
Wellness, **8:**7
Wellness programs, **13:**35
Whitney, Eli, **9:**4
WHO (World Health Organization), **1:**4, **7:**3–4
Wholesale driver, **12:**67 (Route delivery driver)
WHOLESALE SALES WORKER, **10:**77–79 (Profile)
Wholesalers: industry snapshot, **10:**4; overview of, **10:**8–9; trade/professional journals, **10:**28
Wildlife conservation parks, **8:**9
Williamson, Bonnie, **13:**84–94
Winch operator, **12:**39 (Dockworker)
WINDOW CLEANER, **5:**57–58 (Profile)
Window clerk, **11:**46 (Postal service worker)
WINDOW TRIMMER/MERCHANDISE DISPLAYER, **2:**38–40 (Profile)
Wiper, **12:**129 (Merchant marine engineer)
Wire draw operator, **9:**82 (Aluminum industry)
Wire service reporter, **2:**126 (News reporter/correspondent)
Wireless communications, **2:**5–6
WIRELESS COMMUNICATIONS TECHNICIAN, **6:**72–74 (Profile includes: Bench technician, Field technician)
Wish, Fred, **13:**59–67
Women, **8:**8–9; child care, **13:**87; employment trends, **13:**84–86; job discrimination, **13:**19–20; in construction, **4:**9–10; in leadership roles, **13:**86–87; in management, **13:**51; wage gender gap, **13:**85
Word processing, **3:**4
Word processing trainer, **3:**74 (Word processor)
WORD PROCESSOR, **3:**74–75 (Profile includes: Proofreader/format designer, Terminal operator, Word processing trainer)
Work. *See* Jobs
Work characteristics checklist. *See Getting Into section of individual volumes*
Work experience. *See Getting Into section of individual volumes*

Worker Adjustment and Retraining Notification Act (WARN), **13:**22
Worker teams, hotel industry, **8:**4
Workers, food service industry, **8:**5
Workers' compensation, **13:**37, 61
Workforce, **3:**5–6
Working conditions. *See specific job profiles*
Workplace, **3:**14, 15–16
Workplace evaluation. *See Getting Into section of individual volumes*
Workplace trends: change, pace of, **13:**50; education/training and, **13:**52; jobs, new types of, **13:**51–52; lifetime contracts and, **13:**50; management layers, **13:**50; personnel diversity, **13:**51; skills to accommodate, **13:**52–53; workplace methodologies, **13:**51
World Health Organization (WHO), **1:**4, **7:**3–4
World Medical Association Declaration of Geneva Physician's Oath, **7:**2
World trade, **1:**2–3
World Trade Organization, **7:**3
World Wide Web (WWW): occupations related to, **13:**96–97; occupations related to creating/maintaining, **13:**96–97. *See also* Internet
Wrapper layer, **1:**62 (Tobacco industry worker)

X-ray machines, **7:**4

Yard conductor, **12:**104 (Railroad conductor)
Yarder, **1:**47 (Logger)
YOUTH ORGANIZATION WORKER, **11:**79–81 (Profile includes: Activity director, Executive director)
Youth services librarian, **11:**106 (Librarian, public)

ZOOKEEPER, **8:**117–119 (Profile includes: Animal curator, Animal scientist, Veterinarian, Zoologist)
Zoologist, **6:**96 (Biologist), **8:**118 (Zookeeper)
ZOOLOGIST, **6:**175–177 (Profile includes: Animal physiologist, Animal taxonomist, Embryologist, Entomologist, Fishery biologist, Herpetologist, Ichthyologist)
Zoos, **8:**9